# Karate Masters
## Volume 4

# Karate Masters

## Volume 4

Jose M. Fraguas

EMPIRE Books
P.O. Box 491788, Los Angeles, CA 90049

**Disclaimer**
Please note that the author and publisher of this book are NOT RESPONSIBLE in any manner whatsoever for any injury that may result from practicing the techniques and/or following the instructions given within. Since the physical activities described herein may be too strenuous in nature for some readers to engage in safely, it is essential that a physician be consulted prior to training.

First publish in 2010 by Empire Books LLC.
Copyright (c) 2010 by Jose M. Fraguas.

All rights reserved. No part of this publication may be reproduced or utilized in any form or by any means, electronic or mechanical, including photocopying, recording, or by any information storage and retrieval system, without prior written permission from Empire Books LLC.

EMPIRE BOOKS
P.O. Box 491788
Los Angeles, CA 90049

First edition
Library of Congress Catalog Number:
ISBN-10: 1-933901-49-7
ISBN-13: 978-1-933901-49-7

10 09 08 07 06 05 04 03 02 01 00 99 98 97 1 3 5 7 9 10 8

Library of Congress Cataloging-in-Publication Data

Fraguas, Jose M.
  Karate masters / by Jose M. Fraguas. -- 1st ed.
     p. cm.
  Includes index.
  ISBN 1-933901-49-7 (pbk. : alk. paper)
  1. Karate. 2. Martial artists--Interviews. 3. Large type books. I. Title.
  GV1114.3.F715 2006
  796.815'3--dc22
                              2006012533.

Printed in the United States of America.

*"Empty-handed I entered the world*
*Barefoot I leave it.*
*My coming, my going...*
*Two simple happenings*
*That got entangled."*

— **Kozan Ichikyo**

# Dedication

I dedicate this book to the memory of Sensei Dan Ivan, who passed away on November 14th, 2007. His name stands preeminent in the world of Martial Arts.

# Acknowledgments

I gratefully acknowledge the help of a wide range of people who assisted me with great will and generosity,

Special thanks go to designer Mario M. Rodriguez, France's Thierry Plée, long-time friend and president of Sedirep and Budo Editions; Germany's leading martial Arts publisher, Mr. Schlatt (director of Schlatt-Books) for his endless and friendly support to the "Karate Masters" series; Shorin Ryu stylist and writer Jerry Figgiani, who provided additional material to be included in this book; Raphael Levy for his kindness supplying excellent photographic artwork; Okinawa karate great and master calligrapher Tetsuhiro Hokama; Harold E. Sharp, a true legend in the world of martial arts and who kindly supplied great photos from his personal archives; and Oleg Larionov of Moscow, Russia… your amazing talent and heart as karate-ka is only surpassed by your kindness as a friend.

I would foremost like to give my most heartfelt gratitude to all the masters appearing in this book. Not only did they generously give me an enormous amount of personal time for the long interviews, but they also provided me with great pictures to illustrate the work.

And last but not least, to all my instructors, past and present, for giving me the understanding and knowledge to undertake all the Karate projects I've done during my life. My understanding of the art has grown over the years, thanks, in great part, to the questions they made me ask myself. These questions - both perceptive and practical - have sent me further and deeper in search for answers.

—Jose M. Fraguas

# About the Author

Born and raised in Madrid, Spain, Jose "Chema" Fraguas began his martial arts studies with judo, in grade school, at age 9. From there he moved to taekwondo and then to kenpo karate, earning black belts in both styles. During this same period, he also studied shito-ryu karate under Japanese Masters Masahiro Okada and Yashunari Ishimi and eventually received the *Shihan* title from Soke K. Mabuni. He began his career as a writer at age 16 as a regular contributor to martial arts magazines in Great Britain, France, Spain, Italy, Germany, Portugal, Holland and Australia. Having black belts in three different styles allowed him to better reflect the physical side of the martial arts in his writing: "Feeling before writing," Fraguas says.

In 1980, he moved to Los Angeles, California, where his open-minded mentality helped him to develop a realistic approach to the martial arts. Seeking to supplement his previous training, he researched other disciplines such as jiu-jitsu, escrima and muay Thai.

In 1986, Fraguas founded his own publishing company in Europe, authoring dozens of books and distributing his magazines to 35 countries in three different languages. His reputation and credibility as a martial artist and publisher became well known to the top masters around the world. Considering himself a martial artist first and a writer and publisher second, Fraguas feels fortunate to have had the opportunity to interview many legendary martial artists. He recognizes that much of the information given in the interviews helped him to discover new dimensions in the martial arts. "I was constantly absorbing knowledge from the great masters," he recalls. "I only trained with a few of them, but intellectually and spiritually all of them have made very important contributions to my growth as a complete martial artist."

However, there were some drawbacks to his position as a publisher, Fraguas acknowledges, that directly affected his personal martial arts development. "Of course, some people taught me because of my position as a publisher and not because who I was as a person. Even though I recognize that, I'm still grateful for the knowledge they shared with me."

Steeped in tradition yet looking to the future, Fraguas understands and appreciates martial arts history and philosophy and feels this rich heritage is a necessary steppingstone to personal growth and spiritual evolution. His desire to promote both ancient philosophy and modern thinking provided the motivation for writing this book. "If the motivation is just money, a book cannot be of good quality," Fraguas says. "If the book is written to just make people happy, it cannot be deep. I want to write books so I can learn as well as teach. Karate-do, like human life itself, is filled with experiences that seem quite ordinary at the time and assume a fabled stature only with the passage of the years. I hope this work will be appreciated by future practitioners of the art of the empty-hand."

"Regardless of what level the practitioners find themselves in, there really is only one teacher: experience itself. The true karate-ka follows one abiding principle: to pay attention to what is happening in one's immediate experience. And, this is something that cannot be expressed in words. Words and science are one part of the complete process of understanding the art of Karate, but neither one of them can replace what can be discovered by personal physical experience. Only physical experience can fully transmit the true essence of Karate-do from one generation to another.

As the famous Japanese writer Yukio Mishima, practitioner of Martial Arts, personal friend of Karate master, Masatoshi Nakayama and fifth dan in the art of kendo said: "Words are a medium that reduces reality to abstraction for transmission to our reason. In their power, they corrode reality. Inevitably, danger lurks that the words themselves will be corroded, too."

Originally from Madrid, Spain, he is currently living in Los Angeles, California.

# Introduction

Some of my best days were spent interviewing and meeting the masters in this book. There is little I enjoy more than reading a great interview while time slows and sometimes even seems to stop. Having the opportunity to meet and interview the most prestigious martial artists of the past four decades is something that every martial artist doesn't have the chance to do. Hopefully, in some small way, this will help make up for that.

Meeting the masters and having long conversations with them allowed me to do more than simply scratch the surface of the technical aspects of their respective styles; it also allowed me to understand the human beings behind the teachers. Some of the dialogues and interviews began by simply commenting about the superficial techniques of fighting, and ended up turning into a spiritual conversation about the philosophical aspects of the martial arts. Although these masters are all very different, they share a common thread of traditional values such as discipline, respect, positive attitude, dedication and etiquette.

For more than 35 years I've interviewed these martial arts masters, one-on-one, face-to-face, with no place to run if I asked a stupid question. Many times it was a real challenge to not just talk to them, but to make the questions interesting enough to bring out their deepest knowledge. I tried to absorb as much knowledge as I could, ranging from their training methods, to their fighting methods, to their philosophies about life itself. Their different cultural backgrounds never prevented them from analyzing, researching or modifying anything they considered important. They always kept their minds open to improving their arts and themselves. From a formal philosophical point of view, many of them followed classical philosophies and religions—but they all tempered that with vast amounts of common sense.

They devoted themselves to their arts, often in solitude, to the exclusion of other "normal" pursuits. They worked themselves into extraordinary physical condition. They ignored distractions and diversions and concentrated on their mental and physical training. They got as good as they could possibly get at performing and teaching their chosen art while the rest of us watched them, leading our "balanced lives," and wondering how good we might have gotten at something had we devoted ourselves to it as ferociously as these masters embraced their arts. In that respect, they bear our dreams.

If you read carefully between the lines, you'll see that none of these men were trying to become a fighting machine, or create the most devastating martial arts system known to man. They focused, rather, on how to use martial arts to become a better person. There are many principles that once discovered open a wide spectrum of possibilities, not only to martial arts, but to a better existence as individuals.

The interviews often lasted as long as three or four hours. I would begin at their school and finish the conversation at a restaurant or coffee shop. Much of this information had never been published before and some had to be trimmed either at the master's request or edited to avoid misunderstandings. It is not the questions that make an interview. An interview is either good or bad depending on the answers. Considering the masters in this book, I had an easy job. My goal was to make them comfortable talking about life and training—especially those who trained under the founders of original systems. In modern times, there are not many who have had the privilege of living and learning under these legendary founders.

"The masters are gone," many like to say. But as long as we keep their teachings in our heart, they will live forever. To understand martial arts properly, it is necessary to take into account their philosophical methods as well as their physical techniques. There is a deep distinction between a fighting system and a martial arts. Unfortunately, the roots of the martial arts have been de-emphasized, neglected or totally abandoned today. Martial arts are not a sport. Someone who chooses to devote himself to a sport such as basketball, tennis, soccer or football—which is based on youth, strength, and speed—chooses to die twice. When you can no longer do that sport, due to the lack of their required attributes, waking up in the morning without the activity that has been the center of your life for 25 years is troubling and unsettling. In contrast, the martial arts can and should be practiced for life—they never leave you.

A true martial artist is like a musician, painter, writer or actor—their art is an expression of themselves. The need to discover who they are becomes the reason for an endless search for the perfect technique, great melody, inspiring poetry, amazing painting or Academy Award performance. It is this motivation to reach that impossible dream that allows a simple individual to become an exceptional artist and master of his craft.

Many of the greatest teachers share a commonly misunderstood teaching methodology. They know the words they could use to teach their students have little or no meaning. They know that to try "self-discovery" in quantitative or empirical terms is a useless task. A great deal of knowledge and wisdom comes from oral traditions, which martial arts, like every other cultural expression, has. These oral traditions have always been reserved for a certain kind of student and considered "secrets," given only to a special few who have the minds and attitudes to fully grasp them.

Alexandra David-Neel wrote: "It is not on the master that the secret depends but on the hearer. Truth learned from others is of no value, the only truth which is effective and of value is self-discovered ... the teacher can only guide to the point of discovery." In the end, "the only secret is that there is no secret." As Kato Tokuro, arguably the finest potter of the last century, a great art scholar, and the teacher of Pablo Picasso said: "The sole cause of secrets in craftsmanship is the student's inability to learn."

To find out what karate-do means to you, what it does for you, and what it holds for you, is a deeply personal process. Each path is different and we all have to find a personal rhythm that fit us individually, according to what surround us.

As human beings, we are always tempted to follow linear logic towards ultimate self-improvement—but the truth is that there are no absolute truths. You have to find your own way in life whether it be in martial arts, business or cherry picking. Whatever path you pursue, you have to distill the personal truths that are right for you, according to your own nature. The quest for perfection is very imperfect, and not in tune with human nature or experience. To have any hope of attaining even a single perfection, you have to concentrate on a single pursuit and direct all your energy towards it. In this sense, perfection comes from appreciating endeavors for their own sake—not to impress anyone—but for your own inner satisfaction and sense of accomplishment.

It is important to have a feeling of responsibility; and putting yourself into an art as genuinely as you can, without any sense that you are going to get something back in return, reverberates throughout time and space. We need to honor those who came before us, as well as nurture those who will come after, so the art can grow and expand—you've got to send the elevator back down.

Martial arts are a large part of my life and I draw inspiration from them. I really don't know the "how" or the "why" of their effect on me, but I feel their influence in even my most mundane activities. All human beings have sources or principles that keep them grounded, and martial arts are mine. That is when the term "way of life" becomes real. In bushido, the self-discipline required to pursue mastery is more important than mastery itself—the struggle is more important than the reward. A common thread throughout the lives of all the masters is their constant struggle towards self-mastery. They realized that life is an ongoing process, and once you achieve all your goals you are as good as dead. But this process is not all driven by action. Often the greatest action is inaction, and the hardest voice to hear is the sound of your own thoughts. You need to sit alone and collect yourself, free from technology and distraction, and just think. This is perhaps the only way to achieve mental and spiritual clarity.

I don't believe that books are meant to be read fast. I've always thought that writing is timeless and that reading is not a detraction. So take your time. Approach this book with the Zen "beginner's mind" and "empty cup" mentality and soak up the words of these great teachers. They will help you to not only grow as a martial artist but as a human being as well. O

# Gichin Funakoshi

## WORDS FROM THE MASTER

"It is important that karate can be practiced by the young and old, men and women alike. That is, since there is no need for a special training place, equipment, or an opponent, a flexibility in training is provided such that the physically and spiritually weak individual can develop his body and mind so gradually and naturally that he himself may not even realize his own great progress."

"To practice kata is not to memorize an order. You must find the kata that work for you, understand them, digest them and stick with them for life."

"Karate-Do strives internally to train the mind to develop a clear conscience, enabling one to face the world honestly, while externally developing strength to the point where one may overcome even ferocious wild animals. Mind and technique become one in true karate."

"You may train for a long time, but if you merely move your hands and feet and jump up and down like a puppet, learning Karate is not very different from learning a dance. You will never have reached the heart of the matter; you will have failed to grasp the quintessence of karate-do."

"When you look at life think in terms of karate. But remember that karate is not only karate — it is life."

"When two tigers fight, one is certain to be maimed, and one to die."

# Karate Masters

"To search for the old is to understand the new. The old, the new, this is a matter of time. In all things man must have a clear mind. The Way: Who will pass it on straight and well?"

ดั๊ก ดั๊ก ดั๊ก ดั๊ก ดั๊ก

"You may train for a long time, but if you merely move your hands and feet and jump up and down like a puppet, learning karate is not very different from learning a dance. You will never have reached the heart of the matter; you will have failed to grasp the quintessence of karate-do."

ดั๊ก ดั๊ก ดั๊ก ดั๊ก ดั๊ก

"No matter how you may excel in the art of Karate, and in your scholastic endeavors, nothing is more important than your behavior and your humanity as observed in daily life."

ดั๊ก ดั๊ก ดั๊ก ดั๊ก ดั๊ก

"Just as it is the clear mirror that reflects without distortion, or the quiet valley that echoes a sound, so must one who would study Karate-Do purge himself of selfish and evil thoughts, for only with a clear mind and conscience can he understand that which he receives."

ดั๊ก ดั๊ก ดั๊ก ดั๊ก ดั๊ก

"There is no place in contemporary Karate-do for different schools. Some instructors, I know, claim to have invented new and unusual kata, and so they arrogate to themselves the right to be called founders of "schools". Indeed, I have heard myself and my colleagues referred to as the Shoto-kan school, but I strongly object to this attempt at classification. My belief is that all these "schools" should be amalgamated into one so that Karate-do may pursue and orderly and useful progress into man's future."

ดั๊ก ดั๊ก ดั๊ก ดั๊ก ดั๊ก

"Try to do exactly as you are taught without complaining or quibbling."

ดั๊ก ดั๊ก ดั๊ก ดั๊ก ดั๊ก

# Funakoshi

"He who would study Karate-Do must always strive to be inwardly humble and outwardly gentle. However, once he has decided to stand up for the cause of justice, then he must have the courage expressed in the saying, "Even if it must be ten million foes, I go!" Thus, he is like the green bamboo stalk: hollow (kara) inside, straight, and with knots, that is, unselfish, gentle, and moderate."

"True Karate-do is this: that in daily life, one's mind and body be trained and developed in a spirit of humility; and that in critical times, one be devoted utterly to the cause of justice."

"There are many kinds of martial arts, ...at a fundamental level these arts rest on the same basis. It is no exaggeration to say that the original sense of Karate-Do is at one with the basis of all martial arts. Form is emptiness, emptiness is form itself. The kara of Karate-Do means this."

"The correct understanding of Karate and its proper use is Karate-do. One who truly trains in this do [way] and actually understands Karate-do is never easily drawn into a fight."

"To practice kata is not to memorize an order. You must find the kata that work for you, understand them, digest them and stick with them for life."

"Students of any art, including Karate-do must never forget the cultivation of the mind and the body."

"To win one hundred victories in one hundred battles is not the highest skill. To subdue the enemy with out fighting is the highest skill."

"The ultimate aim of the art of karate lies not in victory or defeat, but in the perfection of the characters of its participants."

# Contents

**1** Nick Adler — THE LONG WAY HOME

**13** Richard Amos — SCRATCHING THE SURFACE

**29** Tony Annesi — AN INNOVATIVE TRADITIONALIST

**43** Michael Berger — AN UNLIKELY JOURNEY

**65** Joe Carbonara — I NEVER WON A TROPHY

**71** Hiroyasu Fujishima — THE ROAD AHEAD

**81** Kenneth Funakoshi — TOUCHING BUDO

**99** Paul Godshaw — UNPARALLELED EXPERIENCE

**107** Tatsuo Hirano — THE HEALING ENERGY

**125** Art Ishii — PRESERVING BUDO

**139** George E. Mattson — A LIVING LEGEND

**161** Sam Moledzki — NOT AN ORDINARY MAN

**179** Kunio Murayama — A SOULFUL JOURNEY

| | | |
|---|---|---|
| **187** Taku Nakasaka | **195** Shoji Nishimura | **205** Hiroyoshi Okazaki |
| THE POWER OF KYOKUSHIN | EXCELLENCE IN ACTION | DELIVERING VALUES |
| **211** Richard Rabago | **221** Ted Rabino | **235** Avi Rokah |
| A HIGHER STANDARD | IN THE SPIRIT OF SHITO KAI | IN THE NAME OF THE MASTER |
| **249** Les Safar | **259** Del Saito | **283** Frank Smith |
| A WEALTH OF KNOWLEDGE | A JOURNEY OF WISDOM | A HEART FULL OF FIRE |

| | | | |
|---|---|---|---|
| **299** Gene Tibon | **313** Takeshi Uchiage | **321** Yutaka Yaguchi | **329** Koss Yokota |
| STILL WATERS RUN DEEP | UNVEILING THE MASTER | A CUT ABOVE | CARRYING THE TORCH |

# NICK ADLER

## THE LONG WAY HOME

HANSHI NICK ADLER BEGAN HIS MARTIAL ARTS TRAINING IN 1956, RECEIVING RANK IN JUDO AND JUJITSU AS WELL AS OKINAWAN ISSHINRYU KARATE. HE RECEIVED HIS 9TH DAN FROM BOTH GRANDMASTER DON NAGLE AND GRANDMASTER ANGI UEZU. HE IS THE DIRECTOR OF NICK ADLER'S CENTURIONS, A MULTI-SCHOOL ASSOCIATION WITH BRANCHES THROUGHOUT THE COUNTRY. SHIHAN ADLER IS AN INTERNATIONALLY LICENSED INSTRUCTOR AND GRADUATE OF THE LONG ISLAND UNIVERSITY INSTRUCTOR CERTIFICATION PROGRAM, AND SUBSEQUENTLY TAUGHT A CLASS AS ADJUNCT PROFESSOR. HE HOLDS MENKYO KAI FROM MASTER UEZU, WHICH IS THE HIGHEST LICENSE AN INSTRUCTOR CAN AWARD. HANSHI ADLER IS THE RECIPIENT OF MANY AWARDS AND COMMENDATIONS OVER THE YEARS AND RECOGNIZED AS AN AUTHORITY IN HIS FIELD. USED TO TAKING THE LESS TRAVELED ROAD IN EVERYTHING HE PURSUED IN LIFE, HANSHI ADLER FINDS TEACHING THE TRUE ART OF HIS PLEASANT AND LONG JOURNEY BACK HOME…TO OKINAWA, THE LAND OF KARATE.

**How long have you been practicing the martial arts?**

I started in Judo in 1956, but really started in 1962 with Isshinryu Karate. I began training with a gentleman named Ed McGrath, but mainly with his student Mel Sutphen. I earned my Shodan with both of them. However, both stopped teaching for a variety of reasons, so in 1966 I began training with Don Nagle. I also began my training with Angi Uezu the same year.

**How many styles of karate or other Martial Arts methods have you trained in?**

I trained in many styles: kung fu, jiujitsu, Shotokan, Shorin ryu, Goju ryu, Thai Boxing, Filipino arts, etc. I have had the fortune to train with many different teachers throughout the years. I am basically an Isshinryu stylist; my main teachers in Isshinryu Karate were Don Nagle, until his passing in 1999, and Uezu Sensei. These are the two people I trained with on a regular basis. With Uezu Sensei, I trained every time he was in the United States, which was every year, and on my trips to Okinawa to train, I trained with him as well. With Nagle Sensei, I would take the two-hour drive each

# Karate Masters

"Even though we were from different styles, we used to take techniques from one another or training methods."

way on Saturdays, even though I had my own school, so that I could train with him whenever he was available. He was an undercover narcotics police officer so he basically kept a low profile.

**Who were your teachers and what were their specific characteristics as instructors?**

There were many other people I trained with throughout the years on a pretty consistent basis when I had the opportunity. The list is long but I shall try to name some to give you an idea of the cross training and different concepts. These Sensei include: Osamu Ozawa, Hirokazu Kanazawa, Fumio Demura, Joe Lewis, Bill Wallace, Nakazato, Oyata, Chuck Merriman, Bob Taiani, Patrick McCarthy, and many others. It is very difficult to name them all, but the characteristics of all these gentlemen are their consistency to strive to always get better and better at what they were doing, whether it was as a practitioner or as a teacher or lecturer. It is something I strive for in myself as well.

**Would you tell us some interesting stories of your early days in karate?**

Well, in the early 60s and 70s, traveling across the country and competing in tournaments was different. A whole bunch of people would pile in a car, and if you won any kind of trophies, there was no place to put them. We fought in some of the filthiest places you could imagine. I remember going to places where we had to pick up the debris and glass from parties held the night before. It has changed a good deal today. In the early days of competition there was real camaraderie. Even though we were from different styles, we used to take techniques from one another or training methods. At that time we did not wear much protective gear; my Sensei thought if you wore a groin protector, you were a sissy. Today we gear up as much as we can, which I think is a better idea for the students.

There are many stories; most of them are not printable. There are two stories that stand out in my mind, though. One was when I was judging at the Battle of Atlanta in the Black Belt division and one competitor got up and said, my name is "Jesus Christ," and told what form he was about to do. The judges all looked at one another and Bobby Yarnell said: "I don't know if this is really him but if we give him a bad mark, we're in trouble." Fortunately he was a top-notch competitor and I believe he shortened his name at a later date to "JC." Another time, with Grandmaster Trias on the judging board, a person got up to say he was going to do a "Surprise" kata. He preformed his kata and at the end he pulled out a gun and fired six rounds of blanks. The judges got up and ran behind Sensei Trias. Robert Trias was shocked and said: "You guys are supposed to be here to protect me!" I thought that was really funny.

**In karate, what does kata really represent, and how important is it?**

Kata is very very important, especially to carry on the lineage of your system. Most people don't realize how much there is in kata. In kata you have throws, breaks, traps, all the different things that styles break off into, like ju jitsu does this, kung fu does that. Kata, if you use it correctly, has all your self-defense and applications in it. It teaches you to use your left and right side. It is not basically to go into a sparring match; it is basically used for self-defense and to carry on the movements that the particular person who invented that kata thought were the best essentially for him or her. This will depend on when they learned the kata and who they learned it from. Katas have been changed through the years, depending on how old the instructor was that you studied with. Certain attributes that one had when he was young, he did not have when he was an old man, so there may be a few changes in the movements, but the basic concepts should always be there. Especially for the older generation, kata is very important. If you cannot wrestle on the ground when you are 40, 50, or 60 years of age, are you saying there is nothing else for us to do? I believe kata is very important.

**How has your personal expression of karate changed and developed over the years?**

Basically, when you first start out in the martial arts, you are really young. We had no children in our classes way back then and you did everything on your fighting aspects. You basically were a real fighter; your katas were so/so, your weapons were so/so; but as you got older and more experienced, you found out how important these elements were, and then you got involved with them a lot more than just fighting. When you are training in other styles and with other instructors, you find out all the applications that can be in your katas and your weaponry. So, you go back and do your own research and really start to develop your own personal aspects and ways of doing things. I had to work at everything I learned. There was nothing natural about it to me. I really was a guy who came off the streets of Brooklyn, and we never paid attention to what stances we were in or how you blocked, and so on. Karate changed that and I always had to work very had, but I always felt the accomplishment every time I got better at what I was trying to work on. I learned from Nagle Sensei, who used to take a move and work on it for two or three hours until he felt comfortable with it. Since we are basically the same age, except he was 126 pounds and I was 180 – it was a little different – we were never going to look the same.

**What are the most important points in your teaching methods? And what are the most important qualities for a student to become proficient in the karate style?**

The important points in teaching methods are basically to get what you are teaching over to your students, to make it understandable, verbally and practically. As teachers, we are teaching many different levels; we are going from a beginner class to a little ninja class, advanced junior class, and so on, so the teaching methods are changing constantly. The most important quality of a student is to have that "yes, I can attitude," never give up, and always try to do the best he/she can. One of the codes in our school that we give is: "I will develop myself in a positive manner and avoid anything that would reduce my mental growth or my physical health." This sounds very simple but it is very, very hard to do. We get a lot of people who may be natural athletes, but they are not used to working hard at what they do. Once they start and they can't do it, they usually give it up. The guys who come in and trip and fall but keeps picking themselves up, those are the people that you like to have because they stay with it forever.

**With all the technical changes during the last years, do you think there still are 'pure' styles of karate?**

I never think that there is a pure style of any system. All styles of karate have changed through the years. Here again, everybody is going to put a personal touch into the system he/she is doing. But, basically your A, B, Cs – your kihon – still should be the same. Again, what age was your instructor when he was studying? What rank was he? What was his experience? A lot of times, people learn something and then go on to a different style of training and begin to put their own perspective into what they begin to teach.

**Do you think different 'styles' are truly important in the art of karate?**

It usually depends on the style you are studying, if it fits you as a person. If you are a 100-pound person, you are not going to be studying a hard style of karate because you are not built for it. If you are a 200-pound person, certain styles will fit you. I think you have to go out and see which style fits your personality, build, and athleticism.

Every culture has its own fighting arts; it also depends on which country or what the atmosphere is. If I am training in a jungle, desert, or an urban atmosphere, things change. Things that work in the city may not work in the desert; things in the desert may not work in the jungle. It's like having a Ferrari; it works really well on a highway, but if I take it off road, it doesn't do too well. Everything has its purpose; that is why arts constantly change.

"There really is nothing new in Mixed Martial Arts. It goes all the way back to the Greeks, and they had what we are calling Mixed Martial Arts now."

**What is your opinion of fighting events, such as the UFC and Mixed Martial Arts events?**

I think there are some very talented people in Mixed Martial Arts. It's for certain types of people. It's like wrestling. In school, it usually is the smallest team because these guys work out really hard and are susceptible to a lot of injuries. Unfortunately, there is really not a lot of money to compensate these guys for what they put their bodies through. There really is nothing new in Mixed Martial Arts. It goes all the way back to the Greeks, and they had what we are calling Mixed Martial Arts now. They wouldn't allow it in the Olympics way back then because they would not allow eye gouging and biting – and you still can't eye gouge or bite in this MMA, either.

**Karate nowadays often is referred to as a sport. Do you agree with this definition or is a martial art?**

Well, the sporting aspect is in the martial arts. No matter what we do, to get young people involved, they like a sport. It is like Wushu; is it a martial art or is it a sport? Most of it is sport oriented, even though there are martial arts applications within it. For the younger people who compete in the sport aspect of the martial arts, yes, it is a sport, and we refer to them as athletes and they train very hard on scoring different types of points. But you also have to remember, here again, rules were set to take out the techniques that would really maim or kill somebody. There is the sport, but for people who do not want to compete, we train in our school on the self-defense aspect.

**Do you feel that you still have further to go in your studies?**
I believe you never stop learning and developing new ways of teaching what you are teaching. You can learn something from a person who just started out or a student who just walked in the door. All of a sudden you say, "I never thought of that," and it also keeps you involved, young at heart, and young in mind.

**How do you see Okinawan karate in the world at the present time?**
Okinawa is a funny place. They were never really interested in the sport aspect and they basically taught on an individual basis in most cases. They tried to organize. I believe the Japanese had a big influence on that for the pre-world championships. I co-hosted them in New York in 1990 when the Okinawan masters came over to represent their styles and promote the event.

**Do you think it helps the karate student physically to train with weapons?**
Yes, I believe it's very important if you train with a "weapon." Unfortunately, most people today train with weapons that are not real; they train with ones that are not the right weight. The use of correct weapons develops their whole body, their flexibility, strength, and many things that are beneficial from a Kobudo standpoint. It also helps you out in your fighting. When you train doing weapon drills, if you get punched in the chest, it is one thing; if you get whacked in the hand, it is another thing. It teaches you how to move, it teaches footwork, which is very important as far as defending yourself.

**How does the karate style differ from other martial arts methods when applying the techniques in a self-defense situation?**
The question is "how does karate compare with other martial arts." You can only kick, punch, grab, throw, break in so many different ways, no matter what you call it. Karate has all the arts in it. Here again, depending upon the knowledge of the instructor who is teaching it and how he senses

that the other people who are studying it want to get involved in it as well. I think the arts were broken up into different aspects of what this person did particularly well. I have never seen an instructor get up and teach a seminar on what he couldn't do.

**When teaching the art of karate, what is the most important element – self-defense or sport?**

I teach both. I teach many different age groups and I teach them all. I teach the art of karate as far as the self-defense element, and I also teach the art of sport. My people compete in all aspects: kata, kumite, weapons, and self-defense. Each aspect balances one another. Teaching basic self-defense is important, here again, depending on the age group. Sport always keeps you in great shape working your timing, distance, and so forth. You want to teach self-defense on a basic application of what a person normally is going to run into. I am not teaching self-defense to a person who is going to go over and fight in a war or doing bodyguard service. All these things are separate departments, even though I can teach all of them. Overall, I teach a basic concept of self-defense that comes out of the katas, and I also teach sport.

**Forms and sparring – what's the proper ratio in training?**

Forms are very, very important, as well as sparring. I think both work hand in hand. Depending on the katas that you know, you learn your angles, and weight distribution in stances; you learn timing and different types of technique. Kata teaches you balance. Whether you compete in kata or sparring, you need to have mobility, agility, accuracy and balance. You can't do any of this without balance – physical and mental. Now, when you get into sport karate, there are techniques that are different than your forms, so I think you have to have a good balance of both. But, you always have to have that strong foundation. Remember, when they first started out, they used to start teaching forms. But, you need sparring, which is basically going to teach you your reaction time, your speed, and your distance from your opponent. If you're training and competing as a fighter, you are going to have to spend more time sparring, the same as if you are competing in forms and weapons; then you spend more time in those areas.

**Do you have any general advice you would care to pass on the practitioners in general?**

Don't be closed minded; go out and look at different styles, different type of people who teach it. Does the person who is going to be teaching you have the personality and attributes that you are looking for? For a young

# Karate Masters

"Whatever you do, have your whole "Mind, Body, and Spirit" into what you are doing. Also, there was more discipline in the old days."

person whose parents are involved, they also have to see how that person is teaching on the floor. Are they teaching the qualities not only in the martial arts but as a person in general. If you are an older person, you also have to see if the instructor recognizes that if you are not 20 years old and you are 40 or 50 and older. Is there a place in that dojo for you that will meet your requirements?

**What do you consider to be the major changes in the art since you began training?**

The instructors are more qualified today working with the anatomy, working with people's problems; there are new and better training methods. These methods are better for you as a whole for your body than the old methods, many of which were really detrimental to your health.

I believe in a balance of Mind, Body, and Spirit. Isshinryu means "One Heart Way," which means, whatever you do, do it with all your heart, whether it is teaching karate, studying karate, or studying music. Whatever you do, have your whole "Mind, Body, and Spirit" into what you are doing. Also, there was more discipline in the old days. But most of us were military guys, used to taking orders. Also, there weren't as many young people as there are today.

**Who would you like to have trained with that you have not?**

I think I've been pretty fortunate to have trained with so many different people, in so many different arts that I really can't think of someone offhand. If there would be somebody alive or dead I would like to have spent more time with, it would be my Sensei, Don Nagle, who unfortunately passed on.

**What keeps you motivated after all these years?**

What really motivates me are my students. I have been very fortunate. The people who have achieved black belt level have always gone on to become very successful in whatever endeavor they tried, whether it be teaching, finance, or as martial artists. Just seeing their accomplishments, and have them to come back and say thank you, keeps me going.

**Do you have a particularly memorable karate experience that has remained as an inspiration for your training?**

Well, my most memorable experience is when Uezu Sensei had his stroke and two years later he came back to the United States. He couldn't do any of the things that he could do before very well. He got up and he stumbled and he fell, and he picked himself up and he never stopped trying. I stood there with tears in my eyes. But what he was showing was it does not matter where you are, you do what you can the best way you can, and never

"If you do something with all your heart, how can you go wrong?"

give up. In karate, everything goes back to mind, body, and spirit. It also goes back to all the people you have influenced and set an example for through the years that you have seen gone on to bigger and better things. Whether it is physically, mentally, or financially, everybody has made an improvement. It shows how practicing the discipline you need for karate affects your life.

We should always remember that the most important qualities for a karate-ka or a martial artist, regardless of style, are perseverance, dedication, self-discipline, and never giving up, always continuing to strive and to learn more, to be better at what they do. One of the things you learn, as you get better, you can help other people get better, and now you realize how all of a sudden you can become a mentor to others.

**How do you think a practitioner can increase his understanding of the spiritual aspect of the art?**

It's pretty easy with Isshinryu because everything you do, you do with all your heart. If you do something with all your heart, how can you go wrong? When you are working your katas, you start out very raw, very

# Karate Masters

"As you perfect your form, the better you flow, the more you can visualize, the better your kata becomes."

mechanical, thinking of your right foot, your left foot, how you stand, how you punch and kick, and so forth and so on. As you perfect your form, the better you flow, the more you can visualize, the better your kata becomes. And with this better understanding, you become one with what you are doing—not only in kata but also in life itself.

**What advice would you give to students on the question of supplementary training?**

I believe one of the best things to supplement your training is Pilates. Now they even do it with machines. It works the whole core, the whole flexibility and suppleness of the body. You can't really hurt yourself with this type of exercise, and I think you get a lot from it.

**Why is it, in your opinion, that a lot of students start falling away after few years of training?**

Primarily because the teacher does not know how to teach, he/she does not know how to keep that person motivated. Everybody wants to feel good about him/herself, so if that teacher continued to make the students feel good about themselves and they continued to improve, the teacher would not have that problem.

**Have there been times when you felt fear in your training?**

I felt fear many times, especially when I first started out in the martial arts. My Sensei, Don Nagle, was just a fierce fighter and if he didn't hurt you, he thought there was something wrong. But I think fear is a good tool; I think you have to have it at the beginning. You also have to pay more attention; when you are afraid of something you really begin to focus on it. We used to have inter-clubs way back then that were worse than tournaments. We used to go to Peter Urban's school, Pete Siringano's school, George Cofield, people of that nature. We had to represent our school, and if you lost you had to go back to face your sensei. Things have changed today—I believe for the better.

*"Karate is more than punch, kick, sport, or self-defense, and as people discover themselves through its practice, others will follow."*

**Do you think that Olympics will be positive for the art of karate-do in case that happens one day?**

I think it would be good in some ways and bad in other ways. See what happened to Judo once it became an Olympic sport; the quality of the art really went down because everybody is looking for points and for scores, and the art starts to get watered down while everybody is looking for points that are really not points.

**What are your thoughts on the future of karate?**

The future for all martial arts is very bright. Today we have really good books and good DVDs on the market. Students are able to cross-train and are exposed to some really quality people who they might not have been able to meet because of travel costs. I think this makes the martial arts continue to grow by leaps and bounds. Karate is more than punch, kick, sport, or self-defense, and as people discover themselves through its practice, others will follow. It's no wonder educators and psychologists are sending their children to us. Karate is discipline—it can help all. O

# RICHARD AMOS

## SCRATCHING THE SURFACE

Born in England in 1963, Richard Amos began karate at age 10. By the age of 23, he had competed in England and Europe, gaining numerous championships. After a two-year sojourn in New York, he went to Japan to train at the headquarters of the Japan Karate Association and stayed for 10 years. During that time, he completed the three-year instructor's program of the JKA, placed second or third in the All-Japan Championships several times, taught many classes each week over a six-year period in the headquarters of the JKA, and opened his own school in the heart of Tokyo.

In 2000, Sensei Amos moved to New York again, this time as an established professional karate instructor with an international reputation. He currently is the chief instructor of the World Traditional Karate Organization, heading its instructor program, and teaches everyday at the headquarters dojo in Manhattan. When asked about giving advice, he simply smiled and said: "Be willing to chip away over the years and, once in a while, when you approach a familiar technique, see it as a beginner and ask yourself if you really are applying all that you know into this one movement. After all, we're all just scratching the surface."

**How long have you been practicing the martial arts?**

I started in 1973 in Essex, England, with Charles Naylor and his wife Dot. Charles was one of Enoeda sensei's closest colleagues and students and the secretary of the Karate Union of Great Britain (KUGB).

I have only dabbled in aikido and iai-do, and attended some seminars of Goju-ryu and Shito-ryu. I did judo for five or six years in the early 70s at around the same time I started karate, but found that karate suited me more. Anytime I try something else, however, it's in order relate it to the deepening of my understanding of movement, and how I might apply that into my Shotokan.

# Karate Masters

"I wasn't a natural by any stretch of the imagination, and had a stiff, gangly body as a teenager."

### Who were your teachers?

As I mentioned, my first teacher was Dot Naylor and her husband Charles. They were great with kids: tough Liverpudlians who took no nonsense and developed a bunch of top junior competitors in England during the 70s and 80s. Growing up, I was exposed more and more to Enoeda sensei as well. He was a regular visitor to our dojo and a close friend of the Naylors. I was in awe of him. I think most people were in his presence.

I was on the KUGB team for some time and Andy Sherry sensei was the coach. Prior to getting on the team, I occasionally would take my school holidays and go up to Liverpool to train with him for a week. Those were wonderful chances to train under both Andy Sherry and Frank Brennan. No one else came in the morning sessions, except maybe one of the Poynton brothers. It was an extraordinary experience as they were, aside from Enoeda sensei, the most influential Shotokan karate-ka in the UK at the time. Sherry sensei was a relentless slogger and Brennan sensei was simply the most talented and powerful karate-ka I'd ever seen.

Later on in my teens, I began staying at Crystal Palace, where Enoeda sensei had his spring and summer camps. I found myself always wanting to emulate the various Japanese sensei and the naturalness with which they moved. Enoeda sensei was certainly a huge influence, but visiting instructors such as Yahara and Tanaka were very inspiring too—Yahara for his dynamic movement and presence, Tanaka for the spectacular things he could do with his body.

I wasn't a natural by any stretch of the imagination, and had a stiff, gangly body as a teenager. But I was inspired easily and frequently by stories of those who worked hard or who overcame adversity. I remember being 12 or 13 years old and one of the other kids in the class asking me why on earth I worked so hard. I've never forgotten that and, in my youthful way, I imagined I was struggling against the odds like the heroes in stories I'd read.

**Would you tell us some interesting stories of your early days in karate and your days in the Honbu dojo of the JKA?**

In my youth, I suppose some of the most interesting times were going to Liverpool as a skinny kid of 16 in the late 70s and lining up in front of the toughest guys in England, who were champions (and nightclub bouncers in their spare time), and believing it was completely normal. Retrospectively, I'm surprised I didn't get badly injured, but it certainly prepared me for what was to come later, and I dug into those experiences many times in Japan. I'd be standing there in the Red Triangle dojo with my back to the wall and all these guys were lined up in front of me, ready to attack with anything, in quick succession: daunting Joe Farley glared at me as I sidestepped his massive sweep; Frank Brennan feinted mawashi-geri, only to crack me with an ura-mawashi-geri, which was marginally less painful than the wall hitting the back of my head on the recoil; then Jimmy Poynton finished me off with ushiro-geri at the same moment I kicked mawashi-geri. He managed to hit me squarely in the groin; I was allowed to take a break after that.

Later on, in the Tokyo Honbu of the JKA in 1989 (when no one knew what was to happen in a year or so regarding the political mess), I was probably happier than at any other period of my karate life. I certainly had a sense of fulfilling my destiny (I was young and had dreams). There I was with no other responsibility but to train and get better. This was before I became an instructor trainee, when I would join every class, doing little else but sleeping and eating in between. The great thing back then was that I was under no obligation to do anything else.

**How was the training at that time at the JKA?**

To be honest, it wasn't particularly hard, and the classes were only an hour long. The variety of instruction stood out, however, as it was exceptionally broad. The instructors all tended to do their specialties, so some classes were only gyaku-zuki, or only mae-geri, or simply jiyu-kumite. I don't think this was very helpful for beginners necessarily, or for those who only trained a couple of times a week, but I was a thirsty sandan then, and drank it all in. I regret not making notes on some of the classes but I was doing so much I assumed I'd just absorb it. I wasn't conscious of it at the time but that's really the Japanese way of learning: a sort of process of osmosis.

I lived in the Hoitsugan dormitory on and off for my first year and a half in Tokyo, but trained in every class in the dojo downstairs from January 1989 till September 1990. We would train Monday to Saturday at 7:30 am, with Kawawada sensei teaching Thursday, Friday, and Saturday. The other days were led by whoever was senior, usually Rene Villedorosa, but sometimes Leon Montoya and, later on, me. Kawawada sensei was a terrific instructor and gave the most fascinating classes, usually translated by Leon, in the Hoits. During that period, when I trained with him several times a week, I had not yet learned Japanese. I wonder sometimes how much got lost in translation, as he was surely the most articulate of instructors. Those who trained only a couple of times a week and needed a workout got frustrated when he taught in the Honbu Dojo, as they got cold and fidgety, but we in the Hoitsugan knew what we had and I loved his classes. Outside of teaching, he seemed a lonely and shy man, and never appeared to get the recognition he deserved. Perhaps he has now, though, although sadly I'm not in touch with him.

Anyway, we'd all have breakfast together after the Hoits session and then head over to the JKA Honbu for the 10:30 am class, considered to be the foreigners' class, presumably because there were so many foreigners in it. I always took that morning class as it was just before the instructor's class and we would get to see all the big names come in and loosen up with jiyu-kumite before their own training, which started at 12. More often than not, a few would come early, at 10:30 am, and train behind us as a warm-up, and in order to keep us on our toes, I suppose. It wasn't unusual to have 10 regular students in that class with Tanaka sensei teaching and Ogura, Kagawa, Kurosako, Aramoto, and Naka using us for target practice just inches behind us.

**You were a foreigner training at the JKA Instructor Training Course, how were you received and how were things at that time for a gaijin?**

I think that as long as you try to conform to a certain degree in a balanced way without losing your identity or pretending to be something you are not, you can't go far wrong. That was my attitude then, but in all honesty, I don't think anyone cared what nationality I was. I suppose I was a bit of a novelty and by and large that went in my favor because non-Japanese were uncommon then and people were mildly intrigued and showed interest. There were instances of course that could have been different or easier if I were Japanese, but you could say the same in any circumstance and blame it on being tall, or fat, or one-legged.

In serious training, petty things such as nationality can last only for a short while, perhaps a few months, and then are forgotten. One is lambasted instead for tension in one's shoulders, or one is hit because one blocked too sloppily. Everyone suffered in the instructor's class.

**Have there been times when you felt fear in your training?**
Anxious and nervous yes, but not really fear. I did used to tell myself that no one actually died in the instructor's class, though, and I recited "Henry V" on the way to the dojo to steel myself.

There was one time in a competition that I'd been knocked unconscious for the only time in my life. Apparently I was out for quite a few minutes. I couldn't remember a thing, but I knew what must have happened and stupidly agreed to carry on. I ended up clumsily winning and, in the next round, for the first time I was afraid of getting hit, aware of how dangerous it would be to get hit hard again.

"In serious training, petty things such as nationality can last only for a short while, perhaps a few months, and then are forgotten."

**Why did you leave Japan and how did you feel at that time?**
Things actually were going very well for me in Japan when I left and, to be honest, the only real reason was fear of complacency and the knowledge that I would eventually no longer be an Englishman and yet would never be a Japanese. I very much wanted to reproduce the life I had in Japan in an English-speaking country. I was tired of not enjoying reading all the media available and of never getting 100 percent of the nuance of conversations in groups as well.

I also was restless as a result of the position I'd found myself in. I had a beautiful dojo in an elegant part of Tokyo but had basically hit the ceiling of what I could realistically achieve in karate over there. I saw it would be more of the same for another 10 years. I'd also grown up somewhat and didn't necessarily want to do the same things at 35 that I'd dreamed of at

# Karate Masters

"The whole process of continuing training in karate for me has to be for it to lead to refinement, simplicity, and naturalness of movement."

25. I'd lost my desire to compete and couldn't really see my senpai evolving or being particularly happy or fulfilled into their 40s and 50s, either. Karate in general, but especially in Japan and as a professional, is so hierarchical that there are no interesting career opportunities at all, beyond merely ticking over, for decades.

**How has your personal expression of karate developed after all these years?**

Sometimes I think I teach a little too much on a daily basis, but I only need to have one day off every now and then and I'm refreshed and ready to go again. So I haven't lost the natural motivation and love that I've always had for the art.

Personally, the whole process of continuing training in karate for me has to be for it to lead to refinement, simplicity, and naturalness of movement. I really love Shotokan for that, because its emphasis and source of movement is the center; this is a principle found in every art that involves movement. I think Shotokan is a terrific tool for exploring this, for distilling things down to pure form.

In order to remain motivated, it is of course important not to stagnate, and so exposing oneself to a variety of other arts, whether they are martial or not, helps. Living in a place like New York, where one is exposed to so great a variety of things, is a constant source of motivation. Whether that's from seeing an awful demonstration of someone else's version of karate in Central Park or seeing the ballet at Lincoln Center, it doesn't matter.

I've also had some great teachers and to incorporate some of their best qualities keeps me hungry and motivated. It's wishful thinking, but I'd like to hope that my karate today is heading toward a combination of Yahara's intensity, Asai sensei's sheer joy and freedom of movement, and Steve Ubl sensei's absolute efficacy.

The purpose of karate training should not be to learn to hit someone; it is to refine the body's movements into a pure, uncluttered form, and this is what I try to emphasize in my classes. For example, I've worked quite hard at getting people to cooperate when doing kumite, which, by the way, does not mean sparring; it literally means "exchanging hands." The trouble, of course, is that moving very powerfully, having the potential to pole-axe someone with a single beautiful technique, is an extremely seductive idea. But we should think of hitting hard as an inevitable by-product of timing something to perfection through composure and getting the body to move harmoniously. I like to teach beginners very much because habits are learned very early on, and getting the student to learn to move rather than make shapes is essential for me.

**Do you think different 'styles' are truly important in the art of karate? And how is JKA Shotokan different from other styles of Karate?**

Different styles are not necessarily important, but they are inevitable, and we shouldn't pretend otherwise. Most big styles were named after or by their respective founders, often because they had picked up one kata from this style and one from another. They couldn't very well continue without indicating this distinction by using a new name. However, names didn't matter to anyone until karate came to Japan and encountered the Japanese need to label everything.

As far as movement goes, within Shotokan, you can see clearly that one person's style is different from another's (at a high level). But from either lack of ego, or perhaps from lack of pressure from supporters, they have decided not to call themselves a new style per se. For me, karate is about using the entire body as a potential weapon or means of defense, and the name doesn't matter. Someone can be from any so-called style and if they move in a fine, principled way, they must be doing very good karate.

# Karate Masters

Different emphasis of certain movements is natural because of people's strengths and weaknesses and should be encouraged, but that's not to say they all are of a different "style." Having said that, the JKA certainly does have uniformity, which is extraordinary for such a large group. I know many exceptional instructors who are not JKA, but if I had to recommend a dojo to one of my students in an area where I didn't know anyone personally, my advice would be to find the local JKA dojo for this reason. It must be said that the overall quality is generally there. No one else has achieved that on a global scale.

Pure Shotokan or not-pure Shotokan is just a question of semantics. Is it pure in the sense that it is unchanged from the original teachings of the founder? Absolutely not. Is it pure in that the movements have become much more refined and yet recognizably Shotokan as opposed to another style? I think yes.

**What is your opinion of fighting events such as the UFC and Mixed Martial Arts events?**

They are both fascinating and revolting at the same time. Two thousand years of civilization seem to have passed by since Roman times, and I find it incredible that this stuff is legal today. It is still riveting, though, and valuable for us to see how effective the things we practice with control can be. The bones and teeth I have broken in the past (mostly of others, thankfully) have all been unintentional, but the notion of going into the ring to deliberately knock someone's teeth out is more than a bit distasteful. I find it difficult to watch much beyond a limited viewing of five minutes. But I do like the fact that because it is so real, there's a lot of respect between the fighters.

**Do you consider the art of karate to be a sport?**

Karate is many things to many people, and this is its beauty. Of course it's a sport if you approach it that way, and it's a very exciting sport, too. It is very much a martial art, too, although we lose something with the translation of a term like "budo." Budo is not a means to an end; it's far more than that, as it's a path one takes in order to conduct one's life in a certain way. If that way is maiming people, then that person is pretty low in the great scheme of things. If, however, the way for you is using a tool such as karate (or any other art) as an expression to gain mastery over the self, then we are on very high moral ground. Karate can allow one to access whatever level one seeks, from thug to saint.

**How do you see Shotokan karate in the world at the present time after the death of Nakayama Sensei and the different branches that broke away from the JKA?**

Nakayama sensei appeared to have celebrated in his books and teachings the wide variety of his top instructors, and perhaps that's why there were few splits (relatively speaking) in the JKA prior to his passing. Since then, groups have fallen apart, but that's also due to the age we live in.

We have so much information to tap into these days, and there exists a need to apply it all, finding our own experiences and satisfying our own questions. And that means sometimes one has to leave the nest. Of course, we still have an incredible amount to learn from the old masters. In their approach and commitment to the art, they discovered a certain essence that cannot be conceived of without the experience of it. To not be able to freely tap into all of that is a shame (some groups do not allow visitors to train with them), but the mindset of any group should be one of encouraging diversity, as long as it is logical and sincere.

"There is a lot of cross-fertilization going on now in Shotokan groups and, as a result, there's a terrific energy there that I've not seen since the 80s."

I think that if one is secure about what one is doing, then there is no threat from either visitors to one's dojo/organization or one's students visiting elsewhere. In the first case, it is flattering and in the second it is to be encouraged. Students should never feel they cannot explore.

There is a lot of cross-fertilization going on now in Shotokan groups there's a terrific energy there that I've not seen since the 80s. The JKA now appears to be jealously guarding itself from any influence but a past image, perhaps not recognizing that the nature of human beings is that they are individual and need to evolve constantly.

# Karate Masters

"We have to remember the words of Tancredi in the great novel "The Leopard" – "If we want things to stay as they are, things will have to change"."

We have to remember the words of Tancredi in the great novel "The Leopard" – "If we want things to stay as they are, things will have to change".

**What is you opinion of Nakayama Sensei?**

Something of a genius, bringing stylish, charismatic instructors with effective karate to the world. Like all great historical figures he appeared to be in the right place at the right time…but maybe he created that place and time. In the world of karate, where there are many fragile egos, I've never heard a bad word against him.

**Do you think that the hardcore traditional method (thousands of repetitions, makiwara, etc.) of teaching Karate is still valid nowadays?**

Without question. Show me a world-class anything, from a guitar player to a golfer or a dancer or a basketball player or a karate-ka, who does not do thousands of repetitions. Muscles are stupid and need thousands of reps to learn anything. Some people nowadays are looking for shortcuts and quick fixes. They may think because they intellectually "understand" that they have it. Not true. Of course we should approach our repetitions intelligently and not mindlessly; otherwise we'll get very good at bad technique. This is the only problem.

**What is the most important element: self-defense or sport?**

There's too much going on in the whole process of learning and teaching karate for me to focus on one over the other, but I refer to them in their contexts during explanations of why things are done a certain way. The student may or may not want to lean toward one aspect or the other, between sport and competition or pure application. Remember the sensei's job is not to dictate but to show a path, to show a possibility. I might do a class specifically for one or other of these things randomly to jolt the students out of any impending apathy, though.

**Kihon, Kata and Kumite: what's the proper ratio in training?**

I don't want to sound facetious but we should try to be doing kihon while we're practicing kata or kumite; try to be doing kumite while we're doing kihon or kata; and try to be doing kata while we're doing kumite or kihon. In other words, they must all blend, particularly in terms of mental attitude. The greatest portion of training time, though, will inevitably be spent on kihon.

**What do you consider to be the major changes in the art since you began training?**

I suppose there's a loss of awe about the art and a gain in intellectual curiosity about the nature of technique and why we do it. All this promotes a more knowledgeable approach, which I think is very good indeed. I don't go back that far, but in the early 70s we unquestioningly just slogged away in class. Film I've seen from earlier suggests that things were even less refined in the 50s and 60s. But you have to take these things in context.

On the down side, we now have so much information available to us that we cross-reference and question everything we are told. We must be careful not to over-analyzes, as the mind must be balanced with the body. Otherwise we'll all be armchair experts.

**Who would you like to have trained with that you have not?**

Everyone knows that things were tougher in the old days, but I'm not so sure. I'd also like to find out. That is, as long as I could come running back if I did actually get daily beatings and had to hang outside in the freezing rain clinging to a pole! Nowadays, I'm inspired in many ways, ranging from some of the kids I teach to stories about Yamaoka Tesshu I guess the latter would be my choice to train with if it were possible.

**What is your philosophical basis for your karate training?**

Same as for everything really: apply oneself fully in mind, body, and spirit (even if only for a few minutes at a time) to the task at hard and you will be able to respect yourself. Anything else is a kind of fraud and will lead to regrets.

I tend to play around with my mental attitude in my own training rather more than with the physical content—sometimes being deadly serious, sometimes simply having fun, and sometimes pretending I am one of my sensei or anyone, just to get a sense of what they might sense. All these things help one see a new aspect or discover a new approach and keep things interesting.

# Karate Masters

**Do you have a particularly memorable karate experience that has remained as an inspiration for your training?**

Well, I know that I have trained in some very tough situations in the past, so I know my limits are well beyond what is comfortable. With this in mind, I gain a certain inspiration and resist the human tendency of laziness. As for my experiences, to write them all down would be beyond the scope of this interview. Thinking about some of these questions, I started writing and writing. And then editing and editing. Some things are for private reflection, others are for close friends over dinner. I have my notes, though, so one day I'm bound to want to string the stories together in some form or other.

**How do you think practitioners can increase their understanding of the spiritual aspect of the art?**

Anything spiritual has to be experienced to be understood. Spiritual people are rarely very young for this reason. To seek the spiritual is like seeking happiness—we'll just get frustrated and achieve nothing. Meditation and yoga are great for spirituality, but the most neurotic person I know is a yoga teacher, so one doesn't necessarily lead to the other unless one has a sound philosophy. It matters not what you know; it's acting upon it that makes the difference. That is another reason why karate is so important: forcing oneself to do it is bound to be good for the body and might even lead to spirituality. If someone is seeking an understanding of the spiritual though, that in itself is an excellent start.

**Is there anything lacking in the way martial arts are taught today compared to how they were when you started training?**

If anything there's too much not lacking. If our heads were not so full of our reading and the YouTube clips that we saw from last night, we might just be able to isolate the one task at hand. I mentioned before that there is a lack of awe, though. Awe can be a great inspiration and, without it, the spirit cannot soar.

**What advice would you give to students on the question of supplementary training (running, weights, etc.)?**

All these things are good, but we must know ourselves and not overdo it. So much is available to us today that we want everything. This is human nature. We have to know that we can't possibly have everything and it's a modern curse that we all suppose otherwise.

Having said that, weight training is invaluable for strengthening stressed areas of the body and balancing the muscles. Running helps in general for stamina and rhythm and breathing. Using surgical tubes to stretch out techniques with resistance is something I do once a week without fail. Hitting the bag or makiwara, for obvious reasons, gives feedback on all strikes and kicks. And, perhaps more than anything, a good diet is much, much more than keeping the weight under control—the right food has an enormous effect on performance, mental and physical, both internal and external.

"Students should never feel they cannot explore."

**Why is it, in your opinion, that a lot of students start falling away after two-three years of training?**

Many have a low boredom threshold and are impatient, or they come in with unrealistic expectations. After all, karate is not for everyone. I think that any activity or hobby is probably the same, except perhaps for the ones that are intrinsically social, such as bridge—a pleasant evening with friends that is challenging but not painful. Almost anything physical gets harder as you get better. The pressure grows in order to maintain levels that one achieves on certain days when one is on song.

I think that as long as the students have something definite and logical to work on, and that they know will lead to more and more of those on-song moments, they will stay. I'm not really interested in entertaining to keep interest—to break the ice, maybe, when things get intense, but not to distract them from realizing they are in the dojo to practice karate. And karate is very difficult.

**Do you think that Olympics will be positive for the art of karate-do?**

Yes and no. It will give karate amazing exposure, of course, but it will also reduce it to a spectator sport in which techniques have to be understood by normal people who don't train in the art.

Karate is too subtle and difficult for any but those who really do it to understand when a point is valid. This is why the "Ultimate Fighter" matches are so popular—there's no subtlety whatsoever. It's a spectator sport in which normal people are unable to participate.

# Karate Masters

"Karate is too subtle and difficult for any but those who really do it to understand when a point is valid."

If karate does get in to the Olympics, it should be called something else. This way, everyone can distinguish it from presently known and distinct arts that do not necessarily want the compromise that is inevitable for Olympic recognition. Karate (as happened with TKD) will become virtually unrecognizable if it does get in, so why not start something new? Of course, I would be proud for karate to be an Olympic sport, but I'm afraid to see it get watered down beyond repair.

**What are your thoughts on the future of karate?**
Karate is unquestionably free of the fickleness of fads. It will be borrowed from and fall from popularity now and then, but there is something magnificent about an art that can be practiced anywhere with or without a partner, fast or slow, competitively or meditatively, injured or fit and well, as a sport or a hobby or a form of self-defense, and as a way of tapping into a primordial need to be good at something in which each movement has meaning.

I love the title of C. W. Nicols' book "Moving Zen"—it is perfect for karate. What could be more Zen that spending one's whole life attempting to create a perfect technique when perfection itself does not exist? So much is known about Karate and so much documented. It will always be around; we just might have to search a bit for the ideal version, though.

"Try to find satisfaction in the discovery of nuanced variations of technique and in their infinite possibilities. Even the simplest techniques offer so much."

**What are the goals of the WTKO that you run with Sensei John Mullin?**

The WTKO for John Mullin, Fred Serricchio, and me is really just a platform for those who wish to practice Shotokan karate at the highest level we can offer. The organization grew from a spontaneous and mutual desire to escape the egos and politics that have plagued many karate groups. We have no affiliation agenda and do not canvass new members, but welcome anyone who has a serious attitude and a willingness to try to improve. As such, like training itself, there aren't any specific goals over and above a gradual improvement.

**Do you have any general advice you would care to pass on to practitioners in general?**

Try to find satisfaction in the discovery of nuanced variations of technique and in their infinite possibilities. Even the simplest techniques offer so much. Whatever you read about the greats, they often will urge you not to rush and to focus on each moment at a time. The fable of the hare and the tortoise is never more appropriate than for karate training. Be willing to chip away over the years, and once in a while when you approach a familiar technique, see it as a beginner; ask yourself if you really are applying all that you know into this one movement. We're all just scratching the surface. O

# TONY ANNESI

## AN INNOVATIVE TRADITIONALIST

*Turbocharged with a dry and ironic sense of humor, Sensei Anthony Annesi is one of the few traditional teachers who never refused to continually test and experiment in order to bring a more realistic approach to what he was teaching at a given time. His appreciation for the traditional values and training is visible in everything he does, and his keen sense of "practical functionality" is second to none. Decades of training and research have been distilled in this budo-ka. "Youthful karate is big, gymnastic, muscular, and rather inefficient. Senior karate is unimpressive looking, but very efficient and sometimes nearly invisible. The future, to be healthy, should constantly be aware of its past," he says with a smile on his face. He is the founder of "Bushido-Kai Kenkyukai", a federation for the development of innovative traditional Martial Arts and founder of "Bushido-Kai Budoya", whose goal is to help broaden the martial education of practitioners worldwide.*

**How long have you been practicing Karate, and how many styles have you trained in?**

I started Martial Arts back in 1964 with sport judo, adding ju-jutsu and karate in 1970, aiki-ju-jutsu in 1972, and Aikido around 1974. I've been advocating multiple Martial Arts training for all my life, way back when practitioners were still arguing over which art was better, judo or karate. My initial karate method was Shotokan. I also am ranked in Kamishin Karate and have taken short training spurts in Goju. It's nothing to write home about, just informal training when seminars or training partners presented themselves. When I resigned from the Kamishin-kai International, I founded Takeshin Sogo Budo in order to continue teaching my ideas in karate, aiki, and an in-house art called Seiken Budo. Takeshin Karate uses kata from "the big four": Shotokan, Shito, Goju, and Uechi, with a few family or village style kata thrown in.

# Karate Masters

**Who were your teachers?**

In Judo during my college years, Charlie Chaves (Tohoku Judo Club, Somerville, MA). Charlie, who never let us call him "sensei," was both the workhorse and the drill sergeant of Tohoku. He ran a workout that was an hour and a half of calisthenics, uchikomi (fit-ins), and drills, with 15 minutes of instruction, and another 15 of randori (free sparring.) If you could walk at the end of training, you'd still have to lift your legs into the car to drive home. He was oriented to competition, as most Judo was in those days. I would have preferred concentrating on the details of the art itself. Still, one can't argue about his getting us in shape. At Tohoku, I also was introduced to Aikido and Shotokan Karate, although I did not have time to particiapte in the classes.

After college, I continued training in Judo, Hakkoryu ju-jutsu, and Goju under Shihan Larry Garron, formerly a running back for the Patriots. Sensei Garron was more laid back than Charlie and more eclectic. Our major concentration was Judo, with a minor in Hakkoryu and just a smidge of Goju and Jodo thrown into the mix. Master Garron was, even at that time, well-versed in a number of traditional arts, had trained with Donn F. Draeger and other notables, and was both personable and affable. In Aikido, I trained under Kanai Mitsunari Sensei and thus got a chance to experience different Aikido Shihan, such as Yamada Yoshimitsu, Chiba Kazuo, Tamura Nobuyoshi, Saito Morihiro, and several others. Kanai Sensei kept to himself, almost seeming like a recluse at times, but always seemed to know what was going on. He was generous in allowing me to train with his black belts even though I held no rank in Aikido.

My Shotokan instructor was Sensei Lou Demas who exposed me for a brief time to the teachings of both the JKA under Mori Masataka Sensei and the SKA under Ohshima Tsutomu Sensei. Lou, also opposed to being called Sensei, drilled us in basics, kata, and ippon kumite (one-step sparring.) We free-sparred only after we achieved the rank of gokyu and only once per week. His was a self-defense oriented art. Lou had grown up in a challenging area of Boston so sport was of little interest. He favored hard and fast retaliations to get the job done. I trained in Kamishin Aiki-ju-jutsu and, to a lesser extent, Kamishin Karate under Shihan Albert C. Church Jr. Shihan Church was very relaxed, jocular, and generous with information. He encouraged regular phone communication when I could not travel down to South Carolina to train. Training was simply trying out the technique "du jour" and getting better at it. Like Shihan Garron, Church was a man of many arts, having been ranked in Chinese, Korean, and Japanese arts, weaponry and empty hand arts, hard and soft arts. At the time (late 1970s) his dojo seemed like the Shaolin of the South, with an unbelievable array of possibilities to choose from. Although his regular classes were in karate and aiki, you could get special instruction in any number of other disciplines if he accepted you. My main emphasis with Shihan Church was Kamishin Aiki-ju-jutsu, although I was also cross-ranked into Kamishin Karate.

**Was there any specific reason why you got to train in the Shotokan style?**

I sort of fell into it. I was working in a gymnasium school called The Academy of Physical and Social Development under a groundbreaking teacher of youth by the name of Sumner "Mike" Burg. The Academy sponsored a karate program in the evenings. Because the Judo class I taught met Mondays and Wednesdays, I was able to train in Shotokan on Tuesdays, Thursday, and Fridays. Although I knew the difference between arts, I did not know much about stylistic differences. The fact that my karate was Shotokan was insignificant to me at the time. Much later, I started corresponding with Bernie Weiss, cofounder of ISOK (International Society of Okinawan/Japanese Karate-do), got to know Dr. Elmar Schmeisser, who took over after Bernie's passing, and now serve on the senior technical committee under current director Vince Morris. Although ISOK embraces all traditional Okinawan and Japanese systems, its past three directors happened to be Shotokan stylists.

"Although I knew the difference between arts, I did not know much about stylistic differences. The fact that my karate was Shotokan was insignificant to me at the time."

**Were you a "natural" at karate – did the movements come easily to you?**

I thought I would be a natural because I had two other Martial Arts in my background and because I had trained in gymnastics. However, I found

# Karate Masters

"Many people think that advanced karate is basic karate done faster and harder. I don't think so."

myself not only uncoordinated practicing even simple movements, but also in pain, as my knees did not want to take a back stance.

**How has your personal expression karate developed over the years?**

It has gotten softer and much more efficient. Many people think that advanced karate is basic karate done faster and harder. I don't think so. In one of his twenty precepts, Funakoshi said, "Kamae (posture) is for beginners, Shizen-tai (natural body) is for the advanced." Exaggerated training postures are essential for developing muscle memory, balance, endurance, speed, and reaction, but that is "Aka-chan" (youth) karate, even if performed by a 50-year veteran. I advocate teaching "Ko-jin" (old-person) karate earlier than most instructors. (Both terms are borrowed from Shorin stylist Major Bill Hayes. Neither term is meant to be derogatory; rather they are descriptive.) Youthful karate is big, gymnastic, muscular, and rather inefficient. Senior karate is unimpressive looking, but very efficient and sometimes nearly invisible.

**What do you think are the most important qualities for a student to become proficient in Karate?**

Most important is fidelity to a teacher who will take him/her from Aka-chan to Ko-jin Karate at the right pace. Too many students who are exposed to the advanced stuff want to jump into it right away. This is the downside of introducing senior karate early. If instructors introduce it too late, students have a tough time making the transition from formalized, rigid postures to relatively relaxed tailored-to-the-situation reactions. If instructors introduce advanced material too early, students don't want to spend the time developing a base to build the structure on. Students who are faithful to a good instructor may develop at a pace too slow for their liking, but their trust in their sensei – accompanied by regular training– most often results in talent that is an echelon or two above others of similar rank.

**With all the technical changes during the last years, do you think there still are "pure" styles of karate?**

Yes and no. Clearly there are styles that want people to consider them pure. No Uechi dojo wants to be infiltrated with Goju kata, let alone a Shotokan sense of distance or a Shukokai movement pattern. But, pure styles evolve and are changed even by their strict governing boards or individual inheritors. That is the difference between classical Martial Arts (almost no change at all,) traditional arts (gradual change adhering to timeless principles,) and traditionalistic arts (gradual change that also adopts new complementary principles.) Most of us do not practice pure arts in the "classical" sense, but most of us do practice either "traditional" or "traditionalistic" arts that hail back to and honor their roots.

I think it important to study a specific style in order to concentrate one's mind. How would you get a B.A. in college if you studied biology, literature, math, sociology, psychology, a foreign language, and a dozen other subjects for four years? A B.A. in what? The broad liberal art background is important, to be sure. That's why there are general education requirements for most freshmen. Just as important, however, is concentrating on one subject. That major subject is concentrated even more in graduate school. Logically then, students are best served by studying one discipline in depth after developing a broad foundation. What most students (and teachers) don't see, however, is that depth leads back to breadth. That's why the broad background was important in the first place. Too much depth and one becomes an expert at a sliding side kick, but unable to escape a simple wrist hold. When you leave graduate school, you need to apply your study in a much broader way. Styles, like graduate school fields of concentration, are important while the student is formally developing. However, generic principles are much more important after the specific details are mastered. For the seasoned martial artist, I see the developmental path as follows: specific style (e.g., Shotokan, Shito, Goju, etc.) to broader art (Japanese Karate) to artistic field (Asian Martial Arts) to a rather generic field (Holistic Martial Arts.)

**What is your opinion of fighting events such as the UFC and Mixed Martial Arts events?**

While I appreciate the toughness of the fighters and their dedication to training, and while I can see the attraction, especially to young males, I find the cage matches too reminiscent of gladiatorial events. While the fighters and some fans realize there are several sets of skills to develop, the average spectator is more interested, I think, in the gore.

After decades of introducing Martial Arts to the public as noble, philosophically-based traditions that produce better, more polite, more peaceful people, we are back to where boxing was a hundred years ago: a brutal spectator sport that serves as a way up and out of mediocrity, but seldom as an example for the aspirations of youth or even adults. Also, through no fault of their own, but simply through television exposure, cage fighting under the name of "Mixed Martial Arts" has replaced the David Carradine/Bruce Lee model in the imaginations of non-martial artists. To a large extent, in my opinion, people who might otherwise be interested in studying a traditional martial art, figure that cage-fighting is what all Martial Arts has evolved into. Although they may be happy to rent a pay-per-view grudge match, they are not personally interested in being slammed around, and will balk at their kids considering this type of training. This hurts memberships in schools that emphasize the more traditional self-defense and self-development.

The group of youngsters – and I admit that I would have probably been among them forty years ago – who are attracted to the "mixed Martial Arts" are not interested in traditional training because it does not get down and dirty. Once again, traditional schools suffer. Traditional training does not appeal to those who are looking to be the "baddest dude" in the valley or to older or younger students who confuse it with the TV cage-matches. Traditional Budo, however, is exactly what the vast majority people would benefit most from.

**Karate is nowadays often referred to as a sport ... would you agree with this definition or is "only" Martial Art?**
Unfortunately, karate is as much a sport now as it is a martial art. Sport is a fine venue to test oneself against other unfamiliar practitioners, but I don't see sport as an end in itself. I think that, for longevity and depth of study, the emphasis is best placed on self-defense and self-development in an ordered traditional setting. For someone to say that a martial art is "only" a martial art suggests that he/she is missing both the art's history and its personal development potential.

**Do you feel that you still have further to go in your studies?**
Only about a lifetime or two.

## Annesi

**How do you see karate in North America and around the world at the present time?**

Through the myopic perspective of my own prejudices. I see many physically talented practitioners who do not understand much about the body, about human reactions, or about subtle, efficient technique. Those are my emphases, however, and certainly everyone should study for his/her own reasons.

**Do you think that the amount of Kata of the style has relevancy in the mastery of the art of Karate?**

Yes, but only if the kata is understood in depth. Without application and variation, kata is nothing more than an aesthetic exercise in good body control. Bunkai is the most important part of kata. Without it, you have a teacher without a voice or text in a foreign language. In fact, I would gamble that most of us have the emphasis backward.

"Without application and variation, kata is nothing more than an aesthetic exercise in good body control. Bunkai is the most important part of kata."

Where we, as karate students, logically learn kata before oyo (application), the creation of kata came from applied self-defense. This is a point often emphasized by Sensei Patrick McCarthy. The artistry of those who created great kata was, in my opinion, in making specific movements generic enough so that they could be seen to have many possible applications, thus producing a concrete with many interpretations. This is like studying Shakespeare. No one knows for certain what the author's intended interpretation of *Hamlet, Macbeth,* or *King Lear* was. Students see the same words and follow the same story, then write centuries' worth of doctoral theses, many of which look at the plays with fresh eyes. That would have been impossible if Shakespeare were a dime-novelist. His genius is in the richness and suggestiveness of his material. So too with traditional kata. That richness is drawn out through analysis or bunkai.

35

**When teaching the art of karate – what is the most important element; self-defense or sport?**

Self-defense and, as an adjunct, the personal development that occurs when one faces the challenges of making self-defense functional. In my book "The Road to Mastery", I talk about how Martial Arts "trick" a student into self-development. The goal of self-protection folds into the wider goal of self-improvement via the challenges of training.

**Kata and Kumite, what's the proper ratio in training?**

For most people, "kumite" means jiyu kumite (free sparring) which I think should have relatively little emphasis in self-defense. However "kumite" as engagement drills (one-step sparring and various other self-defense drills) is of prime importance. In my teaching, I introduce two types of self-defense: SAD (Sudden Attack Defense) and CAD (Combat Attack Defense.) Most karate-ka (probably because they training in tournament sparring) think that a self-defense situation will resemble a one-on-one encounter like Bruce Lee vs. Chuck Norris in the coliseum in "Return of the Dragon". Although faceoff situations (CAD) can happen, I think them less likely than a surprise attack or attacks that start off being a single person's threat and end up being many-against-one (SAD). In short, SAD is one-step sparring in a more realistic context while CAD is realistic free-sparring that the defender needs to convert back into SAD as quickly as possible in order to dominate the situation.

**Do you have any general advice to pass on to anyone who wants to teach the art of Karate?**

Making a living on just Martial Arts will never be a secure living unless one is willing to cut corners here and there. If you are like me – unwilling to compromise quality – you will have to endure students flocking to the MacBudo dojo down the street in large numbers. Popularity pays the bills. Uncompromised standards leave one with elite students and a stack of unpaid bills. I would suggest a two-tier system – popular martial arts in the front room and traditional in-depth training in the back room. Serious front room people can qualify for back room instruction or, if they want to move on, can take their MacBlackBelt and toddle on down to the local bar to brag.

**What do you consider to be the major changes in the art since you began training?**

Bruce Lee led us to a more realistic training regimen. Unfortunately, this also led us through full-contact karate into cage-fighting. Both are very athletic and the dudes who train in them are as tough as they come, but neither is geared toward self-defense or self-development. Even among non-traditionalists I have talked to, like Bruce Juchnik (Kosho-ryu,) Joe Cowles (Wu-wei Gung-fu,) and Bill "Superfoot" Wallace (Full Contact Karate), there seems to be an uneasiness that Martial Arts, in trying to innovate, may have left the idea of "martial art" and have gone down the path of prizefighting. Traditional or traditionalistic arts need to embrace the concept of "Mixed Martial Arts" while distancing themselves from the current cage-fighting manifestation of that concept.

**Who would you like to have trained with that you have not?**
Sokaku Takeda. However, I feel that I was lucky to have a balance of conservative and liberal training that held high standards and still exposed me to several martial disciplines.

**What would you say to someone who is interested in starting to learn karate?**
Shop, shop, shop. I don't want to imply that a potential student should be concerned only with choosing the correct school, however. After that choice is made, the way one conducts oneself and what one contributes to the school and one's own training is equally important.

**What keeps you motivated after all these years?**
My own ignorance. Still more to learn. Still better ways to be more effective and efficient. I'd also like to see several of my long-term students rise to the level of *Shihan*.

**What is your philosophical basis for your karate training?**
Constant never-ending improvement (kaizen) toward the goal of efficient efficacy. I also favor the best defense with the least damage to the opponent whenever possible. The meaning is within each practitioner. I recall the climactic scene of "The Silent Flute", written by Bruce Lee. It was a hockey production, but the concept of the movie is that the big secret all martial artists are striving for is hidden in a book. When you finally earn the right to open the book, there it is, what you've been training for all these decades — a mirror.

**Do you have a particularly memorable karate experience that has remained as an inspiration for your training?**
The untimely passing of Shihan Church at the age of 50 made me realize a few things: (1) even masters are mortal; (2) make your contribution now, for tomorrow may be too late; and (3) try to maintain your honor "despite the slings and arrows of outrageous fortune." I know it is not your typical

# Karate Masters

"If one has an attitude of wanting to learn, everything else will fall in place."

action-oriented karate vignette, but it is the one that keeps occurring to me when I think of inspirational experiences.

**How do you think a practitioner can increase his/her understanding of the spiritual aspect of the art?**

By understanding training analogies. Every training drill, skill, interaction, etc., can have an analogy to everyday life, if one thinks metaphorically. This is one of the essential paths to a deeper philosophical understanding of Budo.

**Is there anything lacking in the way Martial Arts are taught today compared to how they were in your beginnings?**

The popularization of karate in the late '60s and early '70s produced a glut of belt factories that lowered the standard of training. At the same time, technical improvements in communications (videotapes, then DVDs, and the Internet, for example) made sharing information easier. As a result, karate got better technically among the few as it got worse normatively among the many.

Outstanding karate-ka usually are masters of their limited systems. They look great in a kata, in tournament competition, in their own dojo, but exposure to other systems also have made karate-ka aware that there is more to master in order to be competent at self-defense. It is a very difficult challenge to develop an art or combine several arts toward self-defense and not be overwhelmed by the demands of the training. Overwhelmed martial artists turn out to be "jacks of all trades and masters of none." Skilled martial artists, on the other hand, tend to be masters of one trade and jacks of many. Neither, in my opinion, is ideal. I am in favor of understanding your own martial art in such depth and breadth that you easily see overlaps with arts that, at first, seem totally different; in other words, study in depth for the purpose of creating knowledge in breadth.

**What do you consider to be the most important qualities of a successful karate practitioner?**

Showing up to train consistently with an attitude of wanting to learn. If one has this and a good school, everything else will fall in place.

**What advice would you give to students on the question of supplementary training?**

Do whatever makes you feel you are bettering yourself, but do not let supplementary training substitute for learning concepts and principles in the dojo.

**Why do you think that preserving the cultural values of Martial Arts is important in our modern society?**

The dojo, dojang, or kwoon is an oasis in a desert of what often seems to be disorganized, disagreeable, and disruptive daily living. Asian Martial Arts present supportive, ordered environments in which students can take a breath of fresh air and concentrate their minds while they exercise their bodies. Without certain cultural traditions (admittedly adjusted for a Western society), we are left with values similar to group sports or an exercise program. To get the maximum salutatory effects from Martial Arts training, I think one needs three items: (1) a knowledgeable teacher to set an example, (2) an organized environment with behavioral guidelines, and (3) a path to constant, never-ending improvement. The traditional Martial Arts offer all three.

**Have there been times when you felt fear in your training?**

Never. I have felt exhaustion, pain, and injury, but never fear. I don't think this is because of my bravery; rather it is because I trusted my instructors.

"Do whatever makes you feel you are bettering yourself, but do not let supplementary training substitute for learning concepts and principles in the dojo."

# Karate Masters

"The future, to be healthy, should constantly be aware of its past. This includes the ancient past, recent past, and contemporary history."

**Do you think that Olympics will be positive for the art of karate-do in case that happens one day?**

No. Look at what happened to Judo. Vastly popular in the early '60s, it sacrificed popularity to Martial Arts less interested in achieving international competitive status. Olympic arts are overly specialized arts that per force draw fewer people. Sport karate is popular enough so that it probably will become an Olympic event, but that will change the common person's perception of what traditional karate is. Dojo will overemphasize sport to adapt to the new Olympic sheriff in town, thus limiting new memberships to those looking for sport. Traditional self-defense and personal development will lose even more emphasis and karate's unique benefits will be further diluted or lost.

**What are your thoughts on the future of karate?**

The future, to be healthy, should constantly be aware of its past. This includes the ancient past, recent past, and contemporary history. We have gone from strictly structured self-defense taught privately in the backyards of Okinawan masters to semi-privately taught physical education and cultural discipline taught in the gyms of Japanese universities, to post WWII sport, to exported self-defense art hued with the mysteries of the Orient, to contemporary sport/self-defense/self-development that homogenizes items from each phase. I suggest that the future of karate will see a broader interpretation of karate so as not to lose the attention of those adherents who want contact, non-contact, sport, non-sport, self-defense, and aesthetics, all within an Asian *uwagi*. The benefit is that karate will be more holistic; the deficit is that the depth of detail will be lost even more than it already have been.

**What are your personal future plans in the Martial Arts?**

I am developing a course of concentrated study to help experienced martial artists – who feel their training has been incomplete – reach their full

"Get a dependable job. Settle down with a dependable mate. Train in a dependable dojo with the goal of being an exemplary human being."

potential. I hope to help traditional martial artists see that their traditions do not have to be limiting. In addition, weekend seminars across the country might help turn students on to the unlimited possibilities of principle-oriented instruction.

**Any accomplishments you feel particular proud of?**

I tend to look forward and not back. People have to whack me on the shoulder and point to the books I've written, the DVDs I've produced, the teaching concepts I've created, and the students I've taught to remind me that Gosharootie, I really should be proud. Somehow, I always think the next project will make me proud, but that lasts just long enough to think about the next one and the next one.

**Any final advice that you'd like to give to martial artists in general?**

Get a dependable job. Settle down with a dependable mate. Train in a dependable dojo with the goal of being an exemplary human being. The first two will help the third. O

# MICHAEL BERGER

## AN UNLIKELY JOURNEY

MICHAEL BERGER BEGAN HIS OFFICIAL TRAINING IN 1979, FOLLOWING A SUCCESSFUL WRESTLING CAREER AS A COLLEGE SCHOLARSHIP ATHLETE AT A NATIONALLY RANKED PROGRAM. IN 1983, HE RELOCATED TO JAPAN, WHERE HE EVENTUALLY WOULD SPEND A CUMULATIVE PERIOD OF MORE THAN THREE YEARS TRAINING. AFTER ENDURING THE ARDUOUS SEVERAL HOURS OF DAILY TRAINING AT A SMALL COUNTRY DOJO IN RURAL JAPAN, IN 1984 HE RECEIVED HIS BLACK BELT FROM THE LEGENDARY CHIEF INSTRUCTOR MASATOSHI NAKAYAMA AT THE JAPAN KARATE ASSOCIATION WORLD HEADQUARTERS IN TOKYO. THAT SAME YEAR, HE WOULD QUALIFY FOR AND COMPETE IN THE ALL-JAPAN KARATE TOURNAMENT HELD AT THE FAMOUS NIPPON BUDOKAN, WHERE HE WOULD RETURN TO COMPETE AGAIN IN 1986 AS PART OF AN ELITE INTERNATIONAL TEAM REPRESENTING THE WORLD HEADQUARTERS.

DURING THAT SAME TIME PERIOD, HE WAS ACCEPTED TO TRAIN, AS ONE OF FEW FOREIGNERS EVER, WITH THE TEAM AT TAKUSHOKU UNIVERSITY, RENOWNED FOR ITS RIGOROUS KARATE PROGRAM AND ALMA MATER TO NEARLY ALL OF THE JKA LEGENDS. IN ADDITION TO THE PREVIOUSLY MENTIONED LEGENDARY MASTERS, MICHAEL'S OTHER INSTRUCTORS HAVE INCLUDED HIDETAKA NISHIYAMA, HIROSHI SHOJI, MASAHIKO TANAKA, KEINOSUKE ENOEDA, TAIJI KASE, YOSHIHARU OSAKA, MIKIO YAHARA, MINORU KAWAWADA, TADAASHI ISHIKAWA, AND A HOST OF OTHER GREAT LEGENDS IN THE ART OF KARATE.

HE HAS HAD ADDITIONAL TRAINING IN JUDO, KENDO, TAI CHI, KOBUDO, JU-JITSU, GRAPPLING ARTS, AND IS A ZEN PRACTITIONER. HE CONTINUES HIS STUDY REGULARLY UNDER THE TUTELAGE OF GRANDMASTER TAKAYUKI KUBOTA OF THE INTERNATIONAL KARATE ASSOCIATION.

**How long have you been practicing the martial arts?**

My father taught me how to box when I was about five, in the early sixties, so I suppose in some ways you could say most of my life. I always was fascinated by martial arts, and in about the mid-sixties I started practicing from whatever books I could find. I remember buying a used book on Judo by Bruce Tegner. I would practice the throws onto an old mattress with my brother. I remained very active in boxing and wrestling throughout high

# Karate Masters

"I received my shodan from Nakayama Sensei in 1984 at the JKA World Headquarters."

school, and went to college on a wrestling scholarship. During the off-season, I was recruited by the judo club and began my real formal introduction into martial arts. So, I guess my formal training began at that time.

**How many styles have you trained in?**

As I mentioned, I began in judo in the late seventies. Not long thereafter, I began training in Wado-ryu, but only very briefly and somewhat hesitantly. Somehow, at that time, I never really believed in the effectiveness of martial arts over boxing and wrestling, although I had learned very quickly that judo could be great. I had made it to the finals in a large multistate judo tournament, and was ahead on points with just a few seconds left before getting choked out. It sold me on the chokes, at least. The karate guys that I had seen up until that time didn't seem that strong to me. Then I discovered Shotokan karate. I was so impressed with the power of the techniques. It looked like it really would work. Since then, I have practiced kendo, iaido, some aikido, tai-kyoku-ken, tai chi, qigong, Brazilian ju-jitsu, a little baji chuan ... and with Soke Takayuki Kubota, where I have learned Soke's Go Soku Ryu , kobudo, Kubota style Ju-jitsu, etc...

**Who were your first teachers and under what other people have you trained?**

My first real karate instruction was under a guy who had trained in Vietnam. I trained there very briefly at his home, and then again very briefly with Toshio Osaka in Wado-ryu. Then I met John Linkletter, who was a senior student of Nishiyama Sensei. This would have been around 1980 or so. At that time, Nishiyama Sensei used to come to Salt Lake City to teach us about three or four times a year, or he would send Sensei Robert Fusaro from Minnesota to teach us. Then, in the summers, we all would attend the Summer Camp in San Diego, where I trained with Nishiyama Sensei,

Enoeda Sensei, Kase Sensei, Shirai Sensei, Okamoto Sensei, and others. I received my brown belt from Nishiyama Sensei in about 1982 or 1983, and left for Japan very shortly thereafter. It had always been my dream to train in Japan, but when I arrived there I was in a small city in the countryside and did not know if I would be able to find a place to practice. My first teachers there were Mr. Teruo Honda, and his teacher Mr. Minoru Akita at the TDK company dojo in Narita. They were so strong! Mr. Akita was a direct student of Shirai Sensei, and Honda Sensei was his senior student. They taught me privately every day in a small tatami room at the factory after work, until we wore out the tatami mats. It was only kihon! Everything had to be big and powerful. I feel so blessed to have them as my first teachers. After that, I began training in a very small country dojo in Narashino, with Ishikawa Sensei, who at that time was a rokudan (6th dan) and former All-Japan Champion in kata. Some of the other dojo members included Yoko Nakamura, a many time JKA All-Japan and World Champion, Ohta Sensei, assistant to the late Enoeda Sensei of KUGB in England, and Kokubun, another eventual JKA All-Japan and World Champion, who was a white belt and my kohai at that time. Another very influential teacher there at the Shotojuku Dojo was Sensei Watanabe, who was a 4th dan student of the great Sensei Shoji. I also was training then at the old JKA Hombu in Ebisu, where I trained with Nakayama Sensei, Asai Sensei, Osaka Sensei, Tanaka Sensei, Ueki Sensei, Shina Sensei, Yahara Sensei, Abe Sensei, and many others. This was before the JKA had split, and there were so many strong teachers there. Then, I also trained with Shoji Sensei and Yoshioka Sensei about that time. I was with Iida Sensei at his dojo in the early nineties.

I received my shodan from Nakayama Sensei in 1984 at the JKA World Headquarters. In about 1986, I began training, through a special recommendation from Sensei Shoji, at Takushoku University under Tsuyama Sensei. Naka Sensei, the current JKA great, was the sub-captain there. After the program at Takudai was banned due a training related death, I trained at Komazawa University under Sensei Ohishi. Between my residences in Japan, I trained in the U.S. with Sugiyama Sensei in Chicago, Mikami Sensei, Yaguchi Sensei, and Sensei James Fields in Santa Monica. In Hawaii I trained with Kenneth Funakoshi for a short time in the eighties, and later with Ed Fujiwara there. Sometimes George Sasano would teach, and every year Asai Sensei would come; sometimes Akiyama Sensei as well. At that time in the eighties, he was an 8th dan in the JKA and original student of Gichin Funakoshi as well.

I was fortunate enough to have met Soke Kubota in about 1995 and have been training there since, returning to Japan to train and compete periodically. I have visited the Kodokan and have trained with an Olympic Gold medalist in Judo. In grappling, I have trained with Gene LeBell and his protégé Gokor, as well as Pedro Sauer in Salt Lake City at his Brazilian Jiu Jitsu Academy. I am sure that there are others that I am leaving out...

**Would you tell us some interesting stories of your early days in karate training?**

Probably the most memorable of my training experiences were in Japan, during the cumulative period of about four years I spent there over a ten-year period. Most notable was the rigorous, dangerous training at Takushoku and at Komazawa Universities, and then of course with the hombu dojo instructors at the old Ebisu dojo, the JKA World Headquarters at that time. There were a lot of trips to the hospitals in those days. It was real budo. There were many occasions when people were looking for teeth or carrying someone else out of the dojo. The training included a lot of kihon and body conditioning. Often it was carrying people on your back in zenkutsu-dachi or holding them for long periods in kibadachi. We did so much usagi-tobi (rabbit jumping) that your knees would become so swollen that you could hardly walk. I am surprised that any of us have knees left after all of that.

At Takushoku, it was all kumite. We would train from 4 pm to 7 pm six or seven days a week. We usually did about 20 minutes of kihon, and then it was all yakusoku kumite or jyu kumite. Sometimes right from the start without warmup, we would hear the command to face each other, and "Hajime!" We would go for about five minutes, then shift left, and continue this for an hour and half before we took a break. There were no pads used and no protective equipment, unless someone got hurt very seriously, I mean something much worse than broken out teeth, at which time we would put on kensuppo, which basically was nothing more than something like an ace bandage. It was brutal training, and every day was just trying to stay alive and survive. I would get there an hour early just to prepare my mind for what was to come. It was very dangerous.

**Had you heard of Takushoku University's reputation prior to going to Japan?**

I only knew that it was where all of the JKA legends had trained, and that it was tough. I wanted the toughest training. That's what I was there for ... but I had no idea just how tough and how brutal it really was. You have to remember that you have a lot of ambiguous feelings being a gaijin in Japan.

**Please tell us about your training in Takushoku University and your experience with Nakayama sensei?**

I first met Nakayama Sensei in the very early part of 1984 at the old JKA Headquarters in Ebisu. My first teacher in Japan, Mr.Honda, took me to the hombu to watch the dan testing one Sunday. At that time, the JKA probably was at its peak, and there were about 150-200 people there for the dan testing. We waited as Nakayama Sensei walked into the dojo. He was so imposing and had such an indomitable presence. Not long thereafter, when I would train at the hombu, sometimes Nakayama Sensei would teach the class. He was very strict about kihon and bunkai. My most memorable experience with him was at the 1984 All-Japan tournament at the Budokan, where I was a contestant in kumite. During one break, I spoke with Nakayama Sensei and he signed his book and a piece of his calligraphy for me. The kanji character read "Ken Zen Ichi" (Fist and Zen becoming One). I have named my dojo in his honor according to that saying. I also have a photo of me with Nakayama Sensei, something that few people, even senior members, of the JKA in Japan, have!

"The training at Takushoku was the most unbelievable thing that I have been a part of."

The training at Takushoku was the most unbelievable thing that I have been a part of. I was the only foreigner there, and had to have a suisen-jo, a recommendation from Shoji Sensei to attend. All of my friends who were training at the hombu then thought I was crazy to try to go and train there. They said that those guys were going to try to kill me. You have to remember Takudai is the "alma mater" of all the JKA legends. like Nishiyama, Okazaki, Enoeda, Shirai Shoji, . . and had a long reputation as being the toughest, most brutal and strongest dojo in all of Japan. arrived there the first day one hour early with all of other kohai, to clean the dojo and to

# Karate Masters

"I still have many scars and injuries from the training there, but I loved it so much, and I am so proud to have had the opportunity to have trained there."

stand at attention and wait for the captains and the sempai to arrive. Almost all of the guys there had no front teeth and faces like boxers.

When the captains arrived, it was very intimidating. They swaggered in and looked for any reason to beat someone. The first day that I was there, before the training, one of them found a tiny spot on a mirror that hadn't been cleaned. He was furious, and the guilty party was kicked in the head with *mawashi-geri*. After he didn't move for a few minutes, the sempai walked slowly toward me smiling. It was a scary welcome, and I wondered what I was doing there.

Before I went, Shoji Sensei and Watananbe Sensei had told me that it was important that I show no fear and never go backward or retreat for any reason. There were no gloves, no mouthguards, cups, or any other kind of protection allowed. It was basically full contact. We trained for three hours a day, with a short break after the first hour and half. That first day, at the break, I was taken by one of the captains to the first aid kit where something was put on my knuckles, which were covered with blood from hitting guys in the teeth. It was pure survival, every single day, anything goes. It was real fighting. As a foreigner, they really went after me. Every day, I was really scared that I could get seriously injured. I saw a lot of broken and knocked out teeth and all kinds of other injuries. They didn't want me there. I think that if I had not made friends with Naka Sempai, one of the captains then, they would have killed me. Naka looked after me pretty well and told the other captains to take it easy on me. I still have many scars and injuries from the training there, but I loved it so much, and I am so proud to have had the opportunity to have trained there. I improved so much, and there was an indelible effect on the forging of my spirit, something that never ever leaves you.

One day in the summer of 1986, my friend from the Takudai team called me and told me that there had been a death of one of the members and that the Japanese Ministry had banned all further karate training there. It was a big blow to me, so disappointing.

**You, of course, did leave with your teeth. To what do you attribute your survival there?**

Well, I do have my teeth, but I did have some cracked that broke later, and made many trips to the hospital! I used to go to Takudai an hour early just to get my mind ready. It was like ... every day I would think, I could get killed. I could really get killed. So it became a kind of a kill or be killed attitude. We all used to do whatever we could to win, including just about every dirty trick you can think of. I had to cut off all my hair after the first day, so they couldn't get a grip on it. Kicking to the groin was not uncommon. Cheating on the techniques or on *yakusoku* kumite was to be expected. I guess I just went in there each day and thought, well, it is either them or me. If you got a tiny window of opportunity, you seized it and tried to end it fast. It was really like facing an opponent in a life-and-death moment, like facing an opponent with a live sword. I learned to fight with what I call "patient urgency." The whole experience was really kind of addictive.

**How did you find the Westerners respond to traditional Japanese training?**

In my opinion, most Westerners did not respond well to the very rigorous hard training in Japan, although there were some who really endured. You have to remember, at that time, the training went far beyond being called hard training. It was almost suicidal, certainly not smart training or scientifically beneficial training. Squat jumping around a dojo for up to an hour at a time, and up and down flights of stairs, still squat jumping, cannot have been called smart training. I remember sometimes doing crazy makiwara training, or suddenly going on a run around the Olympic Stadium in our gis and wearing rubber slippers. Everyone had chronic fatigue, but you were not allowed to quit. There was a run at Komazawa that they did every year in the springtime. I think that was injured or something and was not required to do it, but it was a 20-mile run to the top of a mountain and back. It was kind of a spirit training. There was a lot of that kind of training in Japan. It really, really tested you, and above anything else, forged your spirit so that if you made it through without injury, you felt invincible., that you could do anything.

# Karate Masters

**Were you a "natural" at karate – did the movements come easily to you?**
Absolutely not. Although I had been a college scholarship athlete, I think that was what intrigued me the most ... that I just couldn't get it right! It made me mad, and I used that anger to fuel myself to go further when I was tired. I used to try to make myself pass out from training so hard so that I could rest, and prove to them that this training was ridiculous! After having since taught professional athletes, I am convinced that no one is really a natural at karate. Some people have athleticism and a good knowledge of their bodies, but no one seems to be a natural. The movements are unlike any others....

**How has your personal karate has changed/developed over the years?**
I think that over the years, karate has become my own karate. I have adapted it to my body, to my personality, and to my spiritual beliefs. I think that it has become softer, yet stronger, more relaxed ... more calculated, more precise, more compassionate and yet more ruthless – very refined. I think that I have grown to appreciate the subtleties and to strive to find the hidden deeper meanings, even as they present themselves in a Zen sense as lessons in life. I feel that I am more of a beginner than I ever was, and am constantly amazed at how little I really know.

**With all the technical changes during the last 30 years, do you think there is still "pure" shotokan, shito ryu, et cetera?**
Well, to begin with, I think that when you study karate, you really are studying only the karate of your teacher. If you look at great masters, even within the same ryu-ha or system, you see dramatic differences and interpretations of technique, in accordance with body type, philosophical interpretation, and personality. They have made karate their own, too. Look at the great masters ... If you watch Asai Sensei and Tanaka Sensei of the JKA, would you ever guess that they were from the same style? Their own interpretations and ideas have influenced their techniques to the degree where they appear vastly different. Asai Sensei and Kanazawa Sensei, for example, have a great deal of Chinese influence, whereas someone like Tanaka Sensei or Kase Sensei or Iida Sensei is more power oriented. Soke Kubota has his own uniquely powerful and comprehensive style. I guess it depends upon your definition of pure. I am more prone to identify style with the name of the teacher, as was done in early times.

**Do you think different "ryu" are important?**
Well, yes and no. On one hand, I think that karate is karate. I don't think that it is necessarily the ryu-ha themselves that are as important as where

"There are numerous paths to the same mountain peak, but if we all arrive at the same destination, it doesn't matter much how we got there."

we are trying to go and what we are trying to achieve with the training. There are numerous paths to the same mountain peak, but if we all arrive at the same destination, it doesn't matter much how we got there ... there are longer routes and shorter routes, paths with different aspects to them, ones that are very rugged and ones that are quite gentle. In the end, what is more important is which peak we are trying to climb, and ultimately to realize that the journey is the destination.

**What is your opinion of Full Contact karate and Kickboxing?**

I have great respect for them for what they are ... but I am not sure that they can be called martial arts. They are athletic sporting endeavors, and their contestants are competitive and talented athletes, some with great fighting ability. They are successful in attracting those kinds of individuals who are in search of that aspect, which is wonderful because that sometimes leads those people to another dimension, the art side, the spiritual or "do" side.

**And what about other fighting events such as the UFC and Mixed Martial Arts events?**

The advent of the UFC events was revolutionary in some ways. It revitalized interest in the martial arts and gave martial artists a means of testing their skills in a more realistic kind of setting. This, in and of itself, is wonderful. Many people who become involved in training initially to be strong eventually find a different path, after they have nothing more to prove. Most of the true masters of martial arts whom I know would not participate in this type of event. They are training for other reasons – reasons that strive to kill the ego and find the self through losing the self ... something that is not philosophically aligned with this kind of event. I am not saying that these events do not have value for some people, and I am not saying that do not attract great fighters and masters. I guess it all goes back to "Why are we training? Which peak are trying to climb?" It is an individual choice.

**Do you think that karate in the West has "caught up" with Japanese karate?**

I would say yes and no. In terms of physical ability, perhaps yes. But there is something inherent in the development of spirit in Japan that cannot be duplicated and never will be duplicated ...

**Do you feel that there are any fundamental differences in approach or physical capabilities of Japanese karateka in comparison to European or American karateka?**

As I said, it may have caught up in some ways. It depends on what means you are using as a measuring tool. Is it competition? Then, yes. Does success in competition equate to real karate proficiency? Maybe ... maybe not. It is one tiny aspect of karate. Other factors, perhaps more significant ones, are less discernible, and not as easy to measure. Again it goes back to "What are we striving for, why are we training...?" I don't believe that there are significant physical differences that would be a factor, although it has been suggested that Asians may have more of a genetic propensity for flexibility, particularly in the hips, and that may be true, perhaps partially due to cultural differences over generations. I believe that Westerners have the same potential to be superior, and we are seeing it more and more in a measurable sense, like competition.

There are significant differences. Japanese tend to trust, not to question ... they don't need to know why. They simply respond with "Osu!" or "Hai!" – not only in karate, but in life. There is great faith. This is one big difference. So even when they are told to do something that sounds impossible, they just say "Osu! " This applies not only to training, but business and life as well. They have the ultimate respect for their teachers, and undying loyalty. To give you an example, years ago, I went back to Japan for the first time in many years. When I met Naka Sensei, who had been the captain at Takudai when I was there, I didn't know if he even would recognize me. But he instantly did and was so happy to see me. They had big parties for me with Takudai members, and I was treated with such great honor and respect, because I had been at Takudai…

I believe that the Japanese mind also is more visual as far as learning goes. This may be due to the early study of kanji characters or … I don't know. But in Japan, you see a technique demonstrated once, with no explanation. If you miss it, you lose; that's it, you don't get it again. The Japanese also are more concerned with forging that indomitable fearlessness. This probably is the most significant difference in approach. Attack, attack, attack! Even though this can tend to make them more predictable as fighters, that training has a far-reaching effect in terms of developing fighting spirit. The thousands of hours of crazy ridiculous training that leaves only a few left to train has a lasting effect on spirit, as well. I remember them holding a shinai while standing behind you while you were doing jyu kumite, and screaming at you that if you took a step backward you were going to get hit … so you would rather die going in than going back. This is Japanese spirit … I think that this is the fundamental difference between Western karate ka and the Japanese.

**Karate nowadays often is referred to as a sport… would you agree with this definition?**

To me, karate is not a sport, although there is an aspect of sport within karate. There is an important reason for competition, but it has nothing to do with winning. I prefer to use the Japanese term of *shiai*. SHI means basically to *test* in this regard, and the kanji for *ai* means harmony or together. So, it is a way of testing our skills with each other, to be used as a learning tool for further growth. Karate do is a *way*, a *path* to achieving some sense of greater understanding of universal truth, of generating love and compassion. For me, it is a physical bridge to the study of Zen.

**Do you feel that you still have further to go in your studies?**

Absolutely. In fact, again, it is what I love about the practice of karate-do, and similarly, the practice of Zen. The more you think that you begin to understand, the more you realize you don't really know My Zen teacher once told me that Zen is a constant practice of stepping off the edge, of

# Karate Masters

"The status of Japanese karate, real Japanese karate in the U.S., is more of a concern in some ways, but actually less of a concern in others."

grasping and letting go, of being stuck and getting unstuck, of getting it and dropping it, of life and death, moment to moment ...

**How do you see Japanese karate in America at the present time?**

Well, the state of Japanese karate on the whole is somewhat of a concern to me, not only in America, but in Japan as well. Over the last 20 years, there has been a real decline in interest in traditional endeavors in Japan and elsewhere. "Furukusai" is a slang term in Japanese that means, "it stinks of old." These days, youth are more interested in soccer, baseball, and video games. On my trip to Japan in 2001, I taught at several dojo, and the difference between now and twenty years ago is significant. Kids can't even do pushups anymore. The status of Japanese karate, real Japanese karate in the U.S., is more of a concern in some ways, but actually less of a concern in others. Fortunately, in the early sixties, many of the top of instructors from Japan, like Soke Kubota, Sensei Nishiyama, Okazaki, Kanazawa, Shirai, Enoeda, and others, relocated overseas to places like America and England, France, Italy, and elsewhere. On the other hand, others arose claiming to be legitimate instructors, who were less than so, and consequently, the art of true Japanese karate became somewhat diluted. These days, it seems that everyone is a black belt, so it undermines the value of having received one (if that is why you are training), unless it is from a respected instructor..

**Do you think it helps karate physically to train with weapons - kobudo?**

In a general and tangible sense, I would say no. In some other ways, it depends on how one trains. I think there are certain benefits to the further understanding of ma'ai (distance), and to the development of chi (ki), but in a general physical sense, I don't see a lot of direct relevance physically to karate. I will say, though, that I have gleaned some ideas for kumite from the practice of kendo and fencing. So there are principles that do have crossover effect, and things like zanshin. I do think that after 3rd or 4th dan, it is important to have a fundamental knowledge of the traditional weapons of Japan, as many of the kata bunkai involve defense against those weapons.

**What's your opinion about "makiwara" training?**

I think that makiwara training is the most undervalued and underestimated training device in karate. It is the single most important training tool to develop kime, accuracy, precision, distance, zanshin; to understand the relationships of speed to power, of relaxing/tensing, expansion/contraction, etc. Furthermore, it allows one to enter a state of mushin, of samadhi, which is another level of mind/spiritual training akin to Zen. In Japan, it always is part of the training. Proper instruction really is important, however, as is the proper construction of a makiwara. Most people fail to understand that it is not used solely to develop calloused knuckles, but rather teaches kime, hip rotation, use of the back leg, and the other elements that I mentioned above.

**When teaching the art of karate – what is the most important element: self defense, sport, or tradition?**

For me, the important thing is the *do* aspect of the training, a means of following the *way*, of striving for some deeper form of understanding, of attaining some kind of satori or kensho, or rather realizing that perhaps there is nothing more to get, so to just surrender and appreciate your life for what it is.

**Kata and kumite: what's the proper ratio in training?**

The simple answer is one-third kihon, kata, kumite. However, kata is the soul of karate. I think that kata and kumite are the like the waves of the sea, separate and yet one. Ultimately, I believe that karate is a fighting art, and that kata, when done correctly, is kumite.

**Do you have any general advice you would like to pass on the karate-ka?**

Well, there is so much ... but I often think of a Japanese proverb with regard to my training: "Soshin wasereru bekarazu" or "Never forget the beginner's mind."

Some people think going to Japan to train is highly necessary. Do you share this point of view? Absolutely. Until you have witnessed karate in Japan, you cannot capture the true essence of the art. The whole culture is steeped in tradition, and Zen and martial arts are infused into the entire culture and society. Until you train there and experience this, you cannot understand the real essence of the art. There are aspects of life that go beyond rational understanding, beyond words, knowledge, or conventional understanding. They simply must be experienced. Training in Japan provides a totally different perspective of the essence of karate-do, and training there is a must for the serious student. I am working on putting together an annual trip for a select group tour that would give one this chance.

**What do you consider the major changes in the art since you began training?**

Well, I think that there is less emphasis put on power and kime, less focus on *ikken hissatsu* (one killing technique), and more emphasis on aesthetics and the sport element. Even the kata have been modified to look nicer for presentation, and in some instances, the real bunkai is compromised for the sake of appearance. I also think that a lot of reigi or etiquette has been lost, and a certain spiritual dimension has been sacrificed.

**Who would you like to have trained with that you have not?**

That's a tough question. I would love to have trained with O-Sensei, Ueshiba Sensei. I think that he really was one of the greatest who has ever lived. I also love Tesshu, the great Zen warrior swordsman and calligrapher. Certainly there are many others, but I feel so blessed to have trained with the great legends that I have trained with and continue to train with.

**What would you say to someone who is interested in starting to learn karate-do?**

The most important thing is to find a good teacher, someone who is legitimate and shares the same philosophical viewpoints as far as the reason for training. I feel so blessed to have been able to have trained with those who I feel were the greatest of the masters. I feel that I was destined to meet them…people like Nakayama Sensei, Shoji Sensei, Asai Sensei, and Soke Kubota. There were so many and I wouldn't want to miss recognizing any of them, but find a good teacher and make a commitment to yourself.

**What is it that keeps you motivated after all these years?**

Well, it no longer is a choice for me. That is like asking what motivates one to eat … you just do it. You wonder if you are doing it or it is doing you. I guess I just have an image of how karate is supposed to be done, and I want to do it the best that I can on that level. But, there are many different levels of why. I am continuing my climb. I also continue to make new discoveries and to experiment with new ideas to continue to grow. I appreciate these subtleties and gain more insight to the relevance of Zen and to my life. I want to honor my teachers and preserve the tradition.

**Do you think it is necessary to engage in free-fighting to achieve good fighting skills in the street?**

Not really. I think that one can become a very good fighter through the proper practice of kata, kihon, and yakusoku kumite. That is one-step, three-step, and jyu-ippon kumite. At Takudai, we often would do five-step or three-step or ippon kumite, and to tell you the truth, it was more dangerous than free sparring, because you can't cheat and you can't rest. Ask some of the Takudai *alumni* and I am sure that they will agree.

"The understanding of bunkai brings life and soul to the kata, and it is what separates it from being little more than a performance dance."

**Modern karate is moving away from the "bunkai" in kata practice. How important do you think "bunkai" is in the understanding of "kata" and karate do in general?**

The understanding of bunkai brings life and soul to the kata, and it is what separates it from being little more than a performance dance. Bunkai brings a different dimension to kata, and it is the essential element of kata. Many years ago it was kumite … there was no free sparring. When I speak with Shoji Sensei or Akiyama Sensei, direct students of Gichin Funakoshi, this was their response. Soke Kubota came from a unique background: it was karate to kill; yet, he still trains us very hard in kata, too. I believe that kata is kumite and kumite is kata.

**What is the philosophical basis for your karate training?**

There are many individual reasons for training, and I feel that we should be able to identify our own personal reasons and philosophical reasons. We have to ask ourselves, "Why are we training? To be tougher? To be stronger? For health? Fitness? Spirituality? To foster the ego or to rid ourselves of it and the entire notion of self and duality, thereby generating more love and compassion. I think that perhaps, initially, everyone is interested in the physical nature of budo; they want to be stronger or more confident. I did. They enjoy the camaraderie of training, or are fascinated with Eastern Philosophy. Then, later they discover something more. Martial Arts have the -do element. That is, the element of the way or the path, as a means to some kind

# Karate Masters

"I feel that martial arts, like cha-do (tea ceremony) or iai-do (sword) or flower arranging, all are bridges to the ultimate study of Zen."

of higher understanding or enlightenment. Perhaps even glimpses of *kensho* or *satori*. I feel that martial arts, like cha-do (tea ceremony) or iai-do (sword) or flower arranging, all are bridges to the ultimate study of Zen ... that is to say, I believe it easier for one to have a glimpse or moment of samadhi when it is done through a physical activity, or through movement. It is more difficult for one to go straight to the cushion and sit still for 40 minutes. Aside from that aspect, keep the beginner's mind. Karate is Life. Look for the lesson. Look inward.

**Do you think this tough skill coupled with kindness and compassionate is the very essence of Budo?**

I think that we transcend one to become the other; that we have to experience the fighting completely in order to become more compassionate. By experiencing all aspects of fighting, including getting beaten, we can experience what it is to be truly compassionate, as we identify with it first hand, from an experiential nature, not one that simply is lived vicariously through others ... in this way, the fighting has great value in the end, its greatest values being that it generates great compassion. It reminds me of Zen koan about "Stopping the Fighting across the River..."

**Do you have a particularly memorable karate experience that has remained as an inspiration for your training?**

I have some memories of the very early years that I was in Japan. The first day that I met Mr. Honda, he swaggered toward me with piercing eyes and an unbelievable presence. He seemed to take up the whole room. The first thing he did was grab my wrist and look at my hands for signs of makiwara training. After seeing none, he tossed my hand aside and started to laugh. I felt the same way when I first met Kase Sensei: that indomitable presence.

Nakayama Sensei was the same. They were so imposing; they seemed to be about nine feet tall, but when you got up next to them, they were not big at all.

I also never will forget seeing Watanabe sempai the first time. He was about five feet tall, but he was as ferocious as a tiger. He was a yodan then, and I saw him taking down guys nearly twice his size with tobi-zuki and tobi-geri. He had piercing steel eyes and what a spirit. I was really inspired by him. The other guy I never will forget, because of fearlessness and daring style, was Yahara Sensei. His ferocity and fearlessness always were an inspiration for me. I used to want to be able to fight like him, and would imagine myself as a tiger. That was how I envisioned him. I remember when I participated in the All-Japan team trials at the "Katsuura Gasshuku" in about 1984, I was only a brown belt, and one of only two foreigners there. Everyone was so wound up and the adrenalin was really flowing, and I remember being terrified of Yahara Sensei. He was so ferocious, and his feet were like hands, and he really hurt people. I saw a lot of guys lose their teeth there. I remember Shina Sensei knocking out someone's tooth, and everyone looking around for the tooth on the floor. It was really a brutal event, so that stuck with me.

Then of course, I never will forget Takudai, especially that first day that I was there. After Takudai, I had some great stories from Komazawa. The captain at that time was named *Oi Sempai*. He was so strong, and no dared challenge him. He was about six feet tall and weighed about 230, big for a Japanese person. He used to come to the dojo early and make three or four guys hold the heavy bag for him, with one of them sitting on top of it. Then he would do ashi-barai and topple them all over like bowling pins. Once, he attacked me with that technique and sent me to the hospital. I often think of some of those experiences as inspiration. It is like a flame that stays smoldering inside ... and truthfully, there are too many stories to relate to you in a single article. Of course, the first day that I met Soke Kubota was very special as well. He is truly a samurai displaced in time.

**After all these years of training and experience, could you explain the meaning of the practice of karate do?**

No. I think that the moment we think that we understand that, we have lost the true essence of the training and we stop learning and stop growing. We become stuck again, paralyzed by the ego. It is all about not clinging to anything or any understanding, but rather getting something and letting it go. And, it is so hard for us to let go of our apparent realities or belief systems, because they are what defines us as individuals, and it is how we have been conditioned. It is a strange paradox. I think that in some ways, I have scratched the surface, but continue to bumble along day by day.

**In your book *"Masterclass Karate: Kicking Techniques,"* you state that Sensei Shoji taught you "great lessons of real budo." Can you please expand on this and tell us about Sensei Shoji and his karate? Could you also share some stories you have of him?**

Well, I first met Shoji Sensei through Watanabe Sempai, who I also mention in my book. He was one of my teachers at the Shotojuku Dojo, and became like a brother to me. He had a longtime relationship with Sensei Shoji as one of his students. They invited me to the Chuo University Gasshuku, where Shoji Sensei and Yoshioka Sensei taught. I got to know Shoji Sensei there. After the brutal trainings, he would send someone to my room, and they would take me to Shoji Sensei's room, where he and Yoshioka and Watanabe were all drinking and playing Mah Jong. There, we would talk about budo and Sensei Shoji would teach us many things about karate and talk about his training with Gichin Funakoshi. He told us about the importance of kata, and how the kihon developed. Yoshioka Sensei was a master of the shakuhachi, and he would play for us. Sensei Shoji loved that. I remember the way that his eyes used to sparkle and his would start to laugh. Everyone loved Sensei Shoji. He was so kind, so humble, but so strong. He was very sturdily built, and hit very hard. His sweeps were amazing. He took a liking to me, and would invite me and Nabe Sempai to do other trainings and camps where he was teaching. I was the first foreigner ever to visit his home. He always wore traditional kimono. He was so kind and so unassuming, so humble. Everyone loved Shoji Sensei, but Yoshioka Sensei told me a story of him that happened on a train in Tokyo late one evening. A drunkard was on the train causing trouble with everyone, and approached Shoji Sensei and told him to get off the train. Sensei ignored him, but the drunk continued to scream at him to get off the train. Finally, Shoji Sensei stood up and stared the man in the face, then drew an imaginary line with his foot on the floor of the train. He told the man, "If you can step across this line, I will get off the train." Needless to say, he didn't. I visited Shoji Sensei at his home just a few months before his passing. His wife had passed away, and he really enjoyed having Watanabe san and me visit him. He told us about how the JKA had wanted him to become the Chief Instructor and make him 9th dan, but that he had refused, telling them that that was not budo. I always respected him for that. I think about him every time I put on my belt, which I am honored to have with his name on it.

**Why do you think he refused?**
Because he was a true budoka, devoid of desires or fame or attention. He didn't need it, didn't want it. I think that he knew that it would create great envy and jealously amongst those who really wanted the fame and the glory, and that nothing good would come of it. Shoji Sensei was a very humble man. That is what everyone loved about him.

**How do you think a practitioner can increase his/her understanding of the spiritual aspect of karate?**
I think that the ultimate training for the martial artist really is Zen training. Throughout history, there has been that inextricable link between Zen and the martial arts. They developed together, interdependent upon each other. It goes beyond description, beyond words or understanding in the conventional and tangible ways that we use to understand. But imagine "doing without doing, thinking without thinking," or in Japanese mushin, or non-mind. The Samurai had practical reasons for Zen training, as well. There was no time to think in battle. Thoughts became hindrances, and would inhibit just reacting freely. Maybe some martial artists have had glimpses of what I am talking about. There are too many deep implications to go into here. Recently, under the direction of my Zen Master and friend, Genpo (Dennis Merzel) Roshi, in Salt Lake City, Mr. Jules Harris (another dear friend – a Zen monk and 4th dan in Iaido) and I taught a seminar at Kanzeon Zen Center on "Zen and the Martial Arts." We were able to convey and link some of the teachings that Roshi had imparted to us and make them specific to martial artists in an interactive way. It was phenomenal. In the future, I hope to be able to share more of this kind of training.

**How much training should a "senior" karate-ka be doing to improve and get better at the art?**
To begin with, I think we have to endeavor to get better and better throughout our lives, and I believe that this is possible. I have seen people like Soke Kubota who just seems to continue to get stronger and stronger. You have to wonder how that is possible. If you ever have the chance to be his uke, you will understand what I mean. There is an entirely different kind of energy behind the techniques. Sometimes, you don't even feel that you are being touched. It reminds me of the time when I was at the Aikido Hombu in Shinjuku to observe a training session there. I saw one of the senior sensei utilize his ki and drop someone ten feet away. I also saw Akiyama Sensei, when he would come to Hawaii each year, at the age of about 70. He would let all of us take turns hitting him in the stomach, and when you hit him you felt like his stomach was knocking you back. He once knocked me out when I was his

# Karate Masters

"If you look at great masters as they age, many of them become softer in technique, many just meditate, and their strength and power still increase."

uke, demonstrating the bunkai of *Nijushiho-sho*. So, first and foremost, we can become stronger. What we lose in physical ability, we can more than compensate for in terms of knowledge and, more importantly, power from other sources, like chi. The power of chi is limitless. That is why even great masters who rarely train, but do a lot of sitting (meditation), seem to get stronger and stronger to the degree where they are really unapproachable. Take O-Sensei, for example.

As we age, we have to train differently; smarter, not harder. I think that after 40, it becomes more and more important to emphasize health, through practice of activities like yoga in combination with smart training. That would include training every day, yes, but staggering a hard training day with something like tai chi, yoga, or qigong training, where the focus is on suppleness and the breath. Zen training. If you look at great masters as they age, many of them become softer in technique, many just meditate, and their strength and power still increase.

**What advice would you give to students on the question of supplementary training – weights, running, stretching, et cetera?**

I like to cross-train more now, but in the early stages of training I would not encourage it. Why? Early on, it is better to focus just on karate training, and the key is consistency. You have to train every day, even if it for only a few minutes. That consistency is most important. To be good at something, just practice it. You will get the ligament and tendon strength that you really need from the training.

**Why do you think a lot of students start falling away after two-three years of training?**

There are a lot of reasons. We have become a society of instant gratification, of instantaneous results. People fall away for the same reasons that they fall away from marriages and fall away from school and their jobs and their family. They are not willing to put forth the effort to endure hardship for the reward in the long term. This is yet another way in which we differ from the East. We think short-term, and they are always thinking long-term. In general, we have become conditioned not to have to have perseverance or to be disciplined to get what we want. We are a push-button, find the easier way society, which is good and bad. We are not hungry, but rather have become complacent and lazy. People give up when things require patience or commitment. They are not as willing to work. Furthermore, they can get a "Black Belt," in many cases without the commitment and hard work. Why are they training? They only will get something far more dangerous if they are not careful – a false sense of security. If they only realized that the real enemy is the self! If they are interested only in fighting or in a belt, I encourage them to go elsewhere. I am teaching something entirely different ... with those aspects as side benefits."The Way" has nothing to do with rank, but a lot to do with commitment and letting go.

"Ultimately, Karate is a fighting art, and kata, when done correctly, is kumite."

**Have there been times when you felt fear in your karate training?**

Yes, basically, every day at Takudai and Komazawa, or with the JKA instructor trainees..I think that fear has great value; but when you are afraid, be afraid. Be it completely. Use it as a tool to get better and appreciate it. Fear puts you on the edge, and you become very alert. When you have the feeling of realism that we had at Takudai, you really have a feeling of the essence of budo and of the samurai; that you were facing life and death, that you were facing an opponent with a live blade, and that in one instant, it could be all over. It really heightens your awareness – you learn to defend, and when you see a tiny opening, you are so acutely aware, and you know that you have only that split moment in which to attack, and it must be a killing attack; you may not ever get a another chance, and that in the next instant, if you miss, it could be you. That is the mindset with which we should be training all the time ... like a tiger whose life depends on it. Isn't that the way that we should be *living* our lives, all the time? O

# JOE CARBONARA

## A DEBT OF GRATITUDE

He began studying Matsubayashi Ryu in the early 1960's under Ansei Ueshiro and was awarded Shodan, from the Grand Master Shoshin Nagamine. In 1969, he received permission to open the Budokan in East Northport, NY. It became the U.S. Headquarters while Omine Chotoku Sensei, the chief instructor for the Okinawan Hombu, lived and taught at the Budokan Dojo.

His Karate philosophy is simple: kihon, kata, bunkai, yakusoku kumite, and makiwara. Over the years, you come to understand his opinions of what make a good martial artist. His belief is that karate is not a sport, but a way to self-realization. It was not about playing games but something that should be approached with the spirit of the utmost seriousness to develop both mind and body. He would always say he never won a trophy but that his only competition was himself. His way was practiced as a do — a path to both physical and spiritual development and the human endeavor of the highest order, not as an ego-boosting game. This man has helped shape a path of Karate-do for many martial artists. One of the last of the old timers, his devotion to Matsubayashi remains as strong as ever.

**Sensei, in 2010 you celebrated your 75th birthday and the 40th anniversary of the Budokan Dojo. When did you first start your study of the Martial Arts?**

I started in the early '60s with Joe Johnson and Joe Avela, who were partners in the Patchogue, New York, dojo. They were two black belts under Ansei Ueshiro, who was the first Okinawan sent here by Grandmaster Shoshin Nagamine [in 1962].

**When did you first make black belt and by whom?**

I first made black belt in February 1969 and was promoted to shodan by Shoshin Nagamine at Zenko Heshiki's Dojo on 72nd Street in Manhattan. It was in the middle of a blizzard. I was recommended by Ansei Ueshiro, who was also at the promotion.

# Karate Masters

"Kumite was almost every night, and it was no pads and bare knuckles."

**What was your first impression of Ansei Ueshiro?**

My first impression of him was that he was an outstanding martial artist and very strong. He had outstanding ability.

**What was your memory of the training at that time?**

We mostly trained in basic exercises. The group was always lined up in a circle as we had no lineup at that time. The basics consisted mostly of techniques from kumite [freestyle sparring]. Kumite was almost every night, and it was no pads and bare knuckles. There were a lot of injuries at that time and many people decided it wasn't for them. You had to be in the right mindset for these classes.

**Do you have any other recollections of that time?**

In 1969, the Grandmaster came over from Okinawa, and I was among the group of people who went to the airport and to greet him. As I was still a brown belt at that point, I was not allowed to stay for certain meetings and workouts going on at that time to promote Matsubayashi in the United States. There was a very strict code. It was all about etiquette.

**How did you come to meet Chotoku Omine Sensei?**

When Master Nagamine came over at the time of my promotion to black belt, he brought Omine Sensei with him to become director of Matsubayashi Ryu in America. It was 1969 and already in the Lynbrook, New York, dojo there was a split taking place between the Grandmaster and Ansei Ueshiro. I decided to stay with the Grandmaster and Omine Sensei. Ansei Ueshiro advised me at that time to use my own mind to make my decision. Omine Sensei became the instructor in Lynbrook. I would leave my job cutting slipcovers in the New York City area and travel way out to the dojo. My training there under Omine Sensei was mostly kata, and a heavy emphasis was put on the basics to lay the foundation for our training.

**How did you come to open your own dojo?**

After Omine Sensei came over with Shoshin Nagamine and I became a black belt, I was given permission to open my own school. I attempted to buy the Patchogue dojo and was advised not to by Ansei Ueshiro. I found a location in East Northport and was able to open my own dojo in September 1969. The Lynbrook school was closing and the fate of Sensei Omine was decided at a meeting with major black belts from Matsubayashi, such Frank Grant, Zenko Heshiki, and Steve Corriss. I volunteered to take Omine Sensei with me. I also provided him with money and a job helping me cut slipcovers, which I did for a living, and housed him in the back of my dojo, which was over a Big Apple supermarket.

"I do not train for politics; I train for traditional Karate values."

### What do you feel was a turning point in your studies?

The turning point was when I finally made the decision to stay with Sensei Omine and to start training in the basics and kata of the Matsubayashi system as handed down by Grandmaster Shoshin Nagamine.

### How was it having Shoshin Nagamine's representative, Omine Sensei, living with you?

It was fantastic. I had the opportunity to train every day and really got personalized attention. The downside came in 1971, I received a call to go to the dojo because a fire had broken out, and firemen had to pull Sensei Omine from the flames after stopping me from doing so. That's when my wife and I decided to take him into our home and nurse him back to health. He suffered third degree burns from that fire, and as he recovered he helped my children with their homework.

### What happened after this all took place?

In January 1973, I sold my home in Commack and had a new house built in East Northport with a traditional dojo underneath, including a back room made especially for Omine Sensei. In 1975, the Huntington Town Board decided that karate was not a business that could be conducted in a home and I was ordered to stop. Like days of old, we continued to train secretly until we found a location in East Northport for a new dojo. After his recovery, sensei went back to Okinawa. Eventually, he decided to move to

# Karate Masters

"My promotion was always based on loyalty, commitment, and dedication to the art."

California and to bring his family to the states in 1973.

**What happened when Omine Sensei left you?**
When he left, I continued to structure my classes after him beginning with warm-ups, basics, katas, yakusoku kumite, and heavy arm training.

**What was Omine's favorite kata? Which ones did he teach?**
Naihanchi was Omine's strongest kata and one he heavily influenced me with. Omine taught me all the katas except Kusanku, which I learned at age 52 from the Grandmaster's son, Takayoshi Nagamine.

**How long did you have a relationship with your sensei?**
Up till 1975 when he passed away from a brain aneurysm. He was living in California with his family and teaching at his dojo in San Bruno. I had previously taken students out there to train with him. I flew out there and said the eulogy at his funeral. Ueshiro Sensei also attended and was very kind to me at that time. He understood what Sensei Omine had meant to me.

**Did you go back training with Ansei after the loss of your instructor?**
No. After his death, I was directly associated with Grandmaster Nagamine. I went to visit the Grandmaster for the first time in 1980, which I would follow up with four more visits to Okinawa.

**Did he ever come back to visit you here in the United States?**
Yes. In 1983, the Grandmaster came to visit and held a promotion, and a couple of years later, I was promoted to Godan. I continued to correspond with Okinawa while leading classes at my dojo. Several years later Takayoshi Nagamine made a visit. I was then promoted to 6th dan. Before going to Okinawa in 1991, Takayoshi Nagamine visited and tested me, and the Grandmaster later promoted me to the rank of 7th dan. At that time, Frank Grant and I were the highest Shorin Ryu black belts in the United States.

**I know 1991 was your last visit to Okinawa. I was there with you. What were your feelings with so many of the senior people splitting after the celebration for the Grandmaster's birthday and the transfer of the system to his son?

I still kept in line with the Grandmaster up until his death in 1997. I have always had deep feelings for Matsubayashi Shorin Ryu and Okinawa. However, I do not train for politics; I train for traditional values. There comes a certain point in your training where karate has to come from the heart.

### When did you officially close your dojo?

In 1999, I decided to close my dojo and to continue training my high-ranking black belts. I continued to hold Doshi Kai's every four months to keep the spirit of Matsubayashi Shorin Ryu alive.

### Sensei, in 2005, you were promoted by a high-ranking board of senior karate people here in the United States. What did they base that promotion on?

The promotion was based on my loyalty, commitment, and dedication to the art that I truly love. Unfortunately, it has been going in many different directions, and I truly hope that people can pull it back together.

### What do you feel about the state of Matsubayashi today?

Today, Matsubayashi in Okinawa is divided into factions by karate politics and led by senior representatives who have different divisions and their own directions. Still, I feel it is important to keep the art alive.

### What do you see in the future for Shorin Ryu?

Some senior black belts have ties to Okinawa, but not like it was in the 1960s or '70s, or even up till the Grandmaster's death. There has to be one leader, which today realistically it's almost impossible to have. Hopefully, there can be one person to step up.

### Sensei, I know that you are still very active in your own personal training and teaching. How long will you continue?

As long as the powers up above give me the strength to carry on, I will keep on going. That is the true karate spirit.

### Can you give practitioners any advice?

Try to keep in touch with senior members of your organization. Try to keep harmony amongst the group and, hopefully, a leader with a good strong dojo will emerge. O

# HIROYASU FUJISHIMA

## THE ROAD AHEAD

SHIHAN HIROYASU FUJISHIMA STUDIED KARATE AT TAKUSHOKU UNIVERSITY, JAPAN'S LEADING COLLEGIATE KARATE TRAINING CENTER. TODAY, HE IS A PROFESSOR AT CALIFORNIA STATE UNIVERSITY AT NORTHRIDGE (CSUN), WHERE HE TEACHES KARATE AS PART OF THE UNIVERSITY CURRICULUM AND HIS RANK IS 8TH DAN, THE HIGHEST CLASSIFIED BLACK BELT IN THE CONTINENTAL USA WITHIN THE "SHOTOKAN KARATE-DO INTERNATIONAL FEDERATION."

THE AGGREGATION OF MORE THAN 50 YEARS OF KARATE EXCELLENCE HAS ONLY HUMBLED FUJISHIMA SENSEI FURTHER. "IF YOU DO NOT ASSIMILATE THE DOJO KUN INTO YOUR EVERYDAY LIFE, THEN I DON'T BELIEVE YOU CAN HONESTLY PRACTICE THEM IN THE DOJO EITHER," HE SAYS. IN MAY OF 2002, HE RECEIVED THE TITLE OF "HANSHI" FROM THE JAPANESE GOVERNMENT. THIS IS THE HIGHEST TITLE AWARDED FOR A LIFETIME DEDICATED TO EXCELLENCE IN THE MARTIAL ARTS. IT DENOTES AN EXEMPLARY PERSON, A MODEL TO BE FOLLOWED. HE IS ONLY THE TWENTY-SIXTH PERSON TO RECEIVE THIS AWARD IN HISTORY. HIS PHILOSOPHY IS TO TEACH AND SHARE THE ART OF KARATE WITH EVERYONE, REGARDLESS OF AGE, RACE OR ORIGIN: "IN KARATE, TO KNOW THE ROAD AHEAD, YOU HAVE TO ASK THOSE COMING BACK."

**How long have you been practicing Martial Arts?**

I can't recall exactly when I began training. But as far as I can remember, it was from about the age of 15.

**How many styles have you trained in and who were your teachers?**

Throughout the years I had the opportunity to study both aikido and judo. Judo was a requirement in junior high, but I don't remember the instructors' names. I studied aikido under Sensei Harada while in college. As for Shotokan, my first instructor was Sensei Nakagawa in junior high in Sapporo City. I continued training throughout college at Takushoku University, the university that was responsible for developing almost all the major first generation masters including Nakayama Sensei, Nishiyama Sensei, Okazaki Sensei, Kanazawa Kancho, etc. I trained under Coach Takeuchi, but our program was supervised by none other than Nakayama

# Karate Masters

"I got involved with Kancho Kanazawa through my elder brother, who was a fraternity brother of Kancho's."

Sensei. He was perhaps my greatest influence and happens to have been my son's godfather.

**Would you tell us some interesting stories of your early days in Karate and how did you get involved with Sensei Hirozaku Kanazawa's Federation?**

There are a lot of "incidents" that maybe I shouldn't mention, but in the spirit of the interview, I'll make an exception. During my college years, we tended to be more irreverent than perhaps was in our best interest. Some of my college buddies and I went out drinking at a bar. There ended up being an "altercation" where the unfortunate gentlemen we disposed of happened to be young, lower-ranking yakuza members. We got out of there fine, but someone in the bar informed them that we went to Takushoku. The next day, fifteen or twenty of them showed up at our dorm, and we hid for about six hours until they left. Luckily, one of our sempais knew some of them, and the situation was worked out with no further problems from them, but we absorbed a very painful punishment. We were forced to sit in makuso position with a shinai wedged behind our knees for two hours. Needless to say, no one could walk after that, and that made the whole thing not worth it.

I got involved with Kancho Kanazawa through my elder brother, who was a fraternity brother of Kancho's. Of course I knew Sensei Kanazawa from my student days at Takushoku University, but later on, when I had an independent dojo, my brother encouraged me to join SKIF and to remain committed. And that I have done.

**Were you a "natural" at Karate – did the movements come easily to you?**

With great humility, I would have to say that Martial Arts came quite naturally to me. In my youth, I trained in gymnastics until high school, from which I acquired great flexibility and balance, both of which are essential elements when executing proper technique. Playing baseball and other sports helped with my speed and power.

**What are the most important points in your teaching methods today?**

The foundation of what I teach stems from rigorous and consistent training in kihon. This sometimes seems redundant or monotonous to some who don't understand it, but true understanding and implementation of more advanced techniques are impossible without it, in my opinion. This requires a true desire to learn and unwavering patience.

**What is your opinion of modern fighting events such as the UFC and Mixed Martial Arts events?**

I get asked this question quite often from my own students. I think it's a great forum in which millions of people are exposed to Martial Arts, people who might not otherwise take interest in it. However, one thing I don't agree with is how these events seem to sensationalize one style over the other, as opposed to the individuals competing in them. All these fighters utilize techniques from many styles, so how do you give credit to one in particular? This, along with the rules necessary to get the fights sanctioned, makes it hard to discern which style is truly more effective than another. All in all though, it is good entertainment.

**Karate nowadays often is referred to as a sport ... would you agree with this definition or is it a martial art?**

Karate was not created as a sport, but as a way to defend oneself from harm. In this country, it must be taught within certain legal parameters for obvious reasons and due to the fact that many people train as a form of exercise or weight loss. There is also the sport aspect, in which Karateka are able to compete against each other to test themselves. That aside, it is a Martial Art without question.

**What are the most important qualities for a student to become proficient in Karate?**

Proficiency is attained by training based on the three D's – desire, discipline, and determination. These qualities together with respect and patience are almost certain to lead to becoming proficient.

**When teaching the art of Karate – what is the most important element; self-defense or sport?**

This is somewhat of an awkward question for me because the sport aspect

# Karate Masters

"Kata contains elements of application of techniques as would be necessary when confronted by multiple attackers."

of Karate isn't an element of teaching, but rather a gauge or platform on which to showcase skills and techniques learned in training. You might train specifically for sport, but to me that is only customizing your teaching to accommodate the rules of the sport.

**Kihon, Kata and Kumite, what's the proper ratio in training?**

It's hard to say, but roughly 50% kihon, 30% kata, 20% kumite might be a good benchmark to follow. As I said before, thorough and consistent kihon training is irreplaceable. Kata contains elements of application of techniques as would be necessary when confronted by multiple attackers. Lastly, kumite seems for the most part to be the ultimate proving grounds for whether or not all these techniques are viable in a real situation to most students. We will practice more kumite if students are planning to participate in an upcoming tournament. Of course, younger students like sparring and, depending on the composition of a class, more sparring is done, but Karate is so much more than sparring.

**Who would you like to have trained with that you have not?**

Definitely Sensei Funakoshi. It was the dream of my generation to train with him. Very few of my seniors had that opportunity. Among those who did were Nakayama Sensei, Nishiyama Sensei, Okazaki Sensei, and Kancho Kanazawa. I once had the opportunity to observe Sensei Funakoshi as he presided at the examiners' table during a dan grading.

**How important is competition in the evolution of a Karate practitioner?**

I guess that's relative to an individual's goals. Competition can be an encouraging experience or, in some cases, a tremendous setback. I encourage it to allow students to feel a sense of accomplishment for all their hard training. For myself, it also allows me to, yes, gauge the evolution of their skills when competing against people they don't know.

**How do you think a practitioner can increase his or her understanding of the spiritual aspects of the art?**

By applying the Dojo Kun to life outside the dojo: Seek perfection of character, be faithful, endeavor, respect others, etc. If you do not assimilate these rules into your everyday life, then I don't believe you can honestly practice them in the dojo either.

**Is there anything lacking in the way Martial Arts are taught today compared to how they were when you started training?**

It's very hard to compare the training I experienced back then with how the students train now. There are so many lawsuits, sexual harassment guidelines, and other factors that make that type of training almost impossible. I trained in an era when if your senior struck you in the face during kumite, you thanked him afterward and quietly and tended to your injuries after class. As I'm sure you can imagine, that wouldn't go over so well nowadays. To answer your question, I think perhaps there's a lack of respect for tradition and an attitude that demands instant gratification rather than working for results.

"The mastering of any art never ends. There is always something that you don't know. The study of Karate is infinite."

**Do you feel that you still have further to go in your studies?**

The mastering of any art never ends. There is always something that you don't know. The study of Karate is infinite.

**What advice would you give to students on the question of supplementary training (running, weights, et cetera)?**

I would encourage students to supplement their training with such things as running, stretching, and light weight training. Done correctly, these exer-

# Karate Masters

"I would encourage students to supplement their training with such things as running, stretching, and light weight training."

cises help to build and maintain stamina, flexibility, and strength.

**Why is it, in your opinion, that a lot of students start falling away after two-three years of training?**

Sometimes, life just gets in the way. People's living situations, relationships, finances, and other priorities often alter their capability or desire to continue training. There also is a certain plateau that comes after two or three years. It is at this point that great patience is required. If students can pass this plateau, their mental and physical training will deepen, and their progress will become more tangible.

**Have been times when you felt fear in your training?**

Not really. Have I been frustrated, exhausted, injured? Sure. But I've never had a reason to be fearful because of the way I approach my training. If you get hurt, you figure out what mistake you made that allowed that to happen, and correct it so it doesn't happen again.

**Do you think that Olympics will be positive for the art of Karate-do?**

I have mixed feelings due to the sheer politics involved with the Olympics. It's great for creating an atmosphere of pride for your country, and it may help boost interest in Karate to another level.

**What are your views on kata bunkai?**

It is extremely important because without bunkai, there is no kata. Performing kata allows students of varying levels to visualize the applications. These applications vary depending on the individual's skills level. To me, kata is the dictionary of Karate. Kata makes Karate.

**What are your thoughts about doing thousands of repetitions of one single technique in training as in the old days? Is it a good training method?**

We do this once a year at a New Year's training. It is good for students to have this experience, but not on a daily basis.

**What is your opinion of the direction that the style of Shotokan took after the Nakayama Sensei? How do you think these splits have impacted in the Shotokan style of Karate around the world?**

I think Shotokan changed after Nakayama Sensei passed and the JKA split. Some instructors started their own independent organizations, adapting other styles and teaching methods which vary slightly, and in some cases, quite evidently from what the original JKA system was. As far as the style of Shotokan worldwide, I feel it's pretty uniform and consistent in its teachings.

**How do you see the art SKIF evolving in the future?**

I see a bright future for SKIF as there are many young, strong instructors to insure its future growth, including all three of Kanazawa's sons as well as Sensei Murakami. Global expansion

"Kata is the dictionary of Karate. Kata makes Karate."

has been a main focus of SKIF, which is the reason it is so important to prepare the next generation of instructors to support this growth.

**What is your opinion about the differences/modifications in kata that can be seen in the Shotokan style? Are they really important?**

To me, I see that the sport aspect has had a great influence in these differences or modifications from the original way katas were taught. They seem faster and flashier but in many ways lack the "budo" that defines what Shotokan is in my eye.

**What can Karate offer to the individual in these troubled times we are living in?**

Karate training can offer great personal satisfaction. In the dojo, one forgets about troubles. I have seen students between the ages of 12 to 15 who were very good. They showed great promise. Then they quit. Afterward, they had problems in school, got into all sorts of trouble. They didn't have

# Karate Masters

"My responsibility as an instructor is to teach the concept of Martial Arts, mental and physical development."

the chance to internalize the dojo rules of discipline and patience. In a larger sense, students who train form a part of a larger international community, meeting in peace for tournaments and seminars.

**How do you like to train yourself? Has this changed over the years?**

Yes, it has changed over the years. As the body grows older, it reacts differently and cannot do the same things as a younger body. I have an advantage not all instructors have. I teach Karate in one of the best facilities in the nation, the department of Kinesiology at California State University, Northridge. I can utilize the resources to research ways to compensate for loss or recovery. Every ten years, I change the set of exercises I do to reflect changes in my body.

**Is your style of teaching the same as the traditional Japanese method or do you have your own ideas?**

I have learned a lot from teaching college students at the University for more than 40 years. Many students take Karate to get a unit of credit and have no idea what it means to train in a Martial Art. Many different attitudes are brought in and I have learned to be open to them. My responsibility as an instructor is to teach the concept of Martial Arts, mental and physical development, the dojo kun. Every semester, you face a new group of students and there is always much to learn from them. In the beginning of my teaching career at the University, I was faced with students of so many different levels of understanding. At the same time, I taught students at my dojo. The students at the University were not at the same level with the students at the dojo and I had to be open-minded to learn and discover what aspects of my teaching reached them. According to university policy, all instructors are evaluated annually by their students (and by other faculty members as well). Reading their feedback on the evaluations gave me a lot of insight into what reached them and what did not. Therefore, over the years, my teaching has undergone some modifications for the university students. At the dojo, I am able to maintain more of a traditional style.

**What advice would you give to an instructor who is struggling with his or her own development?**

I would say that perhaps they stopped training and started teaching too soon. This seems to be a widespread problem these days where you have instructors who lack both the knowledge and experience required to properly "instruct" someone else. I would advise them to return to more regimented training so that they can properly understand what it is they are trying to teach.

**What are the real technical differences between the Kancho Kanazawa method of Shotokan and any other Karate styles, including other 'branches' of Shotokan?**

Kancho's style is very traditional. He has created an organized system for SKIF instructors to follow. The curriculum has a sound basis in body movement and structure, and it is accessible to students of all levels and skills and to all for a lifetime.

**Finally, what advise would you like to give to all Karate practitioners and martial artists in general?**

Consistency. Train with consistency. Regardless of what you study, what you train for, or what you desire to learn, there is very little chance you will reach your potential without consistency. O

"Regardless of what you study, what you train for, or what you desire to learn, there is very little chance you will reach your potential without consistency."

# KENNETH FUNAKOSHI

## TOUCHING BUDO

KENNETH FUNAKOSHI STARTED JUDO TRAINING IN 1948 UNDER ARAKAKI SENSEI AT THE FORT GAKUEN JAPANESE LANGUAGE SCHOOL IN HONOLULU, HAWAII. WHILE ATTENDING THE UNIVERSITY OF HAWAII ON A SWIMMING SCHOLARSHIP, HE TRAINED UNDER KAJUKENBO FOUNDER ADRIANO D. EMPERADO FROM 1956 TO 1959.

IN 1960, SENSEI FUNAKOSHI STARTED KARATE TRAINING WHEN THE JAPAN KARATE ASSOCIATION (JKA) ASSIGNED ITS FIRST GRAND CHAMPION, HIROKAZU KANAZAWA, TO TEACH AT THE KARATE ASSOCIATION OF HAWAII FOR THREE YEARS. A YOUNG KEN FUNAKOSHI TRAINED UNDER MASATAKA MORI, ANOTHER SENIOR INSTRUCTOR FROM THE JAPANESE KARATE ASSOCIATION. FROM 1966 TO 1969, HE TRAINED UNDER THE THIRD AND LAST INSTRUCTOR SENT BY THE JKA, THE LEGENDARY TETSUHIKO ASAI, ANOTHER FORMER GRAND CHAMPION FROM JAPAN. IN 1969, AFTER TRAINING 10 YEARS UNDER THREE OF JAPAN'S TOP INSTRUCTORS AND WINNING THE GRAND CHAMPIONSHIP OF THE KARATE ASSOCIATION OF HAWAII FOR FIVE YEARS IN A ROW (1964–1968), SENSEI KENNETH FUNAKOSHI WAS APPOINTED AS THE CHIEF INSTRUCTOR FOR THE KARATE ASSOCIATION OF HAWAII.

SENSEI FUNAKOSHI MOVED TO SAN JOSE, CALIFORNIA TO TEACH KARATE IN DECEMBER 1986, IN 1987, THE "FUNAKOSHI SHOTOKAN KARATE ASSOCIATION" WAS FOUNDED.

**How long have you been practicing the Martial Arts?**
I have been practicing martial arts for 61 years: ten years Judo, three years Kempo, and 48 years in Karate. I began training Judo when I was 10 years old. After attending regular schools, some of the Japanese students went to Japanese language schools. I attended Fort Gakuen Japanese School. After Japanese school, I trained Judo under Arakaki Sensei. My Judo training has helped to make my Karate fighting stronger. At age 18, I trained under Adriano D. Emperado at the Palama Settlement dojo. When I was 22 years old, I started Shotokan under Sensei Kanazawa for three years, under Mori Sensei for three years, and Asai Sensei for four years. They were sent to Hawaii to teach by the Japan Karate Association.

# Karate Masters

"Kanazawa Sensei was a good example because he could knock out an attacker with one punch or kick, which he did on some occasions on the street and in closed door challenges."

**Would you tell us some interesting stories of your early days in karate?**

After the first day of training in Kempo, Mr. Emperado recommended that I train in the advanced class. After training two months as a white belt, I won the first Kempo tournament held in Wahiawa, Hawaii. A week later, Mr. Emperado awarded a blue belt to me.

I taught Kempo at Cannon Air Force Base in New Mexico when I was 21 years old. When I was stationed at Hickam Air Force Base in Hawaii, I started training under Kanazawa Sensei. When I first watched Kanazawa Sensei teaching karate, I was surprised because his classes were slow and easy. I thought the training was supposed to be rough, tough, and hard, like Kempo. I later learned that you don't treat your beginners like advanced students. The training became harder as you got higher in rank. The longer you trained, the more you saw the benefits of the JKA Shotokan system.

When I first trained under Kanazawa Sensei, during the one step kumite practice, I blocked my opponent's punch and performed several punches, back fist strikes, threw my opponent down, and kicked him several times when he went down on the floor (this is the way we practiced in Kempo self-defense). Kanazawa Sensei said, "No, no! You have to block and punch only one time." The reason for this type of defense was that you must have the confidence that you can disable your attacker with one punch in case there are multiple attackers. Kanazawa Sensei was a good example because he could knock out an attacker with one punch or kick, which he did on some occasions on the street and in closed door challenges.

On one occasion, when I had just removed the cast from my right hand (Kanazawa Sensei had broken it during kumite practice), I was driving home one night and I honked my horn at a guy who almost hit my car. He forced me to the side and pulled me out of my car. He was moving around and jabbing his hands like he was a boxer. I think he was showing off because he had two girls in his car. I punched him once in his mouth and, as he was falling to the ground, I kicked him in the head. Immediately he said, "I'm sorry. I'm sorry." He was bleeding a lot from his mouth and I thought I had broken my right hand again, but it was okay. I still have some scars on my right knuckles.

During the 1960s, our tournaments were only for JKA members. The other dojos had their own competitions, which we were not allowed to compete in. One of the other dojos challenged us to a closed door match when Asai Sensei was still our resident sensei. He instructed me on some dirty fighting techniques in case the matches got out of hand. After the last scheduled training was over and the students left, we closed the doors and waited for our challengers to come. They came as promised and we started our matches. At the end of the matches, our challengers left with a broken nose and some cut lips. We never heard from them again.

**Were you a 'natural' at karate – did the movements come easily to you?**

Looking back at my experience in sports, I can say that karate was the most natural and comfortable movements for me to learn. I was a strong Judo-ka, first starter in high school football, captain of the territorial high school swimming team, and first chair trumpet in high school, but karate was the most natural for me. I excelled in the other accomplishments, but it only was because of hard training, not natural movements or talent.

**How has your personal expression in karate developed over the years and what is it that keeps you motivated after all these years?**

When you are young, the most important thing is to improve your competition techniques. After a few years of competition, the goal of winning is not important. Your mind and body feel that there is more in karate than winning tournament. You start to remember what your parents and karate instructors were teaching about perfecting your character. When you become an instructor and parent, you feel the responsibility to teach your students and children about the spiritual development as well as the physical development.

The younger generation needs all the spiritual development it can get. When I began to travel in Europe 20 years ago, the karate students did not know what the Dojo Kun was about. They thought karate was only a sport. I started to lecture about the Dojo Kun and the spiritual training of karate. Now, many of the countries request that I teach them about the spiritual part of karate training as well as the physical training. I teach a good portion about spiritual training in my seminars.

# Karate Masters

The most important point is to emphasize spirit first, technique second, according to Master Gichin Funakoshi. I first explain about spirit, respect, and etiquette; then about punches and kicks.

**What is your opinion of fighting events such as the UFC and Mixed Martial Arts events?**

They are okay because the UFC and MMA introduced a different level of fighting. However, there still are rules to fight by according to the different organizations. I prefer the K-1 competition in Japan, where the fighters must stand up, kick, and punch. Some other martial artists complain that grappling on the floor takes too much time and gets boring. It is okay if an effective submission is executed right away. If you are attacked on the street, you must dispose your attacker quickly with one punch or kick because there might be another one or two attackers behind you. Also, you are at a disadvantage if you are wrestling too long with an attacker who has a knife.

**Karate nowadays often is referred to as a sport... would you agree with this definition or is a Martial Art?**

It is both. Some people train karate and enter tournaments for a few years and some practice karate as a way of life forever. I teach karate more as a Martial Art. Some people begin to train in my dojo as a sport. Gradually, their attitudes change and see my karate as a Martial Art.

**What are the most important qualities for a student to become proficient in karate?**

First, the student must have a qualified instructor who also is a fine human being. The sensei must know how to develop the spirit in the student. Second, the student must have natural athletic abilities and be willing to train forever. If you don't have natural abilities, train as hard as you can and you still will develop physically and spiritually.

**When teaching the art of karate, what is the most important element: self-defense or sport?**

The single most important element in karate, whether it is sport or self-defense, is spirit. Without spirit, you have nothing. A long time ago when there were no tournament competitions, more time was spent in Kata and Bunkai. The katas are based on defending and counterattacking techniques. Now that tournament competition is popular, the emphasis is on attacking to score points rather than defending and counter punching.

Self-defense on the street is more important than sport karate. Karate started for self-defense. Sport karate came much later. It wouldn't be proper for a tournament champion not to be able to defend himself on the streets. On the street, it is your spirit that will save your life, not your tournament record or medals. Two of my high school friends were hospitalized from knife wounds in street fights. One of my Kempo instructors was killed in a bar fight by a knife attack. These incidents happened during the late 1950s when people didn't carry guns.

On the street, I had fought an attacker with a knife and was confronted by a person holding a hammer. I also had one-on-one fights and two gang fights, coincidently with football team members. The gang fights really made me realize later how important spirit is in real fighting, like in the street, where there are no rules.

"Self-defense on the street is more important than sport karate. Karate started for self-defense."

### Kihon, Kata, and Kumite, what's the proper ratio in training?

The most time should be spent in Kihon, about 50 percent, because Kihon is needed in your Kata and Kumite; 25 percent should be practicing kata, 15 percent in Kumite, and 10 percent in self-defense. A long time ago, when there were no tournament competitions, more time was spent in kata and bunkai. The katas are based on defending and counterattacking techniques. Now that tournament competition is popular, the emphasis is on attacking to score points rather than defending and counter punching.

Too much kumite results in too many injuries. Karate training also is a way of developing good health, not injuring yourself.

### Who would you like to have trained with that you have not?

I trained with two of the world's best Shotokan instructors, Kanazawa Sensei and Asai Sensei. I trained for three years under Mori Sensei, another senior sensei from the *Japan Karate Association*. I also trained with Senseis Nakayama, Kase, Enoeda, and Shirai, etc. I would have wanted to train under my fourth cousin, Master Gichin Funakoshi, but when he died in 1957, I was only 18 years old and training kempo.

# Karate Masters

"You must have an instructor who explains every word of the Dojo Kun and gives lectures of what it means in your daily life, not only in the dojo."

**How important is competition in the evolution of a karate practitioner?**

Competition is important because it tests your progress in the fighting category, but the real test is in the streets, where there are no rules. I know because I had many altercations in the streets growing up in Hawaii. The experiences fighting in the streets have made me understand the meaning of spirit. This has been my basis for teaching fighting.

**How do you think a practitioner can increase his/her understanding of the spiritual aspects of the art?**

You must have an instructor who explains every word of the Dojo Kun and gives lectures of what it means in your daily life, not only in the dojo. Don't just repeat the Dojo Kun after every training class, but live it every day outside the dojo. I was brought up by my parents to be a good human being and I learned karate techniques from my instructors.

**Is there anything lacking in the way Martial Arts are taught today in comparison to how they were when you started training?**

The question is, do you want a few strong and dedicated students or do you want many students who are not strong? If you are teaching karate for a living, then you have big expenses to pay every month (rent, insurance, utilities, advertising, etc.). You must teach karate according to what you want to do. Is karate a hobby and you have another full time career? Or, do you teach karate as your only source of income?

I would be the first to admit that the teaching has changed to accommodate the new generation of karate practitioners. Some students want to train once or twice a week for only two months. The average students train for about two to four months and start to lose interest because repetition is boring. They don't realize that repetition is the secret to good karate techniques. Repetition develops patience and perfection. When I was training, we did the same techniques and kata over and over again. We never questioned why; we just did it.

**Do you feel that you still have further to go in your studies?**

You never stop learning. Generally, you learn in three phases. The first phase is the physical phase, in which you are young and train to improve your techniques for better punches, kicks, kata, kumite, competition, etc. The second phase is the mental phase, when you are older and you start to teach. You become smarter and wiser because of your experience teaching people, knowing them, their different ages, sizes, minds, etc. The third phase is the spiritual phase, because of your experience in karate and life. This is when you are much older and have learned to add different teachings and techniques along the way. I learn something new about life, culture and karate every time I go to a different country to teach.

**What advice would you give to students on the question of supplementary training?**

If you have time, it is okay, as long as it complements your training. Too much lifting or running might work against your karate training.

**Why is it, in your opinion, that a lot of students start falling away after two or three years of training?**

Actually, they start falling away sooner. First it is our culture, the American way. If you get bored, it is okay to quit and do something else. In Japan, you are considered to be a quitter if you quit training. Second, the parents of the children think it's okay to quit. Third, there are many distractions or other activities for the children to try. Today, if you fail a student for a karate exam, he will quit. The true spirit of karate is to try harder the next time. If a student tries again after I failed him/her two times, I will pass him/her the third time because of his/her spirit. I grade my students on their spirit as well as their physical level.

**Have there been times when you felt fear in your training?**

Again, I must stress the importance of spirit in karate training. If you have the proper training, you never will be afraid while training or while competing because everything is supervised and controlled. Of course, accidents will happen. There should be a little fear while fighting in the streets because there are no rules.

**Do you think that Olympics will be positive for the art of karate-do?**

It will be good for the sport of karate, but not good for the art of Karate-Do. It is two different things. Olympic karate will encourage more students to train but only for the purpose of winning, which inflates the ego. Karate-Do is to deflate the ego, be humble, and perfect your character.

# Karate Masters

**What are your views on kata bunkai?**

I always have stressed bunkai after learning a kata. It gives you a better insight while doing the movements in a kata. You have better meaning and movements when you understand the bunkai. However, kata and bunkai will not replace kumite. You must train in kumite because you have an attacking opponent and the movements are not rehearsed.

**What is your idea about incorporating kata from other styles in Shotokan Karate?**

I think it should be kept separate because that's what makes karate unique. It is difficult enough to teach a student one style; why confuse or add another kata from another style? It is okay to fight the same way in kumite because the rules and requirements are the same.

**What are your thoughts about doing thousands of repetitions of one single technique in training, as in the old days?**

Repetition is the secret to success for traditional karate. However, many stories about thousands of punches and kicks are exaggerated. Every January for the past 15 years at my main dojo, we have training called the "Month of 2,000 Punches." During the first week of training, we punch 250 left and right punches. During the second week, we do 500 punches from each side. The third week, we do 750 punches from each side. The fourth week, we do 1,000 punches from each side. It takes one hour to do the "Night of 2,000 Punches."

Of course, these punches are done in a relaxed, snapping manner. Doing only 100 kicks from each side is difficult. I remind my students that it is physically hard to do the "Night of 2,000 Punches," but it is more spirit training because when the body gets tired and wants to give up, the spirit pushes the mind to continue. Repetition teaches you to relax and use only the necessary muscles to do an efficient technique. Using too many unnecessary muscles only slows your movements. Speed is more important than power.

**What is your opinion of the direction that JKA took after the death of Nakayama Sensei. How do you think these splits have impacted the Shotokan style of Karate around the world?**

JKA is a large established karate organization, so it will continue no matter who leaves. Whenever the head instructor dies, some of the remaining senior senseis will leave. In the JKA, the three most senior senseis – Nishiyama, Okazaki, and Kase – were established outside of Japan. I think it

"Unfortunately, politics is very involved in Karate these days and politics is the worst things that can happen to the art."

would have been difficult for any of them to move back to Japan. My two senseis, Kanazawa and Asai, already had left JKA because of political problems. In my opinion, after Kanazawa Sensei left the JKA, Asai Sensei should have been appointed as Chief Instructor, but older senseis thought Asai Sensei was too young. I think Kanazawa and Asai Sensei both had the technical abilities, personality, and tournament reputation to be the Chief Instructor of JKA.

Unfortunately, politics is very involved in Karate these days and politics is the worst things that can happen to the art. At the upper level of the Associations and Federations, there are interests and political attitudes than prevent students at the lower level from competing and participating with other groups, and this puts a lot of restrictions on what they can and can't do.

**What is your opinion about the differences in kata that some masters have introduced?**

I am sure that the other masters who have changed the katas have their reasons. We must respect them for whatever they do. I, myself, want to change some movements in our katas, but for the sake of Shotokan stan-

# Karate Masters

"If a student is loyal and stays with his sensei for a long time, he can be trusted over new students."

dards, I never will change anything. It is better to add katas, but to change the existing movements of a kata would only confuse the students around the world. It is difficult enough to standardize the existing kata. Why change them? One of the formulas for having a successful world karate organization is to standardize all of the katas. The changes in Shotokan politically and technically will be for the best. Asai Sensei introduced many advanced techniques that I have been teaching in my system. I have not changed the basic Shotokan techniques. I just have added the advanced techniques to my training curriculum. The basic kihon and kata have not changed. I have added my own advanced techniques and my students have done very well in competition.

**We know loyalty is an important aspect in your teachings; how does this principle affect the character of the practitioner?**

Loyalty in the Samurai Class was the most important element to his Lord (Shogun), because life or death for his Lord was his responsibility. This element "To Be Faithful" is handed down in the Dojo Kun. This also is practiced in the daily lives of the Japanese. This is the reason the Japanese are loyal to their employer forever. Loyalty in the Martial Arts still should be practiced today.

If a student is loyal and stays with his sensei for a long time, he can be trusted over new students. Nowadays, you have high ranking students or instructors transferring to other organizations. You don't know if they can be trusted or awarded higher ranks. They may leave your organization soon after they receive their promotion from you. We learn this from experience.

I think that this lack of loyalty is more widespread now because we have succeeded in teaching the techniques of Karate but obviously we have failed to emphasize enough the values of *Seeking Perfection of Character* and *Being Faithful*. The importance of Dojo Kun is not explained enough these days and people don't understand how valuable these principles are for our lives.

Two of my most proven, loyal, and best competitors and instructors are my two sons. I can see why in the past other senseis have handed dojos to their sons. They can be trusted. I have experienced situations in which some of my high-ranked instructors seemed to be loyal but planned to open their own dojos without my knowledge. In this day and age where loyalty doesn't mean much, you just go on with your life. In the Samurai Age, this would have been dealt with differently.

**Etiquette is a very important element in Budo; how does this affect the arts of Budo?**
There are three elements that form what a Karate dojo is about: etiquette, respect, and courtesy. You erase one of these principles and there is no dojo anymore. Etiquette in the dojo comes from the respect for rank. Karate dojo is based on rank and the etiquette is respect for rank. These three elements are very important in developing the spiritual aspect of Karate, and the lack of teachings from instructors to students is one of the biggest problems that I see in the art of Karate around the world.

**Then, do you think that spirituality can be taught through Karate training?**
Yes, it can, but the dojo shouldn't be the place where this spiritual training must start. The spiritual training of any child must start with the parents at home. What we see today is that parents fail in teaching any spirituality to their children and then pass this "responsibility" to the school teachers. School is the place to learn academic issues, not spiritual matters. The spiritual aspects are supposed to be taught at home, and enforced at school and at the dojo. The result is that we see parents expecting the Karate teacher do all the disciplining and teaching that they don't do at home.

**What can karate offer to the individual in these troubled times we are living in?**
Whatever the problem an individual may have, karate training can have many benefits. After a rigorous workout, it can make your body relax. You forget the stress of your work or problems. You can sleep better and wake up the next morning refreshed. It can develop your spirit to never give up. Your health also will improve. You can be among friends whenever you go to the dojo. You can discuss problems with your sensei and other senpais. Many students have told me that karate training was the main reason that they got through a crisis.

If you practice the Dojo Kun to be a better person, you have peace of mind knowing that you are an honest and humble person. You have peace and harmony within yourself. Wisdom is when you know others. Enlightenment is when you know yourself.

**After so many years of training in Shotokan, what is so appealing for you in this style of karate, and why?**
When I began training Shotokan almost 50 years ago, I didn't know if there were different styles or the size and history of the Japanese Karate Association. I only had to compare it with my training and exposure to Kempo in Hawaii. I realized that to be a karate-ka, you don't have to be macho and strong outwardly. In Shotokan, you learn to develop your character, to be humble and courteous. You don't have to be a naturally gifted athlete. Anyone can develop and improve his or her techniques. The JKA had a good system of training, examinations, tournaments, and organizational structure. My parents used to talk about Gichin Funakoshi but I didn't know he was connected to the JKA or Shotokan.

**Americans generally are physically bigger than Japanese; how do you think this has affected their karate?**
Americans are bigger than the Japanese, but the Europeans are bigger than the Americans. The Russians are bigger than the Europeans and they train the hardest. Size does have its advantages in kumite but not in kata. In Japan, kumite competition does not have any weight categories like we do. So, everybody is in the same division. Boxing, wrestling, and Judo (even in Japan) have different weight categories.

The Japanese do not concentrate on size or strength. They emphasize speed, distancing, and timing. Even though the Americans are bigger than the Japanese, the Japanese competitors still do well against bigger opponents. There should be weight categories.

**How do you see your own karate as opposed to, say, twenty or thirty years ago?**
Due to aging, my own karate techniques and reflexes have gotten slower. My basic kihon, kata, and kumite are still the same as the traditional method but I have added and changed the middle and advanced techniques to my curriculum. When I was appointed JKA Chief Instructor of Hawaii more than 40 years ago, I used to train with my advanced students every day for 25 years. As I got older, I traveled more and trained less. I try to train while I am teaching.

At my age, I don't have the condition and stamina to train as much as I like. However, experiencing the different phases of karate and in life, this has enabled me to broaden my teaching philosophy. I understand how the human body ages and how slow the reflexes become. Through the years, I have become more tolerant, more understanding and more patient. However, my teachings have gotten much better due to experience and travels. The older I get, the more requests I have for seminars and magazine interviews. My main goal is to teach Shotokan Karate-Do. I want to continue in Gichin Funakoshi's path. You become more philosophical in your teaching and personal life as you become older.

**You have had a very impressive competition career. Could you please give us some of your highlights?**

I competed for only five years, 1964-1968 in the JKA Hawaii Championships, All America Karate Federation and JKA Championships in Japan. I won 1st Place in Kata five

"If you practice the Dojo Kun to be a better person, you have peace of mind knowing that you are an honest and humble person."

times, 1st Place in Kumite three times, and 2nd Place two times in the JKA-Hawaii Championships. In Nishiyama Sensei's All American Karate Federation Championships, I was awarded 2nd Place in Kata and Kumite for three years. I was appointed as the Chief Instructor so I did not compete after 1968, but my kumite got better after I started to teach.

My most memorable match was in 1965 when the Hawaii Team competed against the All Star Collegiate Team from Japan. The team from Japan had just beaten Nishiyama's team in Los Angeles the week before coming to Hawaii. After four matches, the score was tied at two wins for Hawaii and two wins for Japan. Since I was the Captain of the Hawaii Team, I went up last against Mr. T. Ozawa, the Captain of the Japanese Team. I won the match with a "gyaku-tsuki" scoring an "ippon" to win the team title for Hawaii. I learned a lot from this match and still think about it.

In 1966, four senior instructors from the JKA stopped in Hawaii on their way to Europe. The instructors were Senseis Kase, Kanazawa, Enoeda, and

# Karate Masters

"I enjoy teaching karate anywhere, especially where the students are eager to learn."

Shirai. There was an exhibition team match between the JKA instructors and a select team from Hawaii. The JKA instructors all won their matches except my match with Sensei Shirai, a current JKA Kata and Kumite Champion. Our match ended in a draw.

In 1969 when I was the instructor for JKA Hawaii, my team won the All Star Collegiate team from Japan again. I also competed in the JKA Championships in Japan many times beginning in 1963 which was a good experience.

**What advice would you give to an instructor who is struggling with his or her own development?**

Before becoming a sensei with one's own dojo, you must have trained and assisted under a qualified sensei for a long time. Even after you were given permission to be an instructor, you still must train at the main dojo and be supervised how to teach by your sensei. Too many young karate-ka are too inexperienced and not qualified to teach properly independently. Some recreational centers offer only introductory classes to children and beginners so you don't need a high ranking sensei. I understand this kind of situation. If you feel that you need more development, see a qualified sensei.

**You do a lot of traveling. Do you enjoy this aspect of karate?**

I enjoy teaching karate anywhere, especially where the students are eager to learn. The problem I have with traveling is the long plane rides and the jet lag from the different time zones. I don't like delayed flights and cancellations.

**Which teachers influenced you the most?**

All three of my Shotokan senseis influenced me at different times of my training. I was a white belt when I first saw Kanazawa Sensei. He was currently the Kata and Kumite Champion for several years from the JKA, so we were all impressed with his strong and beautiful techniques. He emphasized big windups and kime. He broke one of my knuckles during kumite when I was a brown belt. Kanazawa Sensei had a nice personality and everyone liked him.

In 1963, I attended the JKA Championships in Fukuoka, Japan. Kanazawa Sensei picked me up at the train station. During the tournament, Enoeda Sensei broke the neck of another tournament favorite, Nakaya Sensei, who still is paralyzed today from the neck down. Sensei Enoeda threw Sensei Nakaya to the floor while competing in the semi-final matches. I was a young shodan at that time, so I sat in the back of the hospital meeting room while the senior JKA officials and senseis headed by Nakayama Sensei changed the kumite rules to eliminate the throwing techniques.

After the tournament, Kanazawa Sensei gave me a memorable tour of Japan, visited Mori Sensei's wife (Mori Sensei was in Hawaii at the time), all the tourist places, etc. As busy as he was, Kanazawa Sensei still made the time to take care of me. I still have good memories of him.

My second sensei was Masataka Mori. He was a strict disciplinarian and he insisted on long and low basic stances. Some students didn't understand him because he was strict, serious, and didn't smile in the dojo. I knew him as a fine person because I taught him English every Saturday morning and he treated me to a beef teriyaki lunch afterwards. I received my Nidan from Mori Sensei.

Asai Sensei was my third instructor. He introduced us to his advanced techniques that nobody taught. He amazed everyone with his speed and techniques that nobody could do. His feats were legendary even when he was competing in Japan. He stressed speed, timing, and body shifting. I learned not only speed by practicing kumite with Asai Sensei, but the importance of accuracy. I also learned a lot from Asai Sensei because I was a sandan at that time.

"Sensei Masatoshi Nakayama, Chief Instructor of the JKA, also had a big influence on me because he was a few of the remaining senseis who trained under Master Gichin Funakoshi."

In 1984, when I visited Japan, Asai Sensei, his wife (Keiko) and his daughter (Hoshimi), picked me up at the airport. I spent two weeks at his home and he treated me like royalty. I was his student but he didn't let me spend even one yen while I was there as his guest. We trained at 6:30 in the morning in his backyard before his wife prepared our breakfast. We went to train again at the Instructor's class at the JKA Main Dojo. This training schedule continued for two weeks and we reviewed the changes or back to basics katas that I incorporated in my kata and bunkai videos when I returned to Hawaii. Asai Sensei was the Chief Instructor for the Instructor's Class at the JKA Main Dojo.

Asai Sensei's wife is originally from Taiwan and her family has a long history of Gigong and Kung Fu experience. Her brother was a Kung Fu Master and he trained with Asai Sensei to exchange their techniques and ideas. Unfortunately, Asai Sensei passed away in 2006. I had not seen Asai Sensei and his family for more than 22 years so I attended his funeral with my two sons. Mrs. Asai visited me in California the following year. We still keep in touch and write or talk on the phone. She is a remarkable and talented woman.

Sensei Masatoshi Nakayama, Chief Instructor of the JKA, also had a big influence on me because he was a few of the remaining senseis who trained under Master Gichin Funakoshi. He developed the Japan Karate Association to the worldwide organization that it is today. He also continued Gichin Funakoshi's teaching of perfecting your character through karate training. He awarded me a godan at the JKA Main Dojo.

Most students only see their senseis at the dojo during training sessions. I was fortunate to spend a lot of time with my senseis in their homes, traveling with their families, and having long conversations after dinners. It is important to see them in normal situations at home and seeing them as a husband and father as well as a sensei in the dojo. I always talk about my experiences with my senseis to my students. I also want my students to know me as a person outside the dojo but still maintain the student–instructor relationship and respect.

**What are the real technical differences between the Shotokan method and any other karate styles?**

Nowadays, kumite methods are the same because of the requirements in scoring techniques in tournaments. The biggest differences would be in kata, because of Shotokan's long and low stances in the kihon and kata. I would say that it is suited for conditioning the body for fighting. My FSKA organization style of kata is the same as JKA but the footwork in advanced kihon and kumite is different. We stress a lot of footwork in attacking. You must train in my seminars to understand what I am talking about. I haven't trained in other karate styles so I cannot criticize or elaborate about them. We must respect all other styles of karate and martial arts. That is my teachings.

**Do you practice any other art in conjunction with karate?**

No, I am too preoccupied with teaching and researching Shotokan karate. I find myself spending more time behind the desk than teaching on the dojo floor. I spend more time writing and answering e-mails and writing articles for magazines. I have been requested many times to write a book on karate techniques. If I should write a book, it will be about my training, teaching, travels, and experiences in life. It will not be about winning tournaments.

**Where do you see your Organization going in the future?**

My organization, Funakoshi Shotokan Karate Association (FSKA), is growing steadily every year. There are many karate organizations that need training and guidance from a parent organization like mine. There also are many organizations and instructors that want to get away from political problems with their dojos. I stress a non-political organization because all affiliated dojos report directly to me. There is no one person who is the country or district representative of FSKA. My affiliates can write or phone me directly at home if they want to talk to me.

**Finally, what advice would you like to give to all Karate practitioners?**

First, find a qualified sensei. Second, stay out of politics and just train as hard and as often as you can. Third, practice the Dojo Kun to perfect your character. O

# PAUL GODSHAW

## UNPARALLELED EXPERIENCE

PAUL GODSHAW IS THE CHIEF INSTRUCTOR OF THE MISSION VIEJO BRANCH OF THE JAPAN KARATE-DO FEDERATION AND HAS ONE OF THE MOST IMPRESSIVE BACKGROUNDS OF MARTIAL ARTS EXPERIENCE IN THE UNITED STATES. HE STARTED TRAINING IN 1965 WITH DAN IVAN AND FUMIO DEMURA, AND IT WAS UNDER THEIR TUTELAGE THAT HE EARNED A YON-DAN (4TH DAN) BLACK BELT. BY STRICT EXAMINATION OF THE MASTERS OF THE INTERNATIONAL MARTIAL ARTS FEDERATION, PAUL GODSHAW ALSO HAS BEEN AWARDED A HACHIDAN (8TH DAN BLACK BELT IN KARATE-DO).

HE BEGAN TEACHING KARATE IN 1973 AND BECAME A RESPECTED COMPETITOR FOR MANY YEARS. TODAY, SENSEI GODSHAW MAINTAINS THE VERY HIGHEST STANDARD FOR OFFICIATING AND TEACHING THE TRADITIONAL ART OF KARATE. THESE STANDARDS AND RESPECT IN THE MARTIAL ARTS WORLD HAVE EARNED HIM THE TITLE OF DIRECTOR OF THE INTERNATIONAL MARTIAL ARTS FEDERATION (IMAF) FOR THE UNITED STATES OF AMERICA.

**How long have you been practicing the martial arts and who are your teachers?**

I have been training in the martial arts for more than four decades. I have trained in two styles of Japanese Karate-do extensively, Shotokan and Itosukai Shito Ryu. Also, because of my membership in the Kokusai Budoin, the International Martial Arts Federation, I have several years of training in Nihon Jujutsu and in Kobudo. I have been extremely fortunate to be a student of Dan Ivan Sensei, who is regarded as one of the pioneers of bringing and teaching Japanese Budo to the United States after World War II. Also, I trained under the tutelage of Fumio Demura Sensei, who is one of the top Shito Ryu and Kobudo instructors in the U.S.

**How it was the training at that time?**

In the early days of karate training, we weren't concerned about liability insurance. As a matter of fact, if you couldn't take the training, you could move on. It was quite common for outsiders to want to come and train or test our abilities and the dojo was receptive as long as one was respectful.

# Karate Masters

"The early training was extremely vigorous. That is the way they trained in Japan, so we did the same here."

On one occasion, a person asked to train with us, but shortly after sparring started he became abusive, especially to junior belts and female students. So when he rotated to me, Ivan Sensei gave me the look – to kick his ass – and I did. He never returned.

The early training was extremely vigorous. That is the way they trained in Japan, so we did the same here. Kihon was practiced constantly and it was commonplace for us to start a class with five hundred punches and five hundred kicks from various stances. Our conditioning was excellent and we executed good techniques because of all of the repetitions of the basics.

**Were you a "natural" at karate – did the movements come easily to you?**

I was very fortunate that I was a pretty good athlete. I played all major sports in high school and played basketball and threw discuss in college. I don't necessarily think that Karate movements came naturally, but my athletic background helped. From the first day I started training, I knew I had found something that I was passionate about. I never felt like quitting, I just wanted to learn more and get better at what I had learned.

**What are the most important points in your teaching methods?**

For me, the most important points to stress are good form, execution of technique, physical fitness, mental toughness, and a correct attitude.

**With all the technical changes during the last years, do you think there is still "pure" shotokan karate?**

It depends on your definition of "pure." I think Karate-do in general has evolved. We have a better understanding of body dynamics, and training methods have improved. The constant factor is that Kata has remained essentially unchanged. Kata is what distinguishes the styles of Karate-do. It is not necessarily the "style" that is important to the art. But the fact is that, historically and culturally, we have styles of Karate-do. I think that each of the four major styles of Karate-do all brings something a little different to the table.

**What is your opinion of fighting events such as the UFC and Mixed Martial Arts events?**

I personally have nothing against the UFC or Mixed Martial Arts events. But, as a traditionalist, I believe that we should teach our students to learn how to defend themselves and not go into the arena to fight.

**How do you see the art of karate in the world at the present time?**

Karate-do today is international. I would guess that all major cities around the world have Shotokan Karate-do. Especially, sport karate has become an international event. I believe Karate is a Martial Art first and foremost, and there is a sport aspect to it. Budo is not sport-based, but the sport of Karate gives young people the motivation to train. I seldom use the term "sport"; therefore, every technique should be practiced as if it were being used in a self-defense situation.

"Ivan Sensei was my primary teacher, mentor, and friend. I always will remember him as a humble man who allowed others to become greater or more famous than him."

**How do you remember Ivan Sensei?**

Ivan Sensei was my primary teacher, mentor, and friend. I always will remember him as a humble man who allowed others to become greater or more famous than him. He was the toughest man I ever met, and I am not talking about fighting but about his attitude of never quitting. He is truly missed.

# Karate Masters

"The main goal of IMAF (Kokusai Budoin) is to promote and help popularize the Japanese Martial Arts (Budo) throughout the world."

**Do you think that the hardcore traditional method (thousands of repetitions, makiwara, etc...) of teaching Karate is still valid nowadays?**

Yes. However, most people today would not subject themselves to that type of training. The modern Karate-do teacher must be able to vary techniques and incorporate speed, power, strength, and flexibility training within the class or instruction.

**What are the most important qualities for a student to become proficient in karate?**

Dedication to commitment to train. To be able to accept criticism and to be highly motivated and goal oriented.

**Kihon, Kata and Kumite: what's the proper ratio in training?**

I am not sure you can ration out Kihon, Kata, and Kumite. The fact of the matter is that everything starts with Kihon. It has been said "that Kata begins with Kumite and Kumite begins with Kata." In other words, you must practice both equally to be successful in either.

**You have worked for many years in IMAF...what is IMAF's goal in the world of martial arts?**

The main goal of IMAF *(Kokusai Budoin)* is to promote and help popularize the Japanese Martial Arts (Budo) throughout the world.

**What do you consider to be the major changes in the art since you began training?**

When I first started training in Karate-do, Judo was more popular. There were few children and women involved in training. The methods of instruction have become less severe, and the understanding of body mechanics has improved tremendously.

## Who would you like to have trained with that you have not?

I feel so fortunate to have had great Karate-do teachers in Ivan Sensei and Demura Sensei. In addition, through my membership in IMAF, I have trained with Kanazawa Sensei in Shotokan, Yamaguchi Sensei in Goju Ryu, and Ohtsuka in Wado Ryu – plus several renowned instructors in Budo, including Shisuya Sato Sensei in Judo and Nihon Jujutsu, Shioda Sensei in Aikido and Yamaguchi Sensei in Iaido.

"My philosophical basics are that strong physical training helps form a strong mind."

## How important is competition in the evolution of a karate practitioner?

The subject of competition often leads to interesting debate. I believe competition can be used to motivate your students to train harder. I am not necessarily concerned with aspects of winning and losing, but hard training and the preparation it provides is invaluable.

## What is your philosophical basis for your karate training?

My philosophical basics are that strong physical training helps form a strong mind. You need both to be balanced in today's world – the attitude of hard work and doing one's best in the dojo and in one's everyday life. The spiritual aspect is an individual phenomenon. One has to have the attitude to be willing to train hard and have a high sense of integrity. We need to strive for balance in our lives, and when we can achieve balance we move to the spiritual plain. One of the major factors that has kept my passion for Karate-do is that you never stop learning. They day you think you know it all, you might as well retire. The challenges of Budo to continue to improve in the Dojo and in one's life are very fulfilling.

# Karate Masters

"I believe in supplemental training, but if it takes time away from your training at the Dojo, you need to adjust your priorities."

**Do you have a particularly memorable karate experience that has remained as an inspiration for your training?**

We lost Ivan Sensei to a battle with cancer. I relate the following experience: For more than three years he not only fought off the pain of the disease, but he would not submit to it. He kept emphasizing to me that the Budo way is to fight to the end. His body shut down, but his mind and spirit became stronger. I hope that I have that courage as I reach the end of my mortality.

**Is anything lacking in the way martial arts are taught today compared to how they were when you started training?**

I don't think lacking is the correct term, but the intensity of training for the average student in the dojo has been compromised quite a lot over the years. Also, the martial arts have become more of a business, and I believe many teachers compromise their values for money.

**What advice would you give to students on the question of supplementary training (running, weights, et cetera)?**

I believe in supplemental training, but if it takes time away from your training at the Dojo, you need to adjust your priorities. Also, the instructor should be included in setting up a supplemental program so that the correct exercises and training methods are being used to help the student improve.

**Why do you think a lot of students start falling away after two or three years of training?**

Several things appear to happen around this time of training. First, I believe that they realize that there is tremendous commitment to the good of Budo. Secondly, the responsibility of more extra training and helping others to develop leadership in the Dojo. Those can be some of the reasons why people stop training, but I am sure there are many others.

"The life skills involved in teaching Budo are priceless and need to be emphasized. Our greatest fight is with ourselves."

**Do you think that Olympics will be positive for the art of karate-do?**
No. I think the traditional Karate-do will be tremendously compromised to make it as a spectator sport. Tae Kwondo is an example of a martial art that has become a sport.

**What are your thoughts on the future of karate?**
I see more and more people around the world getting the opportunity to train in Karate-do. My hope is that we maintain the traditional aspects of Kihon, Kata, and Kumite and that the teachers emphasize the art not for personal profit.

**Do you have any general advice you care to pass on to practitioners?**
A: Karate should be practiced with discipline, good manners, and respect. Without those attributes we are only teaching and/or learning fighting. The life skills involved in teaching Budo are priceless and need to be emphasized. Our greatest fight is with ourselves. O

# TATSUO HIRANO

## THE HEALING ENERGY

BORN IN KUMAMOTO, JAPAN, TATSUO HIRANO BEGAN HIS MARTIAL ARTS TRAINING MORE THAN 40 YEARS AGO AND HAS TAUGHT FOR NEARLY 30 YEARS. HE WAS FIRST EXPOSED TO ENERGETIC THERAPEUTICS IN 1968 BY HIS SHORINJI-KEMPO GRANDMASTER, REVEREND YAMAMORI, OF THE KONGO ZEN SECT. YAMAMORI TAUGHT SHIATSU, ANMA AND ANMO-TUINA FOR TRAUMA IN MARTIAL ARTS TRAINING. HIS CHI-KUNG TRAINING CONTINUED WITH GRANDMASTER KAM YUEN AND GRANDMASTER JOHN SO OF THE NORTHERN SHAOLIN CHUAN UNTIL 1989 WHEN HE BECAME A STUDENT OF GRANDMASTER TAKAYUKI KUBOTA AND EARNED THE TITLE SHIHAN.

ALTHOUGH MEDICINE AND MARTIAL ARTS MAY SEEM TO BE VERY CONTRADICTORY ACTIVITIES, HIRANO SENSEI EXPLAINS THAT "THE OPPOSING NATURE OF THE HEALING ARTS AND THE MARTIAL ARTS REPRESENT THE FUNDAMENTAL YIN YANG NATURE OF LIFE AND BECOME A MEANS TO DEVELOP A HOLISTIC UNDERSTANDING OF SELF AND THE UNIVERSE IN WHICH WE LIVE."

IN FACT, IT WAS IN THIS CONTEXT THAT HE BEGAN TO "COMPREHEND THE LIVING DYNAMICS OF ENERGY IN RELATION TO THOUGHTS, EMOTIONS, SPIRITUALITY, AND ITS PHYSICAL EXPRESSIONS AND MANIFESTATIONS." AS A RESULT OF BEING A DOCTOR OF ORIENTAL MEDICINE (D.O.M.), A LICENSED ACUPUNCTURIST (CA) AND BEING INVOLVED WITH THE HEALING ARTS FOR MORE THAN THREE DECADES, HIRANO SENSEI IS ABLE TO OFFER A UNIQUE PERSPECTIVE OF THE PRACTICAL RELATIONSHIP BETWEEN KARATE AND KI.

**How long have you been practicing the martial arts?**

More than 40 years ago. In 1960, one late afternoon, dad tossed a brand new judo gi on my lap and said, "Yoi-shite, iko." That means, "Get ready. Let's go." I looked back at him with delight because I knew what this meant. That short moment was to be one of the greatest highlights of that year. The dojo was only a few blocks away, but the ride somehow felt long. We turned into this really small alley, drove toward the end and stopped in front of a small building that appeared to be a modified garage. "We're here," he said. This confused me because all I saw was a garage. As we got out, I

# Karate Masters

"I started with judo because there is a popular belief amongst Japanese fathers that judo will make a better initial conditioning [style] for young boys."

could hear loud sounds of impact and kiai throughout the alley. When we entered, the strong smell of sawdust definitely caught my attention ... only to be interrupted by my dad tapping my shoulder. "Bow and suit up in the restroom/locker room," he whispered. As I started to change, I looked at my feet. They were dark with dirt so I stuck my feet onto the sink and washed them. Isn't it strange what one recalls on their first trip to the dojo?

**In how many styles of martial arts have you trained?**

I started with judo because there is a popular belief amongst Japanese fathers that judo will make a better initial conditioning [style] for young boys, familiarize them with falling, grappling and all around tussling. However, periodically we would receive supplementary karate training to round out judo's edges. A few years later I enrolled in a shorinji kempo school at Konko-kyo Buddhist temple. The teacher was a newly arrived Kongo Zen priest, Rev. Hirokazu Yamamori Sensei. In 1970, I studied under Sifu Kam Yuen's Northern Shaolin tai-mantis kung-fu in the Alpine Gymnasium in Los Angeles' Chinatown. Yuen provided my first training in the Chinese version of Northern Shaolin chuan. Later I trained with Sifu So Bin Yuen in Northern Shaolin chuan mon, and I have trained in hung-gar and wing chun, two Southern kung-fu systems noted for strong hand techniques. These balanced out the leg work for which Northern Shaolin kung-fu was famous.

**How did you get involved in karate-do?**

By 1980, a good friend of mine, Guy Kurose, a 6th Dan goju-ryu seito of Kenzo Uchiage Hanshi of Tenri University in Japan, relocated to California to teach karate at the Tenri Dojo. Guy stood out in Japan karate competition because he was Japanese-American, and he had a style of fighting that had a Muhammad Ali twist to it. As a Tenri University team member and competitor, he had won many titles, including the International Championship in the 1970s. As an adult, Guy first introduced me to Japanese karate, and we trained hard by exchanging instruction with one another. By then, we each had our own schools. He had many visitors from Japan, including the All-Japan Karate champion, Shuji Koshimizu, who added more hard dynamics to our mutual training. There weren't many students who would want to continue training under such rigorous conditions, but those who stayed did become excellent students.

**When and how did you meet Soke Tak Kubota?**

In 1988, Guy was at a very difficult point in his life and [had been] rapidly experiencing a decline in health. As a doctor of Oriental medicine, I treated him. This helped him tremendously, yet I felt he also needed to train under traditional circumstances with a Shihan. I believe martial arts training is a medicine that can reach another dimension that is not obtainable by any other means. I had read about Tak Kubota in Black Belt magazine in the 1970s and somehow his name always stuck in the back of my mind, so I thought about the idea of taking him. After one Tuesday night training, I shared this idea of visiting Soke Kubota with Guy, and to my pleasant surprise, he agreed to visit him the next morning. We arrived at the IKA dojo about 8:10 a.m., and the class was already in session. The dojo was filled with black belts, and the atmosphere was electrifying. We sat down on a wooden bench and watched intently as Soke finished a series of drills. I immediately knew we were in the presence of the very man I was hoping to meet. In a strange way, it felt like I was coming home.

In the front of the class, Soke Kubota had this "huge man" (Val Mijailovic) who glided across the floor with incredible speed and power. I had never seen a non-Asian perform at such an advanced level. However, what impressed me the most was that there was a string of black belts, all strong, many around my age, still pounding the floor and following this enormous smaller man. They were all drenched in sweat and executing strong kiai, a sight only a martial artist could appreciate. Soke Kubota had Shihan Val take over the class and then came over. As I introduced us, he immediately smiled and recognized the situation. "[Did you] bring [your] gi?" he asked. Guy responded "Osu" and went in to suit up. I did not bring a gi so I declined. During the rest of the class, I wrestled alone with my own personal dilemma, for I was now seriously contemplating closing my school and joining the IKA to train fulltime. It didn't take long for me to decide, but it took two months to close my school. The rest is history. Although Guy was the reason I visited Soke, I feel it was fate that led me there. One of the hardest things I found as a teacher was the ability to continue growing in all dimensions as a martial artist. Guy and Shuji had filled some of that void in our exchange training, but enrolling with Soke Kubota was just like hitting the jackpot.

**Was the transition from a Chinese martial art to a Japanese style difficult?**
The transition from kung-fu to karate was not easy, but it was very rewarding. Soke was most generous with me, and he did not tell me what I could do or not do. He allowed me to train mornings and nights with his outstanding students. He watched from a distance, but he also taught the art very closely with the rest of his excellent class of topnotch karate-ka. Soke has an incredible talent to adapt, both with society and in combat. He once told me that karate must be different outside of Japan. People are larger and stronger, so karate techniques must reflect this. This is one of the reasons why Soke's waza is not like other Japanese karate traditionalists' styles with their straight in-and-out linear methods. Instead, he incorporates circular offensive and defensive methods that can easily topple larger opponents with extremely hard and fast tactics and strategy. Fighting a larger, stronger opponent without sidestepping increases your chance of being "run over" or trapped. Studying this hard and fast method with circular movements made me feel good because I was able to nourish my previous training, as well as further advance my karate.

**How has your background in medicine influenced your training?**
I train differently than most people because of my Oriental medical background. You could say that I see everything from the standpoint of ki (called chi in Chinese) in relation to the physical, mental and spiritual realms. I know how ki develops and circulates, as well as how stagnation of ki affects the mind, body and spirit. Organ dysfunctions reflect everywhere, and you can examine the body in a manner that is similar to a farmer who can observe nature and interpret it. This approach also guides [a student] where to strike in karate. It is hard to speak to others about this, but that is not the case with Soke Kubota. This is what makes training with IKA all the more gratifying. We connect on many levels, especially through his landmark development of anso no kata the ki development exercise, which I feel is central to all of his teachings and is his unique contribution to the martial arts.

In modern times, the martial arts are different from yesteryear. Although good hard training is the center of it all, building strong character and peaceful, respectful relations through karate is now the hallmark. In the past, the emphasis was on injury and killing for superiority.

**Sensei, who were your first teachers?**

I was lucky enough to have my father Futoshi Hirano and Ryusei Inouye Sensei of Sen-Shin Judo dojo as my first teachers. You never realize what you have at a young age until later, but these two men set the good hard work ethics in training that is still with me today.

**Would you tell us some interesting stories of your early days in karate training?**

I'm not sure about interesting because it was all remarkable. I hope it's OK, but I would like to share a non-karate experience that happened during a shorinji kempo class. One summer night when I was about 14, Yamamori Sensei had the class kiai 100 times while we stood in heiko-dachi shizen-tai yoi position. Sensei must have noticed me feeling faint because he guided me to the side and had me lie face down on the wooden dojo floor. He applied his family style shiatsu along my back and within a few moments I felt a profound sense of calm and renewed energy. From that moment on, I knew there was much more to life than what I knew existed. That motivated me to research healing, ki and Budo.

"In modern times, the martial arts are different from yesteryear. In the past, the emphasis was on injury and killing for superiority."

**How did the Westerners respond to traditional Japanese training?**

It appears that every decade there is a major cultural broadening here in the U.S. From Japan being an enemy to the incarceration of Japanese-Americans into concentration camps to the acceptance politically, economically and culturally. You now see people wearing fashion clothing with Japanese characters (kanji) and eating sashimi and sushi as if they had been doing it all their life. I find most Westerners are deeply moved and affected by the depths of Japanese traditional culture in general and Budo in particular. Many have become not only great students but great masters and teachers as well.

# Karate Masters

"I always felt that the martial arts are in my blood. I'm not sure if it's due to the fact that both of my parents have a samurai lineage or that I was just an average nihon-jin boy."

**Were you a natural at karate? Did the movements come easily to you?**

By the time I started karate, I had already studied judo, kempo, and played organized baseball and basketball. I always have had a good physical "IQ." However, my mental and spiritual IQ was a different matter and that did not come easy. So, was I a natural at karate? No. Although I was physically coordinated and strong, to be a natural with karate, you have to be natural with yourself. Stiff self equals stiff karate. Movement is life and life is movement and my criteria for being natural with karate movements are under constant scrutiny and construction. This process required me to find more ways to be natural with the movements of daily life and work, integrating them with ki and karate in mind. When its time to train in karate at the dojo, I feel natural with the movements, but it is not something I turn on.

**How has your personal karate developed over the years?**

With karate, motivation was a big factor. I think every Japanese boy grows up watching *Chambara* (samurai sword stories) and *Ninja* (Japanese language) movies and most certainly I was one of its most devoted fans. I always felt that the martial arts are in my blood. I'm not sure if it's due to the fact that both of my parents have a samurai lineage or that I was just an average nihon-jin boy. All I knew is that it lights me up. When my father encouraged my brother and I to study judo, my brother hated it, but I loved it.

My father had obtained his godan in pre-war Japan when judo was very different and much tougher. He was born in Los Angeles in 1916, raised in Japan from the time he was 8 years old and moved to Manchuria during the Japanese colonization of the Pacific rim. He became a judo grand champion in 1940. The atomic bombs were dropped in Hiroshima and Nagasaki,

Japan surrendered and there was a mass escape. He was captured by Chiang Kai-Shek's army in 1945 and held in a prison camp where he was tortured then placed on the firing line to be executed. One of the prison personnel stepped in and stopped it because he personally knew of dad's compassion and good deeds towards the Manchurians and Chinese. He was miraculously released to return to a devastated Japan. Talk about post-traumatic stress disorder (PTSD). Pre-WWI and WWII martial arts were a lot different than now. My father was a samurai in modern times, and I grew up very differently than my peers. Having been born in Kumamoto, Japan, we moved back to L.A. in 1959, and I spent my early years living in a gang-infested area of East L.A.

A school of "hard knocks" is another word for it … both in the neighborhood and at home. By the time I was 6, I had my first street fight. I was a wild boy and confused about humanity and who I was. I spent my early years in East L.A. where the only variance of racism I experienced was Mexican prejudice. I didn't know why I was picked on then, but it was clear that it had to do with my race. I defended myself constantly and never relented to this cruel childish treatment. I changed quickly from an innocent Japanese boy to a untrusting fighter. Because of my fighting spirit, I became popular and soon became friends with the tougher street fighting elements. This became one of the motivating factors to learn martial arts. As a result, I became competitive rather than training to perfect my character. Do you think a kid like me would want to empower himself to be twice as strong with martial arts? You bet! I continued judo training, but kicking and punching somehow seem more attractive to me, especially while attending grade school that had five or more schoolyard fights a day.

At 17, I searched hard for my identity. I trained for realism yet my personal life felt disconnected. This was a critical period for me and it was then that I consciously made the commitment to search for answers. A mission and plan now guided my martial art training, and the key was ki integration. The more I trained, the more hungry I became for the mystical side of ki and the years of training slowly paid off; I felt more peaceful and clear. By 20, I moved to New York City to study Chinese medicine at Lincoln Hospital. This study had a profound effect on my understanding and awareness of the interrelationship of self and nature and my concept and practice of ki application grew simultaneously with karate and Chinese medicine.

My training went through more modifications when I got married in 1978. Issues of sharing space, time, accounts and children — on top of our friendship — added more dynamics to clearing and directing my mind and [added] ki to karate. Mental and spiritual challenges added more dynamics as I matured through the process of having children, [allocating time for] practice and the study of Chinese medicine, martial arts training and deepening my connection with humanity.

My training in the past 10 years has delivered the fruits of my labor, and I now see ki radically different from before. Ki is energy that is a universal information structure that shares a major part of the original intent of creation itself. It can be accessed and used to gain insight as well as to change things for the better. It is a major part of my healing work. It is now commonplace to restore health and strengthen karate through modern medical chi kung and various mental methods. I can honestly say that I feel a oneness with ki and use it in all aspects of my life, including family, work, martial arts, play, study, communication and arts in general.

**What are the most important points of your training philosophy?**
At face value, karate appears to be about fighting an opponent, but it is far from that. You should know goodness from bad because fists of justice are much stronger than fists of injustice. You should also get out of your own way by not fighting yourself. This is something most people do [fight themselves], and this permits internal conflict to prevent pure concentrated movement. One hidden power of karate is its potential to develop you into a natural, uncomplicated being. Come from goodness and integrate the mind and spirit with the ki of the universe. Train for simplicity and do less to achieve more.

**With all the technical changes during the last 30 years, do you think there are still pure styles of karate?**
I don't believe it's been pure since the beginning of martial arts because that is the evolutionary nature of all things. Even the kung-fu that was taught to non-monks during the time the Shaolin Temples were attacked from feudal lords was modified. Those in Okinawa who learned Fukien kung-fu modified it to become Okinawa-te. With each generational lineage, modifications, as well as new kata, are created to further enhance and fill the gap within each style. How many interpretations of san-chin kata do we see now? In the last 30 years, instructors are using science to explain, deepen and strengthen karate. I support this, however, what I believe must remain pure are the "inner ki works" and the fundamentals (kihon) that are essential to excellent karate, regardless of style.

**Do you think different ryu are important?**
Different ryu are a fact of life. It is beyond important; it just exists.

**What is your opinion of full-contact karate and kickboxing?**

I participated in full-contact in the 1960s and 1970s, and it does have its value. I had my first street fight when I was 6, and there were many more during grade school. I am fully aware of the dangers — from severe crippling to possible death. To fight in those circumstances has the potential to awaken you. However, it is not a sound way to teach on a mass scale. Today, we have full-contact karate and kickboxing, and there is a place for these, but they are not for everyone nor are they a way or arts with which to grow old.

**And other modern events such as the Ultimate Fighting Championship?**

The UFC has had a positive affect on the martial arts community because it revealed to the world the value of tactics, techniques and styles compared to others. [In this event], we have seen such things as high, middle and low kicks; jabs, crosses and combination punching; sweeps, throws pins and chokes; combinations; attack areas, et cetera. These were all were very enlightening and educational. I like to watch sumo, judo, jiu-jitsu, kung-fu, karate, boxing, wrestling and the sort. It all has its place. However, I have seen people die or get crippled from all-out fighting. If we are to discern that this is not war but only a sport, then careful attention must be given to protect competitors without compromising the purpose of that sport.

**Do you think that karate in the West is at the same level with Japanese karate?**

Karate in the Western world is not even close to the level of Japan. In Japan, the martial arts are under the authority and direction of the Ministry of Education, thereby creating a huge structure for study and practice. Their teachers all have exceptional qualifications and experience and are directly connected to top instructional lineage and schools. Those attending univer-

"Today, we have full-contact karate and kickboxing, and there is a place for these, but they are not for everyone nor are they a way or arts with which to grow old."

sities like Waseda, Tenri, Meiji, Nippon and Takushoku train morning and afternoons with periodic intense training sessions. However, considering these differences, the West had excelled beyond what I believe to be many of karate's pioneer vision.

**When you compare Japanese karate-ka to European or American karate-ka, do you feel that there are any fundamental differences in approach or physical capabilities?**

The primary fundamental difference is that the Ministry of Education governs Budo, and that is a big plus for the Japanese. I don't believe that the Japanese have any physical or fundamental differences or advantages ... unless being smaller is an attribute. However, I do believe their work ethics are stronger and their training schedule certainly reflects this. One remarkable training point is their emphasis on strong leg conditioning, which is essential to strong karate.

**Karate, nowadays, is often referred to as a sport. Would you agree with this definition or do you think it is only Budo?**

After Japan lost the war, it had officially signed a treaty pact in which it had forsaken war forever. I believe this position had a significant role in toning down all Japanese martial arts and encouraged the promotion of sports for goodwill and global friendship. The theoretical and philosophical properties are there, but the old feudal structure that utilized Budo for authoritative rule will never again be used or promoted.

**Do you feel that you still have further to go in your studies of Budo?**

Yes, most definitely so. My challenge now is furthering my studies with the aging process that will unfold, and this is not necessarily a bad thing, I feel stronger now than [I did] 20 years ago.

**Presently, how do you see karate in the rest of the world?**

It's truly amazing how karate has grown internationally. I see karate continuing to grow with many sensei hungry for the next level. From seminars to special training, there are now high-ranking masters in most developed countries and they will try to emulate Japan's achievement in karate.

**Do you think it helps empty-hand karate physically to train with weapons?**

Weapons training will help the general conditioning of the body, but there is also a danger [that may arise]. This occurs if a student relies too much on the weapon for power instead of continuing his ki training. The power should extend through the weapon ... not from it. Weapons training can also help you understand the various angles of attack and defense and circular techniques. On the other hand, anything can help empty-hand karate training. For example, Chogun Miyagi used to go to a river and throw large rocks. This would not only strengthen his stances, torso and arms, but [it would strengthen] his mind and spirit as well.

**What's your opinion of makiwara training?**

Makiwara training gives stances and strikes purpose. This training aid has the potential to strengthen and perfect stances and unite the whole body, mind and spirit. A karate-ka can learn proper tension and positioning by placing his fist on the striking pad and pressing. Kicking and punching without contact often leads to bad kata and waza and possible injuries. Many students who have not trained with the makiwara often experience elbow and knee pain when striking, and that is because their hands and feet are not contracting (shime) properly. Striking with loose fists and feet will jar the joints because there is no end point or destination. So, the joints become yanked or outstretched. There are some dangers to makiwara training, and the joint structure can become damaged and arthritis may set in, making the aging process more difficult in the later years. [In addition to this], reckless pounding can damage the synovial membrane or shatter the fibrous capsule that protects the joint.

"I would encourage students to supplement their training with such things as running, stretching, and light weight training."

**To progress in the arts, how should a teacher prepare his personal training? What elements should be more emphasized once he becomes an instructor?**

I am from the old school, and that means that I believe basics are key from the beginning to the end. All preparation must be on the basics (kihon), and it should always take center stage, regardless of what level you have reached. Breathing and kiai, stances, timing, ability, strength, speed, alignment, delivery, coordination, agility, calmness, awareness and connection are things to perfect when doing a single punch or movement. You can multiply and expand that, but these considerations are basic, regardless of how advanced you become. However, even with basics, I see steps with karate

# Karate Masters

"Do it to discover the mind and spirit through the body; do it to discover life through facing danger. Train to be whole."

advancement. The first step is to develop physical IQ with kihon. The second step is to develop mental IQ with kihon. The third step is to develop spiritual IQ with kihon, but these steps often overlap as you advance.

**When teaching the art of karate, is self-defense, sport or tradition the most important?**

The art of karate is best taught and understood through tradition, but it must shine through sport activities as well as self-defense.

**In training, what's the proper ratio between kata and kumite?**

This critical question goes back to the days when Gichin Funakoshi was alive and teaching. I believe 50/50 is the right ratio because application with an opponent will reveal more about yourself and karate. Although the various stages of aging may require different emphasis, the ratio should still be even.

**Sensei, do you have any general advice you would care to pass on to the karate-ka?**

Be true to yourself, your family, your country and humanity. Do not separate karate from your life. Find what lights up your life and link karate to it.

**Some people think going to Japan to train is highly necessary. Do you agree?**

No, I do not think it is highly necessary. However, if you can afford it and have the time, then it will be good. In the U.S., we have had many masters from Japan establish schools and organizations, and this has been going on since the 1960s. Many of their students now have master students who have schools and this creates a wonderful training and tournament environment. There is a tendency to belittle U.S. karate development by those who are associated with Japan's karate organizations. In reality, what these individuals are doing is belittling what these pioneering masters had developed here in the U.S. Grandmasters Kubota, Nishiyama, Ohshima, Demura, Enoeda, Kanazawa, etc. have done exceptional lifetime work in the establishment of karate outside of Japan. In a traditional Japanese dojo, the training is hard and potentially brutal, but it has all the respect and structure of the traditional honor system in place. Men, woman, children and seniors pound the dojo floor until the once stiff and hard wooden floor has "training character." Yes, training would be a plus in Japan, but it is not highly necessary.

**What do you consider to be the major changes in the art of karate since you began training?**
The biggest change is the direction towards making karate a sport. The "pros" are the sportsmanship and the international goodwill and exchange that result from sport karate. The "con" is the overspecialization of sports versus training in the whole art.

**With whom would you like to have trained with that you have not?**
Chogun Miyagi, and I may eat my words if this ever happened because the socioeconomic period of that time, the language and the culture were much different then and training under their conditions of Japanese rule may be too much to bear for this modern man.

**What would you say to someone who is interested in learning karate-do?**
Don't do it if all you want is a workout. Do it to discover the mind and spirit through the body; do it to discover life through facing danger. Train to be whole.

**What is it that keeps you motivated after all these years?**
The unfolding of the truth through karate.

**Do you think it is necessary to engage in free fighting to achieve good self-defense skills for a real situation?**
Yes. On one hand, you can't dance until you get onto the dance floor and do all the steps. The importance of free fighting is spontaneity, and it is there that Mushin (mind/heart/awareness) in the infinite source is tempered and developed in combat. On the other hand, free fighting is very different from real situations, and opponents must be accessed quickly for their intent. Real situations should be viewed with human eyes because the person may be a good person who is drunk, saying mean things and demonstrating poor judgment without inhibition. On the other hand, the person may have been unemployed for a long time, depressed and mad at the world. Or perhaps

he just broke up with his girlfriend and is venting wildly. Would you demolish that person? Alternatively, he may not be a good person, and his intent is to create great harm to you or your family or friends. Then self-defense must be strong and unwavering. Can free fighting training help you for those situations? Only a portion, but it is a portion more than not.

**What is your opinion about mixing karate styles? Does the practice of one nullify the effectiveness of the other? Or on the contrary, can it be beneficial to a student?**

It can be counterproductive if you mix styles without understanding and mastering one style first. There are strengths in all styles that can complement other styles. For instance, the linear movements of shotokan can benefit from the circular methods of goju-ryu. On the other hand, even though there are many styles, there is only one body. In the end, many styles can appear very similar to one another on the advanced level. In that regard, I see all the various styles as different instruments for the same orchestra.

**Modern karate is moving away from the bunkai in kata practice. How important do you think bunkai is in the understanding of kata and karate-do in general?**

Bunkai is essential to karate. This tendency to move away from bunkai represents separating sport karate from the whole traditional system. Kata contains waza and its teachings of waza are done with bunkai training. You can take each kata application segment and turn it into a waza drill for kumite.

**What is the philosophical basis for your karate training?**

I did not start with any philosophical basis, but as I matured and studied, philosophy became my beacon. It's been a work in progress that deepens with the years. In short, my philosophical basis for karate training is to become a good man who is one with the energetic realm of the Do, and I apply this way to all aspects of my life.

**Do you have a particularly memorable karate experience that has remained an inspiration for your training?**

It's more than an inspirational memorable karate experience. My training allowed me to practice the proper karate spirit, and that inspires me. Inspiration is my connection to the "Do" each time I train.

**After all of these years of training and experience, could you explain the meaning of the practice of karate-do?**

To become alive. Karate-do is a dedicated practice of a combat system; it is a means and method to clean and clear your mind through the forging (kime) of spirit and body through daily training. It is a way to transcend your immediate surrounding to that of the universal infinite source by facing and accepting death [so that you can] discover life in the energetic realm.

**How can a practitioner increase his understanding of the spiritual aspect of karate?**

This is a choice and not a belief that can be imposed upon. You cannot even give away teachings on the spiritual aspect of karate without a willing receiver. However, with a willing student, the ancient concept of Asian spiritualism is different from spiritualism today. To apply this question to karate, those who may be a Christian, Muslim or an atheist must take on broader parameters of understanding. Simply, the ancient question of spirit implies something beyond and greater than the individual, the self or the connection to God. Connection to nature and humanity, as well as to the universal creative intelligence and force, perhaps can represent this broader parameter without rubberstamping any religion. In the East, spirit does not imply religion at all. "Shin" has a compound meaning of mind, awareness, heart and consciousness. "Shin" is the connection to the infinite source of all things, often referred to as "Mu" or the infinite "Void." If one is committed, disciplined, loyal and hard working, then perhaps this process of karate training can open the mind enough to get a glimpse of this magical connection and perhaps motivate one to listen to his sensei's spiritual teachings. Often these lessons unfold without warning or announcement, and the wise teacher observes whether his student has the capacity to understand.

**How much training should a senior karate-ka be doing to improve and get better at the art?**

The body changes so quickly that even a week's break often starts to undo the benefits of training. Once-a-week training often will make the senior student sore without sufficient development. Twice-a-week training may be the bare minimum requirement for maintenance, but growth becomes compromised. I believe a minimum of training three times a week may facilitate maintenance, development and growth.

**Is there anything lacking in the way karate is taught today compared with those who were being taught in your early days?**

I am not qualified to say what is lacking in the way karate is taught in

# Karate Masters

"There are many reasons why people study karate. Some join to meet people, others for exercise and some just for self-defense."

other schools worldwide, but I see little tricks such as creating louder snap sounds in kata without the proper power and flicking movements that are intended as power moves. And, I see these more than I would like.

**What do you consider to be the most important qualities of a successful karate-ka?**
Big heart, respect, loyalty, honest, clear mind, hard working, maturity and a willingness to go the extra mile as well as the willingness to transcend beyond one's trophy and accomplishments.

**What do you see as the most important attributes of a student?**
To begin, respect, faithfulness and effort. He should also refrain from violent behavior, strive to be the best, stay playful and follow the way of world karate.

**Why do so many students start falling away after two or three years of training?**
There are many reasons why people study karate. Some join to meet people, others for exercise and some just for self-defense. Unfortunately, they do not transcend beyond that within two or three years of training time, and they lack the understanding of karate's potential to develop them as a whole natural being.

**There is very little written about you. You obviously do not thrive on the publicity like some martial artists. Why?**
My main publicity has been with the healing arts. I am a doctor of Oriental medicine, a licensed acupuncturist in the state of California and I run a clinic in Glendale. I am also an educator and teach modern medical chi kung and Hirano Myo-osteo Therapy in seminar formats. I am perfectly content to teach advanced and intermediate students at the IKA Honbu (headquarters) Dojo in Glendale, California and stay outside of the limelight. However, I am very happy to share some of my views on karate every time I

"The future of karate-do is wide open for substantial growth and development."

have the opportunity. Perhaps my words may help to expand the minds of students and encourage them to become future masters.

**Have there been times when you felt fear in your karate training?**

Different types of fear throughout the years. Fear of collapsing from rigorous training, fear of hurting others, fear of re-injury, fear of not recovering from injury, fear of embarrassment and fear of losing friendships from hurting people. Perhaps there may be more, but all of these points have occurred throughout my lifetime and represent my path to growth on the emotional and spiritual realm.

**What are your thoughts on the future of karate-do, and what's your opinion about karate entering the Olympic Games?**

The future of karate-do is wide open for substantial growth and development. I see karate not only becoming part of the Olympic games but also becoming part of national education. We must create the future rather than let it happen and shorten the borders for international exchange and friendship. O

# ART ISHII

## PRESERVING BUDO

THE PRESERVATION OF VALUES AND ETHICS THROUGHOUT HISTORY HAS BEEN ONE OF THE FUNDAMENTAL PILLARS OF ANY SOCIETY. BUSHIDO AND MARTIAL ARTS IN GENERAL ARE NOT EXCEPTIONS TO THIS RULE. ALTHOUGH TRAINING METHODS AND PRACTICE APPROACHES HAVE CHANGED CONSTANTLY IN THE EVOLUTION OF ANY MARTIAL STYLE, IT IS TRUE THAT THE INTRINSIC CODES OF CONDUCT AND EDUCATIONAL VALUES OF THE MARTIAL ARTS HAVE BEEN NEGLECTED TO THE POINT OF BECOMING A SIMPLE FIGHTING CONTEST AND "BLOODSPORT GAMES," WITH NOTHING ATTACHED TO IT BUT A NONSENSE BRAVADO AND A POOR ATTITUDE.

FOR SENSEI ART ISHII, THE PRESERVATION OF THE BUSHIDO PRINCIPLES HAS BEEN AN IMPORTANT PART OF HIS MARTIAL ART JOURNEY FROM THE VERY BEGINNING. AS DIRECTOR OF THE NIKKEI GAMES, HE UNDERSTANDS THE IMPORTANCE OF MAINTAINING VALUES AND MORALS THAT WILL GROW WITH THE YOUNG GENERATIONS. "PEOPLE TEND TO THINK THAT TRADITIONAL ARTS ARE SOMETHING OBSOLETE, AND THAT IS A TERRIBLE MISTAKE," HE SAYS. "RESPECT, EDUCATION, DISCIPLINE, ETC....ARE TRADITIONAL VALUES. PEOPLE TEND TO MISTAKE THESE TRADITIONAL VALUES WITH THE WAY YOUR TRAIN YOUR TECHNIQUE, AND ONE THING HAS NOTHING TO DO WITH THE OTHER."

**How long have you been practicing the martial arts?**

I've been involved in the martial arts for more than 50 years. My first introduction was to Judo at Hollywood Judo Dojo in Los Angeles. The head instructor was Kikuchi Sensei; other instructors were Frank Emi, Art Emi, Frank Watanuki, and Gene Lebell.

**How many styles have you trained in?**

I trained in Judo well into my 20s, competing in military tournaments while in the Air Force. I was introduced to Randy Williams by a mutual friend. Randy ran the New Chinatown (Wing Chun) Gung Fu Club in Chinatown Los Angeles where I ended up training for about four years. I then trained under Guy Kurose in Goju Ryu Karate at the Tenri Dojo in East Los Angeles. When Guy returned to Seattle, I was referred to Ota's dojo, where I trained in Matsubayashi Shorin-Ryu for more than ten years. For the

# Karate Masters

"To this day, my Judo senseis have made the biggest impression on me. They were all true gentlemen and men of honor and extraordinary character."

past twenty years, I have been operating an independent Matsubayashi Shorin-Ryu dojo in "Little Tokyo".

**Who were your teachers?**

To this day, my Judo senseis have made the biggest impression on me. They were all true gentlemen and men of honor and extraordinary character. As a youth, my only source of income was delivering daily newspapers. There came a point where I could no longer afford the monthly dojo dues so I stopped going. Weeks later, my dojo friends told me that Sensei wanted me to come to the dojo; he wanted to speak to me. In the dojo office, the Senseis asked why I stopped coming and I reluctantly told them that I could not afford the dues. They handed me a brand new gi and told me to return, that dues were not important. To this day, in my own dojo, I provide gis and do not charge dues to those who cannot afford it. It's my way of paying back my Judo Senseis.

Randy Williams and I continue to stay in touch; whenever he's in town, I invite him to teach a portion of our class. I've always admired his dedication to the art as both a student and an instructor. Over the years, I've watched him grow and receive the recognition that he deserves. Randy has great communication skills and can explain technical aspects of techniques and teach them in a way that is understandable to the student. He is a charismatic person with a great sense of humour and possesses all the qualities of a true sifu.

Guy Kurose was a character. Like me, he was a third generation Japanese American, but born and raised in Seattle. He always had a passion for the martial arts and even trained for a short time under Bruce Lee in Seattle. In his early 20s, Guy went to Japan, where he attended Tenri University. He had to learn to speak Japanese and ended up joining the university's Karate team. He trained in Goju-Ryu Karate under Uchiage Sensei. Guy ended up being the collegiate team captain and kumite champion. He and Shuji Koshimizu, another Japan kumite champion, opened up their dojo at the Tenri Temple in East Los Angeles. A typical workout would consist of 15 pushups followed up with two to three hours of jiyu kumite (free sparring). In all the years that I trained under Guy, I never learned one kata but the kumite experience was invaluable. Guy Kurose stories are endless; never a dull moment. We remained friends and stayed in constant touch until he passed away a few years ago.

**Would you tell us some interesting stories of your early days in karate?**

Over the years, the Tenri Dojo had acquired quite a reputation as a fighting dojo. It seemed that every week, visitors would stop by either out of curiosity or to train, sometimes with questionable motives. One evening Guy, Shuji, and I were in the instructor's office when Guy told us that a group had asked if they could train with us. We walked out of the office and, sure enough, on the dojo floor were about eight people in black gis warming up doing jumping, spinning kicks, cartwheels, and a lot of acrobatics. Guy looked at Shuji and me and said, "Pretty cool, huh?" He told us to watch while he started class with them. He immediately had them line up in what we used to call a slaughter line in Judo. He went down the line, sparring each one and physically beating each to the point where they could barely stand. By the time he got to the end of the line, you could see that he had broken their spirit and you could see the fear in their eyes. It was quite a sight to see because Guy was so relaxed, but he had told us how the group had told him about their superior style and were there to show off. Another interesting night at the Tenri Dojo.

After Guy returned to Seattle, I started looking for another traditional dojo to attend. At one, I remember being in the dressing room as a new student....I already was in my late 30s and was therefore the newest and oldest member. I wore a white belt because I had no ranking in their system and was unfamiliar with their style. They had no idea that I had spent a lifetime in the martial arts. I only know that not one person spoke to me or acknowledged me. On the floor, I was treated as a lowly beginner and was virtually ignored. I was surprised and angered by this treatment but hung in there, never saying a word. During sparring sessions, I was never asked if I wanted to participate; after all, I was a lowly beginner. Finally, weeks later, the Sensei asked if I wanted to try sparring. I jumped up and enthusiastically yelled "hai!" I took out all of my anger and frustration on my sparring partners that evening and over the next few weeks was able to formally "introduce" myself to those who had held me in such contempt. In some ways, it was perhaps shameful for me to behave the way I did but have to admit that there was a great deal of satisfaction in teaching those "seniors" not to underestimate anyone. More importantly, when I opened my own dojo I vowed never to have a new member treated that way. I personally welcome all new students and introduce them to the floor to make them feel comfortable and not threatened.

**How can the influence of training in Martial Arts help the young generation in becoming successful as individuals in the future?**

I tell our members, both children and adults, that Karate is also spirit and character training. Long after your youth and athleticism begin to wane, you still can grow and develop in spirit and character. There are sayings in Japanese such as *Gaman* and *Yama* to *Damashii*, which mean to endure, to meet a challenge, and struggle to survive and complete your goal. This philosophy can be applied both on and off the dojo floor throughout our lives.

**Were you a "natural" at karate; did the movements come easily to you?**

I probably am an example of not being a "natural" at karate. I have never been very flexible and it was difficult to translate my judo training to Karate. It was my passion for Karate that allowed me to stay with it. My previous training had taught me the value of repetition, self-study, and practice outside of the dojo. I also always tried not to lose sight of the fact that this was a martial art, with roots in combat. I considered tasting my own blood an honorable part of training in a traditional and cultural martial art.

I once told Guy Kurose that I was discouraged because it seemed that I would never be flexible enough to execute high roundhouse and sidekicks with the ease that others could. He then pointed out that he also was the same body type; no matter how much we stretched, we never would be as flexible as someone who was born that way. So, he worked on being more proficient on his middle range kicks with occasional high kicks. He then told me that I was a natural hand and upper body fighter, and from that time on spent hours and hours with me working on techniques that were more natural to my body type. It was a great lesson learned.

**How has your personal expression of karate developed over the years?**

I spent most of my years in Karate relying upon youth and athleticism. As stated, I was not fearless or reckless, but I wasn't afraid to taste my own blood. To me, it was a sign of honor and a lesson in humility at the same time. I joke that getting old is overrated, but in Karate there have been some true benefits. As my body aged, I no longer could count on speed and agility. To compensate, I literally was forced to improve my techniques and timing...to understand the art more completely. I knew that this different approach to my Karate was working because I often was told that I had gotten faster. Certainly, I was not getting faster. My timing had improved and it had the appearance of being faster and more effective. So, working on technique and timing have proven their value and I now teach younger people to not wait for old age to study these important factors.

**What do you think are the most important qualities for a student become proficient in any art of Budo?**

I think proficiency in Budo comes with a personal understanding of all aspects of their chosen art, whether it be physical, intellectual, or spiritual. A realistic relationship with the art is necessary, rather than some fortune cookie proverb. Budo is martial arts; Bushido is the "Way of the Warrior". To participate honorably in Budo, I believe one must have a personal, twenty-first century code of Bushido. Proficiency is not measured by the number of trophies or medals one acquires along the way. I think one must understand Budo and Bushido and personally define how it applies to them in today's world. A code of conduct for martial artists can bring honor to the student, the Sensei and dojo, and the art.

"Proficiency is not measured by the number of trophies or medals one acquires along the way."

**With all the technical changes during the last years, do you think there still are "pure" styles of karate?**

Technical changes and differences in interpretations are inevitable, even within the same style. However, I think there still are many "pure" styles of Karate remaining. I would define "pure" as maintaining the lineage, intent, and spirit of the founders. If we go back to the Okinawan roots of Goju-ryu, Shorin-ryu, and Uechi-ryu, we can see branches of each. For example, there may be several styles within the Shorin-ryu system but each makes every effort to maintain the uniqueness of their lineage. I'm sure there are Japanese Karate dojos that honor the purity of their founders' intent. I think that even as Karate becomes an international art, as long as there is an Okinawan and/or Japanese presence and influence, purity of each style will remain relatively intact.

**Do you think different "styles" are truly important in the art of karate?**
I think different styles within Karate are important in traditional Karate. Unlike Judo and Kendo, which have consistency and identifiable commonalities within their respective arts, Karate has a variety of roots and lineages with obvious differences in emphasis. The fact that Karate has so many systems and styles makes it a diverse art with rich cultures to draw from. However, the uniqueness of each style makes it difficult, if not impossible, to establish a governing body over all of traditional Karate. At the Nikkei Games, we try to celebrate our common love for the art regardless of system or style.

**What is your opinion of fighting events such as the UFC and Mixed Martial Arts events?**
Mixed Martial Arts events have become huge in a short amount of time, surpassing even boxing in popularity. There is no question that the participants are extremely tough and conditioned. It's big business, with its own participants and fan base, and has become an industry by itself. I've seen a lot of matches but don't really follow the MMA circuit. It's sometimes interesting to see the effectiveness of a well placed punch or kick under real circumstances, but other than that I don't care much for all the bravado and bloodlust. To me, MMA is exactly that without the Bushido, and therefore I don't relate to it within my relationship with traditional martial arts.

**Karate nowadays often is referred to as a sport... would you agree with this definition or is "only" a Martial Art?**
As long as there are tournaments and competitions, there always will be a sport element to Karate. But, to refer to Karate as a sport is not correct, in my opinion. The original founders of Karate never intended their art to be called a sport. Tournaments tend to have a "sport" quality to them but I think the majority of traditional dojos do not identify with Karate as a sport even if they do participate in tournaments. Personally, Karate always will be a martial art to me. I have dojo members participate in certain tournaments, but it's only a small part of our training. I guess you can say I'm an old school guy...as long as I identify Karate with Budo and Bushido it always will be a martial art to me.

*"Even in Japan and Okinawa, it seems that Karate is still evolving, refining itself in many ways in an effort to keep pace with its popularity."*

### Do you feel that you still have further to go in your studies?

To this day, whenever someone addresses me as "Sensei," I turn and look around to see if there is a Sensei in the room. There is so much remaining for me to learn about Karate; it's like I've only seen the tip of the iceberg. Whether it was Guy Kurose, Randy Williams, or Frank Smith, I always am pleasantly surprised to learn more about the art. I try to be unselfish as a teacher and always will consider myself a student with plenty to learn from others.

### How do you see karate in the U.S. and around the world at the present time?

Years ago, I was was able to see the growth and popularity of organized tournaments. Even in Japan and Okinawa, it seems that Karate is still evolving, refining itself in many ways in an effort to keep pace with its popularity. Kata, as seen in tournaments today, is much crisper with more snap than in the 60s and 70s. I wonder, though, if the changes were made for aesthetic effect in tournaments or if it's due to better timing and execution of karate

# Karate Masters

"My approach in teaching Karate is that it is indeed a martial art and a self-defense discipline."

movements. The look of karateka with tailored, heavyweight, white gis looks a lot different than the old days with thinner, lightweight gis that weren't always really white. I think the international popularization of Karate is great as long as the old school values that uniquely identified traditional martial arts remain intact. As Karate gains in popularity, I think the Okinawans and Japanese will have to recognize that although Karate originated with them, they should consider it their gift to the world rather than feel that they have total propriety of the art.

**When teaching the art of karate, what is the most important element: self-defense or sport?**

My approach in teaching Karate is that it is indeed a martial art and a self-defense discipline. I emphasize proper punching, striking, kicking, and blocking supplemented with proper footwork and problem solving via kata, bunkai, yakusoku kumite, and jiyu kumite.

**Forms and sparring, what's the proper ratio in training?**

Kata and sparring…it depends upon the individual student. While we all train together on the floor, I try to establish with every student why he/she trains and what his/her goals are. For example, I have middle-aged women who love the warm-ups and kata training but have no interest in sparring. Meanwhile, I have younger students who want to learn both kata and sparring. So, I first have to establish the wants and needs of the student(s).

Generally speaking, though, I try to never let people lose sight of the fact that this is a martial art. It may sound strange, but I often compare Karate to baseball. I tell our students that there are many people that can tell you all about the game of baseball…batting averages, number of stitches in a baseball, history, etc. But, ultimately, I have to ask the person if they actually play baseball or are they simply a baseball historian and intellectual. My position is this: to be a complete martial artist you should know the history of your style, you should learn kata and bunkai, and prearranged (yakusoku) kumite –

that endless hours of kata do not necessarily make you a better fighter. But, the real test of where you are is accomplished only through free sparring (jiyu kumite). By its nature, jiyu kumite is spontaneous rather than prearranged. You find through jiyu kumite that it takes more than understanding situations intellectually; it forces you to act and react physically without the aid of prearrangement. In other words, can they play baseball?

*"By its nature, jiyu kumite is spontaneous rather than prearranged. it forces you to act and react physically without the aid of prearrangement."*

**Do you have any general advice you would care to pass on the practitioners in general?**

I would recommend taking a moment to ask yourself why you train, what are you looking to get out of it? That way, a student can better define his or her status realistically according to his/her own expectations rather than someone else's. If you train in traditional karate, take the time to learn about the history of your style and the cultural aspects of Bushido. Then, redefine Bushido to fit your needs in today's society. Respect the fact that the origins or your art may be Okinawan or Japanese but that you are uniquely American. Pick the finest virtues of both cultures.

**What do you consider to be the major changes in the art since you began training?**

I think the major changes are exactly that...an evolution within systems and styles. For whatever reasons, students and/or instructors leave their instructors and open their own dojos. Most continue training in the same style but as their own entity. Over the years, I no longer can keep track of who is with whom and the politics involved. It makes me appreciate being an independent dojo even more.

**Who would you like to have trained with that you have not?**

I've been friends with Frank Smith for years. He is a regular guest at my dojo and constantly amazes me with his knowledge of the art. We are exactly the same age and I wish that I could have known and trained with him back in the Sensei Nishiyama days.

# Karate Masters

**What would you say to someone who is interested in starting to learn karate?**

Do some homework first before just walking in to a dojo and signing up. The Internet is a good resource for looking up a dojo, but better yet, try to get a referral from someone you already know. Before even speaking to the instructor, watch a whole class to see the demeanor of the instructor and students. Define your goal, then explain to the instructor why you want to learn Karate. Be realistic in your expectations. Know that it's a commitment; are you willing to give it a real try over a period of time?

**What is it that keeps you motivated after all these years?**

I loved Judo and I love Karate. I never intended to be the head instructor, but sometimes life steers you in a direction that ends up being a pleasant surprise as well as a challenge. I don't run my dojo as a business so I don't have the pressure of having to have a minimal number of students. I don't advertise, and generally our new students come through referrals. There is nothing like watching students learn and grow in the art. I see my dojo as Karate for future generations that now include my own family. Also, most of our students are Nikkei, I constantly remind them of their unique Japanese American heritage and culture and how they are fortunate to participate in a martial art that is part of their cultural identity.

**What is your philosophical basis for your karate training?**

I try to end each class with a discussion about Bushido and/or a character and value related subject. Years ago, I found myself telling the dojo members that "when you bring out the best in others, a funny thing happens... it brings out the best in you." That phrase has become the philosophy of our dojo.

**Do you have a particularly memorable karate experience that has remained as an inspiration for your training?**

Like anyone, there are countless memories over the years. This one isn't inspirational, but it did cause me to take a harder look at myself. I should first say that in the military I found out that I had minor color blindness; I had difficulty identifying certain colors or shades. Once, a new student came to the dojo wearing a faded black belt, typical of someone who had worn one for years. We were paired up to spar but when we bowed in, he attacked me with full force, kicking and punching as hard as he could. Naturally, I was surprised and adjusted by defending to find out if he was going to continue sparring with that intensity. He continued attacking ferociously so I adjusted my sparring to match his. It turns out I may have been angry and ended up beating the guy up pretty badly...making him get up and dropping him again and again. Later, someone mentioned that I was pretty hard on that new green belt. I didn't know that he wasn't a black belt; the shade of green was just the perfect shade that I couldn't recognize and I had thought it was a faded black belt. Plus, his technique was pretty good so I never questioned it. By the time I found out, he had gone and never came back....probably due to his bad experience with me. I wish I could have apologized to him.

**After all these years of training and experience, could you explain the meaning of the practice of karate?**

Just as Judo was, Karate is very personal to me. It gives me a sense of culture that complements my American culture. Also, we live in a fast, computer-based society. We all know the benefits of exercising. Training in Karate allows me to exercise as well as participate in a cultural activity that can last a lifetime.

"My approach in teaching Karate is that it is indeed a martial art and a self-defense discipline."

**How do you think practitioners can increase their understanding of the spiritual aspects of the art?**

I think a karateka can continue to grow in the art long after the body begins to fade. We participate in Karate because we choose to do so; we are not drafted or forced to train. And, we always must be aware that Karate is not a cult, religion, or the military. Others may have the Bible, Koran, or other doctrine to live by, but many others do not. Many people live their lives with no defined set of values or code of ethics or conduct. Karateka can take the best modern day values of Bushido as a personal code of values and conduct – values such as respect, honor, discipline, loyalty, obligation, etc. These are important elements of true Bushido.

**Is there anything lacking in the way martial arts are taught today compared to how they were in your beginnings?**

If there's anything lacking, it would be due to the lack of verifiable, quality instructors. Unlike many other disciplines, Karate has given birth to a

# Karate Masters

"I believe a true Karateka should possess a quality of humility to balance a sense of self-confidence."

phenomenon of the instant instructor, or even instant "master," over the years. Nagamine Shoshin, the founder of Matsubayashi-ryu wrote about instances of the "instant instructor" in the post war days in Okinawa and Japan. He sites an example of a man who learned Karate during the day from a legitimate instructor then taught what he learned in the evenings. I've seen head instructors and high ranking black belts that didn't even know how to throw a proper punch. They are irresponsible and exploiting the art and their students. So, before training under someone I recommend doing some research. Know good technique from bad technique when you see it, particularly in the basics. If the instructor's punch looks like he's throwing a Frisbee get out of there as fast as you can. A person's lineage alone doesn't guarantee that he is a quality instructor.

**Could I ask you what you consider to be the most important qualities of a successful karate practitioner?**

I believe a true karateka should possess a quality of humility to balance a sense of self-confidence. I think we should take our art very seriously but not take ourselves too seriously. We should have a presence that people can feel without being intimidated. A genuine sense of caring about others and a good sense of humor are important qualities – to understand the importance of peace through the study of a warrior's art.

**What advice would you give to students regarding supplementary training?**

I encourage supplemental training if done in moderation. I've found that heavy weightlifting can lead to bulkier muscles at the expense of flexibility. Proper stretching is something anyone can do without requiring too much space or equipment.

**Why do you think that preserving the cultural values of Budo is important in our modern society?**

Just because Bushido was the Samurai's code of conduct doesn't mean that modern day Bushido cannot apply to us. We train in a warlike art, one designed to protect ourselves as well as injure someone else. Having Bushido as a guideline separates us from the thugs of the world who only seek to maim and destroy. Bushido is a way of reminding us of our responsibilities to society and ourselves to live a life of honor.

**Have there been times when you felt fear in your training?**

Yes, many times. But, the challenge is to overcome fear and replace it with calmness and focus. I compare this with fear with pain. Pain can be good, a pain that you feel when you've trained hard or have been on the receiving end of a well placed punch or kick. I describe this as good pain because it comes with what we do; we are indeed martial artists, aren't we? The good pain is an indicator that we are in motion and growing. We train to push the limits of our body and spirit and learn to endure as a means to an end. Bad pain is an injury incurred because of bad technique, an accident, or bad intentions.

So, fear can be good. It can be a character builder if you don't allow it to overcome you. Fear can be used as the button pushed to make you calm down, focus, and be in control of your mind and body.

**Do you think that Olympics will be positive for the art of karate-do in case that happens one day?**

I have mixed feelings about Karate in the Olympics, maybe because I've never seen Karate as a sport. Also, the competitive arena can place too much emphasis on winning at the expense of traditional values that are a part of Bushido.

**What are your thoughts on the future of karate?**

When I think about the future of Karate, I only can think about what I can do about it at my level. So, my concerns for the future of Karate are for my dojo and the students whom I count on to continue the legacy of our dojo and Matsubayshi Shorin-ryu. I want to insure that our dojo trains in good, solid Karate with proper basics and good technique. After all, good Karate is good Karate, regardless of system or style. In addition, I want future generations to understand the richness of training hard to achieve goals that may have been considered impossible before. I will have done my job if future generations remain to carry on our goal of being good, contributing members of society. Bring out the best in others and it will bring out the best in you. O

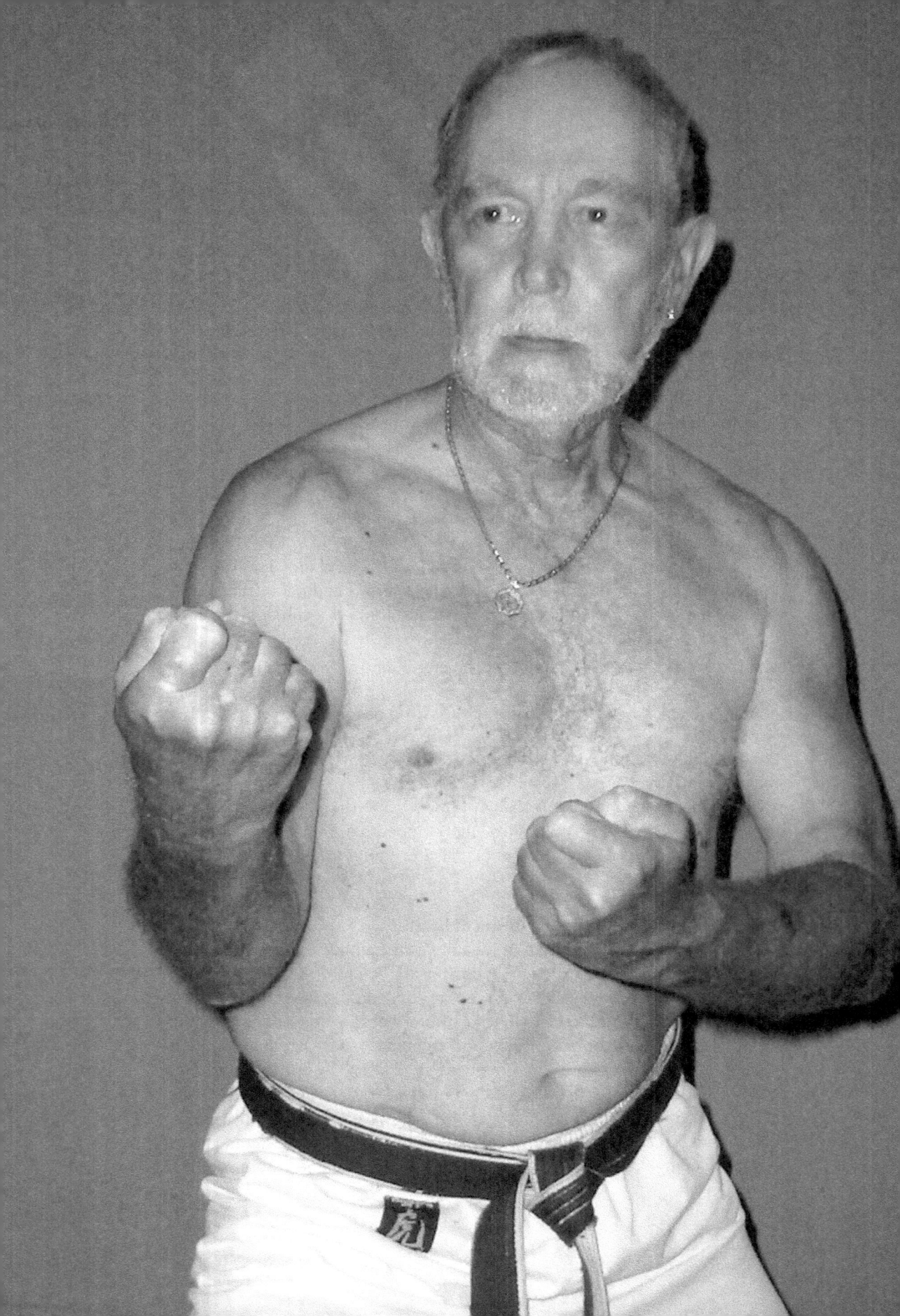

# GEORGE E. MATTSON

## A LIVING LEGEND

IN 1956, GEORGE E. MATTSON WAS SERVING MILITARY DUTY ON THE ISLAND OF OKINAWA. HE WAS A TROUBLED YOUNG MAN AND HIS CAREER WAS ON THE PATH OF DESTRUCTION. FATEFULLY, HE MET A MAN BY THE NAME OF RYUKO TOMOYOSE.

SENSEI RYUKO TOMOYOSE – A KARATE INSTRUCTOR – BECAME HIS FRIEND AND TEACHER. WITH GUIDANCE AND PERMISSION FROM MASTER KANEI UECHI, GEORGE MATTSON WAS GIVEN THE HONOR OF BEING THE FIRST AMERICAN TO BE TAUGHT THE ART OF UECHI-RYU KARATE AND THE PRIVILEGE OF BEING THE FIRST AMERICAN TO RECEIVE A BLACK BELT CERTIFICATE. HE IS THE GRANDFATHER OF UECHI RYU IN NORTH AMERICA AND STANDS AS THE LINK BETWEEN THE OLD TRADITIONS AND THE NEWER GENERATIONS OF INSTRUCTORS.

HE HAS BEEN A PROMINENT WORLD LEADER OF UECHI-RYU KARATE FOR MANY YEARS AND HIS POSITION AS THE HEAD OF THE "INTERNATIONAL UECHI RYU KARATE FEDERATION" REPRESENTS THE SUCCESSFUL ROOTING OF UECHI RYU IN THE U.S.

TODAY, SENSEI MATTSON IMPARTS THE EXPERIENCES AND KNOWLEDGE OF THE TRUE MEANING OF UECHI-RYU KARATE THAT ONLY CAN COME FROM MANY YEARS OF STUDY, DEEP UNDERSTANDING, AND HONEST REFLECTION.

**How long have you been practicing karate?**

I have been practicing Uechi-ryu karate for more than five decades. I have no intention of quitting and I am as active today as I was 50 years ago. I attribute my staying active to the nature of the style and to my tenacity. The system can be practiced in a very physical manner in one's youth and with a more cerebral interpretation as one ages. I am very happy to report that I'm in excellent physical condition and enjoy the practice of a very physical and cerebral form of Uechi ryu. At my age, I remain very active in many businesses, play golf at least three times a week, and work out strenuously in a gym where I supplement my karate with aerobic exercises and circuit training that rounds out and complements my karate workouts. The Martial Arts should be a lifetime activity, not something you do like many Western sports, which are only studied during your high school and college years. The Martial Arts should be practiced as something that involves your

# Karate Masters

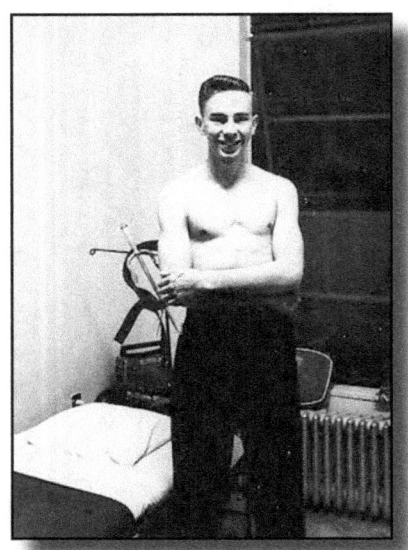

"My primary teacher on Okinawa was Ryuko Tomoyose, a cultural living treasure of Japan."

physical, emotional, and mental maturity.

### How many styles of karate have you studied?

If you consider attending seminars, workshops, and comparing style differences and similarities with teachers from other systems, then the answer to your question is "many!" Seriously though, other than familiarizing myself with many systems, I have only studied Uechi-ryu in-depth.

### Who were your teachers?

My primary teacher on Okinawa was Ryuko Tomoyose, a cultural living treasure of Japan. In 1956, when I first met and began studying with him, we made a pact that he would teach me karate and I would help him with his English. At the time, Tomoyose Sensei worked for the U.S. Government and, even at that time, I already knew I had the better part of this arrangement. Prior to my studying Uechi-ryu with Tomoyose Sensei, other Americans wandered into the Okinawan dojo and tried to learn karate. Typically, they were taught how to punch a makiwara, kick a heavy bag, and perhaps even learn a kata. They only became aware of the physical side of the Martial Arts, and learned nothing about its history or relationship to Okinawan culture. Tomoyose Sensei felt that, besides learning the physical aspects of Uechi-ryu, I also should develop sensitivity to the historical relationship that this art form had with China and, most importantly, the many additional benefits attributed to the training. Every Saturday, he would take me to Kanei Uechi Sensei's dojo for class. This exposure was invaluable, because besides giving me an opportunity to work out with senior students who enjoyed sparring with an American, it also showed this young American how little he knew and what he could attain by continuing his practice. At the time, Uechi-ryu was the only style on Okinawa that practiced freestyle sparring. According to Tomoyose, sparring actually was practiced in China by Kanbun Uechi. I was told by Tomoyose that Kanei Uechi then decided to experiment with different methods of sparring, and this mix-method sparring was soon adopted by most other Uechi dojos.

Due to the hard sparring sessions and the consequent bruises, Uechi Sensei had to administer his healing medicine to me, which miraculously healed the bruising within a day. Supposedly, Kanbun Uechi sold medicine to help support himself during his stay in China. The most famous medicine Kanbun sold was his blood thinning medicine that, when ingested, made bruises and minor injuries disappear. During my stay on Okinawa, I consumed prodigious amounts of this medicine as my body adapted to the hard training. In reality, I guess you could say that most of the senior instructors of the Uechi-ryu Karate Association at the time contributed to my training, and most of them helped me understand the nature of Martial Arts as it relates to different individuals, in different eras, under different and oftentimes unique situations.

### Would you tell us some interesting stories relating to your stay on Okinawa?

The time I spent on Okinawa was filled with visits to other dojos and to the homes of famous artists, potters, and other people who Tomoyose Sensei felt I should meet. One of his claims was that he had cajoled me into buying a painting from one of Okinawa's most famous artists. However, when he asked me what I had done with the painting many years later during his visit to Boston, I had to reply that I had no recollection of either buying it or disposing of it. He smiled and said that the painting today would be worth a great deal of money, and that I should have paid closer attention to his non-karate lessons. He felt I was too one-sided in my exploration of Okinawan culture, and that all I was interested in was karate.

One of the most memorable stories I recall was Tomoyose's tale of Kanbun's medicine. After every class, Mrs. Tomoyose would prepare tea and we would sit sipping tea in the dojo area that doubled as their living room, and I would become hypnotized by my Sensei's words of wisdom he shared with me concerning Kanbun's exploits in China, plus other stories he claimed Kanbun told him. During one session, I asked him what was in the medicine that I was taking frequently to relieve the bruising from pounding on the makiwara and the beating I was taking in class. To my surprise, he showed me a wicker basket filled with roots, along with the medicine in another stage of production that consisted of a gallon jug filled with the liquid. He informed me that Kanbun gave him some roots and the medicinal formula many years ago. Since then, he assisted Uechi Sensei in the preparation of the elixir.

He asked if I would like to learn how to make the medicine and I quickly said yes. He said the climates in Fuzhou and Okinawa were very similar, but he wasn't sure if the root would grow in the northern climates of the United States. He then proceeded to describe the process of creating the elixir, which involved collecting morning dew on the wicker basket, full of cut up roots, for a certain length of time. The process also involved sprinkling mothers' milk on the roots during this first phase of production. When the roots were ready, they were placed in a jug filled with rice wine to ferment for a period of time. Then the elixir was ready to be ingested ... at approximately 1 ounce per day. The roots I brought home died. Apparently they did not survive the cold weather. I often wondered how the Chinese invented such an unusual concoction – I can picture a wise man working on the potion: "Let's see, what if we added some mothers' milk to the dew we collected this morning!"

As the first foreigner to be allowed access to the complete Uechi-ryu system, I found myself being treated in a somewhat experimental manner whenever I visited a different dojo. I also was being watched closely by the Army because there were very strict fraternization rules for members of the Third ASA Division. I had a cryptic top-secret clearance granting me access to information that I had to swear never to share with anyone. I found myself being invited to many socials that, as I learned later, actually were political rallies and gatherings. I recall one coveted event that my Army superiors wanted to attend but they were declared "persona non-grata." When they learned that I was invited, I was questioned by the commanding officer to make sure that I wasn't some type of spy working for the Chinese government. I had to explain what karate was, how I got involved with the Uechi family and, more importantly, the relationship between the politicians on Okinawa and the people who practiced karate.

The bottom line was that the Okinawans, who were treated so badly by the occupying U.S. troops, respected the fact that I appreciated their customs and cultural arts, and that I was making an effort to learn one of their most sacred arts and in the prescribed and respectful manner.

**You wrote, many years ago, one of the first books ever written about karate and Uechi-ryu, "The Way of Karate." What motivated you to do this?**

I wrote "The Way of Karate" to fulfill a promise I made to Tomoyose and Uechi Sensei. Originally, it simply was going to be a book of techniques, but while writing the book between 1958 through 1960, I witnessed a disturbing influx of karate schools with teachers who simply taught Americans how to fight. Worse still, they were teaching fighting skills that were just rudimentary boxing with kicks. This prompted me to refocus the book's emphasis from techniques to the challenge of showing karate's "other side."

The book consisted of the moral lessons Tomoyose Sensei drilled into me during all our after-class chats, and focused on the importance of kata, something that few of the returning GIs learned or were taught. The book turned out to be an important part of not only Uechi-ryu's history, but karate's history, in the sense that it created an interest in karate as an art form and not merely an Asian fighting method. I was told that Americans, after reading the book, began to seek training in kata from the Okinawans, whereas before all they wanted to do was learn how to fight.

**Did the karate movements and techniques come easily to you?**

I was never an athlete in school, nor did I find karate training easy. What I lacked in natural ability, I made up for in patience and hard work. I feel that I'm a good teacher mostly because I'm patient with people who, like me, have a difficult time learning the art. I expanded the curriculum and found ways to make the training both interesting and reasonably easy to learn.

"Practitioners who are successful at learning karate should feel secure in the knowledge that they have an advantage."

At my age, I feel as though I'm in the best shape of my life, and can perform the art in a reasonably competent manner. Although I always could defend myself, I never viewed myself as a fighter and never would pretend to be one. I feel karate is something that should be practiced as an art that just happens to use self-defense movements. Practitioners who are successful at learning karate should feel secure in the knowledge that they have an advantage of going through life with the gift of karate always with them. They also should understand that this gift is something that should allow them to enjoy life to the maximum, while always remaining on guard, be aware of potential danger, and that their first line of defense should be avoidance and caution.

**How has your personal expression of karate developed over the years?**

My personal expression of karate changes on a daily basis. The movements themselves remain the same, but like the artistic expression of the

# Karate Masters

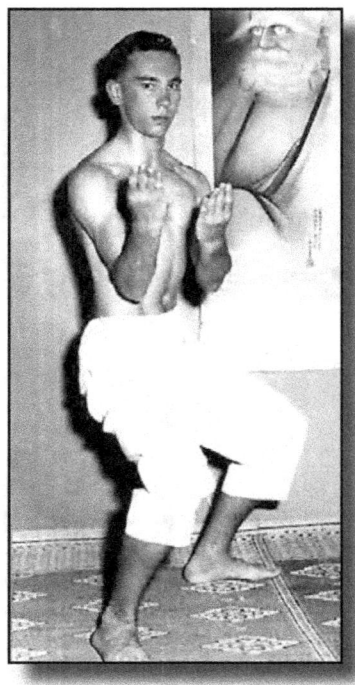

"My personal expression of karate changes on a daily basis."

jazz musician, my karate movements over the years have evolved into expressions, more like performance art than simple blocks, kicks, and gymnastic gyrations. Since discovering this very personalized understanding of my karate, I've actually gained more understanding of the movements and, more importantly, the movements between the movements, which almost always are ignored as people race through their kata and drills.

I get the most from Uechi-ryu through its kata. On Okinawa, during the time I was learning and studying Uechi-ryu, I simply performed the movements, without either understanding or attempting to discover what the movements were trying to teach me. After many years of teaching and experimenting with different ways of presenting Uechi-ryu to the public, I came up with a method of teaching the kata that works for me. I perform three of each kata daily. The first one is done softly, almost in a tai chi-like manner. During this performance kata, I breathe naturally through the nose and attempt to "will" the movements to happen. I want to be aware of my posture, balance, timing, and the elusive "movements between the movements."

The second performance of the kata is conducted with what I tagged many years ago as "dynamic tension." The movements are performed at a speed that approaches but does not reach "full power/speed" dynamics. During this kata, I work on becoming aware of my body and its potential for power, which is released by activating muscles and tendons used for the movements, while maintaining tension throughout the rest of the body that will protect internal organs during the performance of the kata (or fighting). Breathing during this second kata is rhythmic and designed to keep breathing passages open and soft, in spite of the armor-like exterior. The third performance of the kata is where all this training, common aids in what the Martial Arts – especially karate – are noted for. The movements are full speed and power.

This doesn't mean that you must race through the kata. When movements are interpreted to be those that need to be done fast, they are fast and powerful. The breathing at this level is drawn from your practice experiences of both the first and second level of the kata. The goal is always soft breathing with open breathing passages. Another important, yet often ignored, aspect of this type of training is that upon completion of the kata, whether the first or the third method, a practitioner should not be out of breath. With these three methods of performing not only the kata, but all the drills and exercises in our system, I have opened up the opportunity to examine and explore Uechi-ryu in a manner that was impossible during my early years of training.

**What do you think are the most important qualities for students to become proficient in karate?**

First and foremost, you must understand fully that any self-defense method you elect to study will not give you superhuman or magical qualities that will make you immune to injuries or death, either from an opponent or from your inappropriate and dangerous training methods. If you are simply learning karate to get a belt, and are interested in learning as many techniques, drills, or kata as possible, understand this: your ability to use your karate may suffer should you ever have to use it.

If you are studying for the purpose of becoming a serious martial artist, you should be more concerned with mastering a few kata, and the techniques contained in those kata. Mastery is something that takes years to accomplish and only when the right movements are ingrained and imprinted within your mind, and in such a way that they become instinctive, can they be performed without any conscious thought. When needed, they are always there. Once you understand and accept your goals, develop a plan to achieve them. Most dojos that must maintain a large student body just to pay the rent often end up "entertaining" students whose attention span will not warrant the serious type of training necessary to achieve mastery. If you are lucky enough to find a dojo that is capable of helping you achieve your goals, be patient; know that achieving mastery requires three things that my Sensei continuously stressed to me: "Practice, practice, practice!"

**With all the technical changes during the last years, do you think that there still are "pure" styles of karate?**

In Uechi-ryu, how have you seen its evolution? The short answer is "no!" I don't believe it's possible to retain an absolute "pure" style of karate, although a few popular systems attempt to maintain as strong a link as pos-

# Karate Masters

"There is a certain alluring mystique when discipline is applied while studying a traditional art form."

sible with a "version" of their original style, believing there is some type of superiority inherent in that particular combination of movements over what might evolve from those movements.

In the Martial Arts, this purist thinking is not something that came from the originators of the systems, but rather a mindset developed from early Japanese Martial Arts and common thinking in the West among early pioneers of the Martial Arts. This rather cult-like behavior on the part of some teachers stemmed from the belief that simple movements or complex movements within a kata must be performed in exactly the same way that the originator of the kata prescribed, and if it was altered in any way, the application would lose some or all of its efficiency as a martial art. Recently, with the introduction and popularity of Mixed Martial Arts and Extreme Fighting events, the purist myth that its combination or set of movements will enable its practitioners to fight effectively has been demystified and disproved by the modern ultimate challenges that quickly "test the talk."

Certainly, a person trained in any physical Martial Art combined with a healthy amount of conditioning will fare better than most untrained individuals in the event of a physical attack, but few people today will buy into anyone's attempt to acquire some sort of superior fighting ability with merely the traditional/original makeup of the movements. There is a certain alluring mystique when discipline is applied while studying a traditional art form; this makes the study of self-defense particularly appealing when linked to history or to a particular individual. Some of this appeal lies in the fact that the movements, or at least the "core" movements, originated hundreds of years ago and at that time the purpose for performing the movements in a set way was well defined and tested. Nowadays, the cycles of testing self-defense methods last only as long as the methods remain unique and superior to an opponent's ability to cope with them.

Today, anyone hoping to achieve any notoriety within the extreme fighting category must quickly assimilate new methods, techniques, and strategies, and through rigorous training and practice of those methods be capable of matching or hopefully being superior in the use of these methods during his or her next testing in the ring. The longer extreme fighting competition exists, the fewer people will elect or be capable of performing the training necessary to be part of this new tradition. At some point, people will label what they are teaching in facilities as "Extreme Fighting Methods" and, in order to attract as many students as possible, will "dumb down" the curriculum and eventually will create a program based on a core system developed and mastered by the head teacher.

Just as in traditional dojos, where 90 percent of the students are there simply to "get into shape" and learn a little self-defense, this new breed of "traditional" schools will have 90 percent of their students enrolled just so they can say they are learning extreme fighting, and perhaps 2 to 5 percent of their enrollment actually learn and practice for the purpose of testing their skills in real matches. In Uechi-ryu, with its simple kata and no-nonsense applications, most teachers seem satisfied with the makeup of the combinations of movements contained within each kata. Some still hold on to the theory that Uechi-ryu is the ultimate in self-defense, and subscribe to the same misconceptions regarding movement and expectations found in the real world of violence. On the other hand, some teachers retain the basic core movements but are experimenting with the mechanics of the movements and how the movements are performed. Realistically, an honest instructor will not make false promises or give students exaggerated expectations regarding how their Uechi-ryu will fare in a real fight. At best, Uechi-ryu (and all Martial Arts systems) provides the tools that can be used in some measure for self-defense purposes.

Many Uechi-ryu teachers felt that I "sold out" when I proclaimed that the association IUKF I formed many years ago (*International Uechi-ryu Karate Federation*) proclaims that we teach Uechi-ryu as an "art that happens to use self-defense movements." This statement honestly proclaims what our dojos offer to our students. It doesn't imply that our students can't defend themselves but, rather, IUKF doesn't make any special claims or promises that realistically cannot be fulfilled. Our primary reason for studying is to learn the "art" of Uechi-ryu, which is a helluva lot more interesting than running, doing calisthenics, or lifting weights. In 1958, there was an attempt to standardize the kata in Uechi-ryu among the seven dojos on Okinawa. It was during this time that the Uechi-ryu Karate Association was formed. During the first meeting (which I had the privilege of attending), Grandmaster Kanei Uechi's goal was specifically to standardize the style. Prior to this, senior instructors in each dojo pretty much taught from memory of the original movements brought to Okinawa by Kanei's father, Kanbun Uechi. Naturally, each teacher felt honor-bound to retain the Uechi style as they felt Kanbun had taught it. I witnessed each teacher getting up in front of the group, demonstrating their version of each a specific movement in question.

All the teachers were in accord regarding what I call today the "core" movements, but there were obvious variations in certain patterns of movement, extensive hip movement and other technical applications. Today, Uechi-ryu worldwide more or less follows the examples set by other organizations and systems. Ninety percent of the teachers don't have the foggiest idea about why they do the kata or how the kata relates to self-defense, whereas the other 10 percent, the "old school," takes pride in the kata and makes sure that it is taught correctly and that the students understand the reasons behind each movement within the kata. They may perform these movements slightly differently but the overall philosophy for studying their traditional system is retained – as an art that happens to use self-defense movements.

**Do you think different "styles" are truly important in the art of karate?**
Yes, I do think that different styles should be encouraged. As I mentioned earlier, the kata (which forms the heart of a style) contain the tools of self-defense that a competent teacher will use to teach. Without the kata, you simply have a place where people learn to fight by fighting. In a dojo where a style forms the core of the teaching methods, the student builds his or her "inner fighting" skills based on the style's core methods. I describe this learning process using a spoke wheel as an image. The hub is your core methods – kata – and the spokes are the compatible drills, applications, and methods that make the core system practical. There are many other important reasons for maintaining "styles" in karate, but they have more to do with the fraternal aspect of the Martial Arts, and of course rank: the measuring stick used to define the style and to maintain its important traits.

**What is your opinion of fighting events such as the UFC and Mixed Martial Art events?**
These events are great entertainment and provide a testing ground for techniques and methods that traditional martial artists can incorporate into what they do in the dojo. I've found many useful techniques and applications within the Uechi kata by watching these events that were built into the kata during an earlier era when life-and-death struggles were commonplace, but hidden without the roadmap of realistic testing that ultimate fighting events provide. Unfortunately, I see these professional contests evolving in a direction that eventually will destroy the sport as we know it today. The level

of strength, endurance, resistance to pain, and willingness to suffer long-term consequences from such battles will preclude normal people from either participating in the matches or wanting to be associated with its training. Obviously, this will have a negative effect on its relationship with traditional Martial Arts.

**Karate nowadays often is referred to as a sport; would you agree with this definition or is it "only" Martial Art?**

What a dojo teaches can be called anything. I would consider a dojo to be a "sport dojo" if the teacher's primary emphasis is creating students who would compete in tournaments. I consider a dojo "traditional" if the emphasis is focused on development of the system's core values, including kata, bunkai, and drills using the system's unique techniques. Although sparring and competition can be part of the curriculum, the traditional dojo bases its sparring on the core values contained within the system, rather than just using any technique that worked. The focus and goal of a traditional dojo is discovery and through practice, perfection of techniques within the system that can be repeated and reinforced through the kata. This focus and goal is not part of "sport dojo."

"Although sparring and competition can be part of the curriculum, the traditional dojo bases its sparring on the core values contained within the system, rather than just using any technique that worked."

**How do you see karate in North America and around the world at the present time?**

Everything moves in cycles. When I first started teaching, my goal was to introduce something that, at the time, seemed to be a strange and mysterious art form. Once other servicemen returned from Asia and the Martial Arts boom caught on, the emphasis shifted to marketing and building a business out of something that originally was a very exclusive and relatively private activity. There were many secrets that each sensei withheld for fear that the wrong people could gain knowledge from this information and shame the system and the dojo by harming others using the skill learned in the dojo.

As more and more dojo opened, what formally were secrets became com-

# Karate Masters

"There were many secrets that each sensei withheld for fear that the wrong people could gain knowledge from this information and shame the system."

mon knowledge. Emphasis shifted from learning mysterious and formerly secret techniques to earning a belt. Focus continued to shift from self-defense knowledge to motivation skills and confidence-building training. As the dojo's emphasis veered from teaching to building mega-dojos, teachers looked for teaching methods that could accommodate many students instead of developing the core values of their system, which required more time and intense training.

As training suffered, adults lost interest and, in order to keep the business going, many dojos opted to convert their facility into a karate babysitting service with traditional karate training becoming an afterthought. With the advent of Mixed Martial Arts, karate's draw had shifted from its early mystique to the attempt of learning "the ultimate self-defense," which it was believed could be mastered by practicing two hours a week. However, most of the traditional dojos that I'm associated with have reverted back to inexpensive and rather primitive facilities, where they teach a small group of people, with the emphasis on training and mastery of the original system as an art. It will be interesting to watch events like the UFC and the Mixed Martial Arts evolve through their own unique cycle.

**How important is "bunkai" in the overall understanding of kata training in general?**

There are a few ways a student can test the techniques and applications found in the kata. The safest way is breaking the kata down into segments that then are applied against an opponent. The more these applications are practiced, the more the techniques become part of the student's repertoire. In a traditional dojo, advanced students will perform these techniques at full speed and power, which will provide an element of stress along with the power and speed of the technique. I originally was taught that the kata in

Uechi-ryu contain many hidden techniques. Bunkai will explore and perfect the simplest of the applications that are easily visualized by the student. With time and practice, the student will discover many other techniques that were not apparent when he/she first learned of the kata

### When teaching the art of karate, what is the most important element: self-defense or sport?

The Martial Arts are based on self-defense and whether the focus is on scoring a point or defending your life, the techniques and applications are pretty much the same. If a dojo focuses primarily on the sport aspect of the Martial Arts, the focus will be on the competition rules rather than preservation of life. In self-defense, there are no rules. If you are teaching the art of karate, the teacher's first objective should be preservation of the core attributes and purpose of the system being taught. I don't know of any traditional dojo being created for competitive tournament purposes.

### Forms and sparring – what is the proper ratio in training?

An interesting question, since on Okinawa, Uechi-ryu was the only system that had sparring as part of the original style. According to my teacher, free fighting was a part of the training that Kanbun Uechi received in China. During the 50s, Uechi-ryu was the only karate style on Okinawa that believed sparring was a critical part of training. Therefore I only can comment on Uechi-ryu when answering this question. I was taught that a student should first master the kata, so that when it came time to spar, the techniques used were Uechi-ryu based. In a sense, sparring became a test of a student's ability to use his/her Uechi-ryu. In the original black belt tests, sparring accounted for 20 percent of the score.

### Do you have any general advice to pass on to practitioners?

That the student should approach the study of Martial Arts as an art form that happens to use self-defense movements. There are no magic moves or formulas within the Martial Arts that imbues the student with extraordinary powers or skills that will enable him/her to shortcut the process necessary to master this art form. Further, mastering this art form will not guarantee that the student automatically will fare well in an actual confrontation or fight. The beauty of Martial Arts is that they can be studied and practiced for any number of reasons. If health and fitness are your only goals, then the basic training within the dojo should be sufficient reason for coming to class and working out. If you wish to study Martial Arts as a traditional art, then you should spend time exploring other Martial Arts for the purpose of helping you understand your own specific style. This will aid you in your journey of

# Karate Masters

"Uechi-ryu is very much a part of my life. I was fortunate in having an instructor who prepared me for a lifetime of training."

exploration and will make your study far more interesting as you learn to "read" your kata and understand how a single movement can represent an infinite number of applications. If self-defense is your primary goal, you will need to experience elements of stress and realistic scenario applications to unlock practical uses of movements within your kata. Understand, however, that every fight and every attack will be unique and there is no way you can prepare 100 percent for a real fight. There always will be elements of uncertainty, fear, and stress that will accompany any fight that you might find yourself in. At best, your fighting skills based on your Martial Art training will give you an edge only when facing an opponent with less skill and training.

**What do you consider to be the major changes in the art since you began training?**

This is a difficult question to answer, since my training was unique and personal. I was given private lessons in the home of Ryuko Tomoyose during the week and on Saturdays we had small group lessons in Master Kanei Uechi's dojo, which is much different than what students experience today. During the mid-50s, I was more interested in learning about the art of karate in its original and authentic form. My teacher could have told me that jumping off a bridge was part of Uechi-ryu and I would have had no reason to doubt him. I simply listened and watched him instruct and I mimicked what he did and practiced it over and over. Today, everyone has heard of karate, and has a pretty good idea what it's about. Unfortunately, much of the publicity shared with the public relates to aspects of the Martial Arts that are neither relevant nor useful; in some cases, it's not even part of the Martial Arts. In the West, people are eager to extract whatever entertainment value any given art might possess and define this art based on their own interpretations. Elements of the art that are difficult to explain, or simply not entertaining, eventually are overlooked or, worse, eliminated from the instruction. The old methods focused on the core value of the kata. Today, the emphasis is on technique and application. For the most part, the kata has become an iconic ritual that is relegated to be necessary but rather useless.

**Who would you like to have trained with that you have not?**

That is an easy one to answer. I really would have liked to have studied with Kanbun Uechi. After having had experience training with so many different Uechi-ryu seniors and having learned so much from instructors from China who taught systems from the same lineage as Uechi-ryu, I now believe training with Kanbun Uechi would not have been so different as the way I teach today, but … it would be a memorable experience just to take one class with him!

**What would you say to someone who is interested in starting to learn karate?**

Do a lot of homework and research before looking for a school or style. Fully understand what your goals are and select a school and style based on those goals. Some schools will try to sign you up for long-term contracts that exceed what you would pay for a midsize car; therefore, it's only logical that you do at least as much research before selecting a dojo or style as you would in selecting a car. If all you want to do is learn how to fight in as short a period of time as possible, I wouldn't recommend that you choose a traditional dojo. On the other hand, if you are looking for a program that continually challenges both your mind and your body, as well as offering the best opportunity for long-term interest and involvement, then a traditional dojo may be just what you are looking for.

**What keeps you motivated after all these years?**

Uechi-ryu is very much a part of my life. I was fortunate in having an instructor who prepared me for a lifetime of training. He said that as I grew older, my Uechi-ryu would change in many ways. As a youth, I would explore the harder side of the art and later in life, the softer and more efficient side of Uechi-ryu would appear. He also said that I always should focus my training on the kata and allow the techniques and applications to evolve in a natural manner. In a sense, his instruction took away the need to ritualize the style, giving me the freedom to let the style grow and evolve naturally with time. Uechi-ryu, for me, has always been a "lifetime" activity – something that I will always do. At times, practicing is a chore and at times it's a pleasure I look forward to. But, regardless, I practice every day and every day I learned something from this experience. In the West, most people have neither the patience nor the discipline to practice something that will not provide instant gratification or sensory pleasure. The tendency is to look for a new and different product or service, thinking that it is the product that is lacking, when in fact it is our own inability to discipline ourselves to extract the benefits and therefore give up at the first sign of boredom or frustration.

**What is your philosophical basis for your karate training?**

I consider performing kata as "active meditation." I try to prepare my mind and body for whatever happens, in a way in which I will not allow my mind or body to interfere with the best and most efficient action. I am a very simple person with no lofty philosophical goals or aspirations.

**Do you have a particularly memorable karate experience that has remained as an inspiration for your training?**

There are many experiences I could relate, but the one that impressed me the most was the first time I actually had to use Uechi-ryu in a fighting situation. Like most new students, I had my doubts as to how practicing kata would help me in a fight. Just before leaving Okinawa, Tomoyose sensei and I decided we would celebrate my promotion to "sho-dan" by visiting a local bar for a beer. While sitting there, one of the bargirls decided to join us. It wasn't uncommon for this to happen, as the bargirls' job was to make sure that the patrons ordered more beer and, with a bit of persuasion, they would convince the patron to purchase a "short time" in a back room adjoining the bar (prostitution was legal at that time and rampant in all bars). Tomoyose explained to the girl that we were just there for one beer. Before the girl could leave, a soldier who was drinking at the bar came over and started yelling at her. As we found out later, the soldier felt he had the girl on a priority basis.

Tomoyose and I decided to leave and rose to our feet. Without any provocation or warning, the soldier threw a wicked roundhouse punch to my face. Instinctively, a movement from "Seisan" kata materialized. I intercepted the punching arm and connected the heel of my hand to the chin of the soldier at the same time and with the same movement. It was a powerful movement that I never had considered to be a defensive or attacking technique. But when a punch was flying at my face, this imprinted action from the kata materialized without thought or preparation ... just as Tomoyose sensei had predicted. The soldier's knees buckled as he collapsed to the floor. The barmaid told us to leave, and we happily complied. It shames me now to admit how proud I was, and how from that moment on I never questioned the validity of the training or the power of the kata.

**How do you think practitioners can increase their understanding of the spiritual aspect of the art?**

I'm a strong believer in being a religious/spiritual person, yet I do not belong to any organized religion or spiritual groups. Therefore, it is difficult for me to assign a role to the practice of karate that can be defined as spiritual or religious. If an individual truly wants to be a better person, he or she can try to achieve this by practicing karate with both physical and mental harmony in mind.

**Is there anything lacking in the way Martial Arts are taught today compared to how they were in your beginnings?**

Not really, at least not in what I considered to be a traditional dojo. In the early days, there were fewer training options and more emphasis on mastery of the kata, whereas today, teachers spend more time on applications and sparring, which grab students' attention more and therefore retain their interest over a longer period of time.

"I'm a strong believer in being a religious/spiritual person, yet I do not belong to any organized religion or spiritual groups."

**Could I ask what you consider to be the most important qualities of a successful practitioner?**

Patience, dedication, and the willingness to practice on a regular schedule without a thought of missing a training session.

**What advice would you give to students on the question of supplementary training?**

It all depends on how serious the person is about his or her training. Many practitioners believe that their regular karate training is sufficient for maintaining good health, and since they do not plan to compete in the UFC, no other training is needed. I belong to a gym and supplement my karate training with exercises that I don't perform in class and know this extra training in the gym is beneficial to my karate training. I currently teach karate three times a week, go through gym workout three times a week, and go bicycle riding on Sundays.

# Karate Masters

"The traditional and cultural values of Martial Arts are the glue that holds the Martial Arts together."

**Why do you think that preserving the cultural values of Martial Arts is important in our modern society?**

The traditional and cultural values of Martial Arts are the glue that holds the Martial Arts together. People are more prone to stay with a program that is steeped in tradition and history than they would be with a simple program that is just focused on self-defense. The longer a person stays with a program, the better he or she will be at whatever that program aims to accomplish. In a society such as ours, where people constantly are trying to get into condition or lose weight, programs like the Martial Arts that are steeped in tradition are more likely to retain students and help them achieve their goals, whatever they may be.

**Have there been times when you felt fear in your training?**

Interesting question ... there obviously have been times in my life where I felt or experienced fear, but none that I can associate with training. Part of the training that I put my students through are scenario drills in which my team sets up a situation and we place a student under as much stress and fear as possible, to test one's ability to draw on his or her training in order to get out of a particularly nasty situation. These drills help students develop confidence and understanding that what takes place in dojo won't necessarily happen in a real fight. The more experienced the student, the less likely he/she is to experience a great deal of fear or stress in such encounters. They know going into the drill that we aren't going to kill them or inflict extreme bodily punishment on them. In my personal life, I owned a nightclub/restaurant/pub in one of the toughest hoods in New England. For four years, my younger brother and I took turns watching the door and keeping trouble at bay. No question, there were evenings in which I was faced with situations in which if I had the time, I probably would have been scared out of my mind.

**Do you think that Olympics will be positive for the art of karate-do in case that happens one day?**

I don't think traditional dojos will benefit by karate being accepted into the Olympics, but there's no question that sport karate dojos will flourish. Unlike gymnastics, traditional karate kata is too subjective to fare well being judged by officials, even if these officials are trained in traditional Martial Arts. Therefore, the only realistic competition that can be judged fairly will be based on what today is evolving as a competitive fighting sport. I remember early Tae Kwon Do teachers and the sparring taught by these pioneers, and how drastically that art changed once it was considered for the Olympics. Essentially, the Olympics will drastically change and codify all the different and unique systems of karate into a singular, intertwined, sport-based activity. Kids will flock to these new sport-based dojos for an opportunity to be associated with an Olympic sport and, unless the traditional dojos jump on the bandwagon, they will not benefit from the Olympic affiliation.

**What are your thoughts on the future of karate?**

For its continuation, I see the future of karate evolve in the same manner as other activities that rely on the reputation of the teacher more than on the reputation of the activity. Each karate teacher will have to educate the public within his/her marketing parameter regarding what is taught, and why they should want to learn what is taught there. As the newness of karate diminishes and more competition emerges in the Martial Arts field, the public will become less likely to know the differences between a traditional karate dojo, a dojo focusing on competition, or a facility specializing in self-defense. When my dojo was the only one on the East Coast, anyone who had the remotest interest in anything relating to the Martial Arts came to my dojo. Today, only people interested in the specific things that I specialize in and publicize will seek out my teaching. This is a mixed blessing. I no longer have 500 students but, on the other hand, those who end up signing up for lessons are serious and dedicated.

**You are working on a new book project; what can you tell us about it?**

I've written three books on Uechi-ryu karate, each focusing on the art as it was taught to me. My last book, called "The Way of Uechi-ryu Karate" focuses more on my personal experiences on Okinawa and the growing pains I've experienced introducing Uechi-ryu to America.

# Karate Masters

"Practice safely and practice smart! Train your body for the long term and not for what you consider to be immediate or short-term goals."

**Any final advice that you'd like to give martial artists in general?**

I suspect that most readers of your fine magazine already are studying and practicing the Martial Arts, so my comments will be addressed to these practitioners: Practice safely and practice smart! Train your body for the long term and not for what you consider to be immediate or short-term goals. I was taught and I now teach that traditional karate should be a healthful activity, one that conditions and prepares your body for the rigors of life that we all must face, not just for showing off or that possible fight-for-your-life on the street. I think it's important for martial artists to retain a healthy interest in their practice, to be well-rounded individuals with interests that include a wide range of physical, mental, and emotional activities. I've seen too many "former" martial artists who retire at the ripe old age of 35. These are individuals who were super achievers in the Martial Arts at an early age and simply burned out and lost interest in the Martial Arts at the time such activity could play a most important role in their life. When I visited Japan in the mid-60s, I saw what I considered to be a poorly interpreted practice of the Martial Arts in the universities. At the time, karate was practiced as a four-year, very intensive and limited program. Instead of teaching the students a physical activity that could accompany them throughout their working life and even into their retirement years, the programs used models based on other competitive sports where the athletes reached the pinnacle at their senior year, at which time they gave up the sport as part of the graduation ceremony. True, some of the stellar performers were invited to become coaches who would return to the university from time to time to teach and grade students, but otherwise viewed their participation in the

"Regardless how skilled you are in self-defense, without good health and a strong body, your techniques are very limited in value."

sport as something they survived after four years instead of something they learned and could take with them throughout their lifetime.

Regardless how skilled you are in self-defense, without good health and a strong body, your techniques are very limited in value. Weigh the short-term satisfaction found in many of the extreme training methods popular today versus the long-term consequence resulting from this practice. I see too many martial artists relying on modern technology to repair damaged joints and body parts caused by extreme and unhealthy training practices. When students join a dojo, they regard the teacher as the master and therefore will do things they normally would never do. When a practitioner is 18–25 years of age, his or her body will adjust and cope with trauma and punishment, but unfortunately there will be a payback years later. Listen to your body, train wisely and practice often. If you do, you will be enjoying Martial Arts forever, not just during those few years when your body will function regardless how you are abusing it. O

# SAM MOLEDZKI

## NOT AN ORDINARY MAN

CHIEF INSTRUCTOR FOR SHITO KAI CANADA, HIS INTRODUCTION INTO THE MARTIAL ARTS BEGAN IN 1967 WHILE STUDYING BOXING AND COMPETING AS A MEMBER OF THE MIDLAND AVENUE COLLEGIATE GYMNASTIC TEAM. INITIALLY, MOLEDZKI SENSEI TRAINED IN THE CHITO-RYU KARATE SYSTEM FIRST INTRODUCED INTO CANADA IN 1958 BY THE MAN WHO IS REFERRED TO AS "THE FATHER OF CANADIAN KARATE," MASAMI TSURUOKA SENSEI. AFTER MANY MONTHS TRAINING SEVERAL TIMES A WEEK AT THE JAPAN CANADIAN CULTURE CENTRE, PLUS SPECIAL TRAINING SESSIONS AT TSURUOKA SENSEI'S OTHER DOJO LOCATIONS, MOLEDZKI SENSEI SUCCESSFULLY RECEIVED HIS SHO-DAN ON JANUARY 10, 1970.

SAM MOLEDZKI ALSO STUDIED OKINAWAN KOBUDO AS WELL AS KENDO, JODO AND IAIDO, AND HAS TRAVELED EXTENSIVELY TO JAPAN AND HAS TRAINED UNDER SOME OF THE WORLD'S GREATEST KARATE AND KOBUDO MASTERS, INCLUDING THE LEGENDARY RYUSHO SAKAGAMI SENSEI.

HE HAS BEEN A DIRECT STUDENT OF KUNIO MURAYAMA SENSEI SINCE 1991 AND NOW HE HEADS THE SHITO KAI CANADA, A MEMBER OF THE WORLD SHITO KAI KARATE-DO FEDERATION. FOR HIM, SPIRIT AND HEART ARE THE MOST IMPORTANT ATTRIBUTES IN MARTIAL ARTS TRAINING: "IN ORDER TO BE THE BEST." SENSEI MOLEDZKI SAYS, "YOU MUST HAVE THE WARRIOR'S SPIRIT — HEART." QUIET, RELAXED, AND SOFT-SPOKEN, THIS KARATE MASTER EXEMPLIFIES THE TRUE ATTRIBUTES OF A REAL MARTIAL ARTIST.

**How long have you been practicing the martial arts?**

It's been just over 50 years or so, since I first began practicing martial arts. At the time, I was a member of my High School (Midland Ave. Collegiate) gymnastics team and had been studying a little boxing. I was introduced to Japanese martial arts back in 1967, in Toronto, Canada, by a good friend of mine, Bill 'Pinky' Pinkerton. Actually, it was just less than nine years after the initial introduction of the first organized and systemized karate being taught in Canada, in 1958, by the gentleman most respectfully referred to as "The Father of Canadian Karate," Sensei Masami Tsuruoka.

# Karate Masters

"There before my eyes were approximately 100 people wearing funny looking white pajama-like outfits, punching and kicking as loud as they could."

My friend Pinky had asked me one day if I'd like to go and check out a place in downtown Toronto that taught some mysterious Japanese fighting art form he pronounced, "eye-key-dew"!

I must admit I'd never heard of it and, figured it might be interesting to see what it was all about. So, off we went downtown. But, unfortunately, we weren't able to find the exact location. After about an hour of searching, Pinky suggested we try another place he knew of, called the Japanese Canadian Cultural Centre, located in Don Mills, Ontario, (a suburb in the Northeast part of Toronto) where he recently played music at a wedding reception.

We arrived that Sunday afternoon and walked straight into the beautiful architectural marvel of its time, the Japanese Canadian Cultural Centre, and right up to an older Japanese gentleman who was in the reception area, and asked him if he had "eye-key-dew" there!

Well, he then replied, in a very firm but controlled voice, something like "No 'eye-key-dew' here! Is called Aikido and we don't have! We have Judo, Kendo and Karate-do. Come back Monday/Wednesday for Judo, or Tuesday/ Thursday for Kendo and Karate-do."

I signed up that very next Tuesday evening for my first karate class and haven't looked back ever since. Upon opening the big double doors to the JCCC's auditorium dojo, my first impressions was, to say the least, quite spectacular. There before my eyes were approximately 100 people wearing funny looking white pajama-like outfits, punching and kicking as loud as they could. I stood at the back of the dojo and watched the class and thought, "Wow, I can really get into this!" The rest, as the saying goes, is history.

**How many styles of karate and/or other methods have you trained in?**

Well, I first began training in the karate system called Chito-ryu from 1967 until 1969. This, by the way, was the most prevalent system of karate being taught all across Canada by Tsuruoka Sensei and his students. His chief instructor at the JCCC, when I joined, was Sensei Kei Tsumura.

I remember all the training sessions were a full two hours that usually included a ten-minute light stretching warmup before going outside for a two-mile run in bare feet, in the spring and summer months, and with shoes during the fall season.

Usually, after the initial run, we'd do more basic calisthenics back in the dojo, including jumping jacks, 50-100 push-ups (palms, knuckles, fingertips, back of the hands, etc.) and sit-ups, sometimes while applying all the basic blocking techniques. We normally practiced what is usually identified as the 3 Ks—Kihon (basics), Kata (forms), and Kumite (sparring).

After a few minutes break, we usually would line up, ten people deep in seven to ten rows across the dojo floor, and complete the second hour of training.

A point of interest was that we never used water bottles at all during any of the workouts. They just never were allowed. The remainder of the second half of the class was usually reserved for group kata practice by splitting off into belt levels, and one senior belt would lead the group through their designated kata for their kyu grade. Most often, the last 20–30 minutes was the part of the class that was dedicated to free-sparring. In the 60s, we did not use mouth guards, groin protection, or head, hand, and foot guards. Nor did we break up into weight classifications. Usually, you fought everyone in your own belt classification first, then anyone on the floor, including any black belt, regardless of size and weight or their Dan grade.

I also should point out that at this time Sensei Tsumura became the first man to introduce the karate system of Shito-ryu Itosu-kai to Canada, in 1969, (headquartered at the JCCC) after he became increasingly dissatisfied with the whole Canadian Chito-ryu experience under Tsuruoka Sensei. He later chose to travel directly to Japan and begin intensive training in both karate-do and kobudo under Master Ryusho Sakagami, founder of the Shito-ryu Itosu-Kai system. Sakagami Sensei was the most senior student of Grand Master Kenwa Mabuni, the man who created the Shito-ryu style of Karate.

**Who were your teachers?**

My first teacher, of course, as mentioned previously, was Sensei Kei Tsumura, at the Japanese Canadian Cultural Centre, from 1967 until 1981, when, I personally chose to leave the Shito-ryu Itosu-Kai system to further my own knowledge of the martial arts independently. If you will indulge me for just a brief moment, I'd like to say that I remain to this day very grateful

# Karate Masters

to Sensei Tsumura for teaching me the importance of developing good basics, in order to build a strong and firm foundation in karate. In my opinion, I still remember him being a very strict and demanding sensei who always had the best interests of the students in mind, as karate-kas and, even more so, as human beings, whether we knew it or not.

I really learned a great deal about the value of how to persevere and apply hard work, honest effort, and patience in karate and in daily life from Tsumura Sensei, and I always will be thankful for that. As one of his top students at the time, I was afforded the fantastic opportunity to travel to the Honbu Dojo in Tsurumi, Japan (1971, 1976, and 1980). While in Japan, I had the great honor and privilege to meet and receive direct instruction from Grandmaster Ryusho Sakagami in the various martial arts, including, Karate-do, Ryukyu Kobudo, Iaido, Jodo, and Kendo. Sometimes, at the honbu dojo, Sakagami Sensei would simply supervise the karate classes and his son Sakagami Sadaaki Sensei would teach. Other times, he would let the sen-pai of the dojo Ichikawa Fumikaze-san, instruct the classes. Usually, this was the kumite part.

I'd just like to relate what I think is an interesting story of my first training session, at the Japan honbu dojo. During that very first visit in 1971, we started with a brief warm-up, then Kotei kihon, Ido kihon, followed by some basic standard kihon kumite drills, and then what everyone really was waiting for, jyu kumite. At this point in the class, I was sort of expecting to have my personal character and resolve tested right away and I wasn't disappointed. Before leaving Canada, Tsumura Sensei had cautioned me about what to possibly expect. The senpai of the dojo, Ichikawa-san, came right up to me and indicated by hand gesture in my face that we should spar. I must point out that he was then 4th dan and I was a 1st dan black belt.

After the initial salutations, we both assumed a fighting position—he in a classical front stance guard and me taking a more natural, higher left guard, posture. Without hesitation, I quickly snapped up a left front leg roundhouse kick to his face and smacked him flush on his right cheek. Well, he didn't respond immediately, but just looked surprised, so I smacked him again with the same kicking technique. Let me tell you that after the initial shock of the second kick smacking him in the face, senpai Ichikawa launched a tremendous barrage of fists at my face and body (and nearly broke my ribs), which drove me straight back into the dojo wall. And then, the fun began. We just kept pounding on each other, back and forth, tit-for-tat, from one end of the dojo to the other, while the students pretended to spar and looked on in disbelief, until O'sensei Sakagami stopped the class.

"My actual direct relationship with Sakagami Ryusho Sensei really began in 1976, when I was sent to the Japan Itosu-kai Honbu for advanced training by Tsumura Sensei."

By the way, this ritual (sparring between me and senpai) was repeated every class until the time we left Japan almost one month later.

In 1976, on my next visit, Ichikawa senpai and I resumed our relentless sparring sessions and then finally, during 1980, on my next trip to the Japan Itosu-kai honbu dojo, Ichikawa senpai came to the dojo the first night of training and brought his entire family to meet me. He then graciously said that we really didn't need to test each other anymore. It should be pointed out that even at this point in time, we never wore any equipment and every sparring match was bare knuckles.

I have a great deal of respect for him, as he was a tough, no nonsense karate-ka and always a perfect gentleman and my senior who I called a friend. At this time, he was 5th dan and I had received my 4th dan in 1979. My actual direct relationship with Sakagami Ryusho Sensei really began in 1976, when I was sent to the Japan Itosu-kai Honbu for advanced training by Tsumura Sensei. At the time, I had specifically requested to learn more about the martial art of Iaido, and Tsumura Sensei arranged it so.

# Karate Masters

"I lived in an apartment owned by Sakagami Sensei, directly next door to the honbu dojo."

During 1975, in Toronto, I began training in a form of Iaido through a friend of Tsumura Sensei named Claude Vesque, an Aikido-ka and student of Mas Inokuchi Sensei.

When I arrived at the honbu dojo in Japan, Sakagami Sensei asked me to show him what I learned in the past year about Iaido. As I proceeded to show him what I knew, he immediately told me to stop and said that if I wanted to learn Iaido, then I would have to forget everything I had been practicing the previous year and start over in the *Muso Jikiden Eishin Ryu* system taught by him. Of course, I was dumbfounded, but not stupid enough to throw away the golden opportunity to be taught directly by him. From that moment on, I learned directly from Sakagami Sensei privately, every day, a minimum of eight hours a day, and sSometimes ten hours a day, depending on what scheduled classes were being taught during the early evenings. I lived in an apartment owned by Sakagami Sensei, directly next door to the honbu dojo. Each morning my private Iaido training was from 9–12 AM, then, lunch with the Sakagami family, and later, to continue training from 1–4 PM.

Depending on the schedule of evening classes throughout the week, I would attend classes in either Itosu-kai Karate-do, Shindo Muso Ryu Jodo, or privately with Sakagami Sensei in Ryukyu Kobudo, or sometimes part of Sakagami Sensei's Kendo class. Then, it usually would be back to Iaido training from 10 PM–midnight.

After approximately a solid month of this strict, daily disciplined training, Sakagami Sensei asked the Chief Examiner of the district, Ishido Sensei of the Muso Shinden Ryu Iaido system from Kawasaki, to come over to his dojo and check out my form. After performing everything I was taught for Ishido Sensei, Sakagami Sensei informed me that I now was ready to try my test for black belt in Muso Jiki Den Eishin Ryu Iaido.

We were to leave early the next day for another city and Sakagami Sensei was scheduled to be part of the five-member judging panel of examiners that consisted of three 8th dan plus two 7th dan. Sakagami Sensei was a Kyoshi 7th dan in Muso Jikiden Eishin Ryu Iaido then.

That day, approximately 250 people tested for various dan levels from 1st dan to 5th dan. I believe I was one of only two or three foreign (non-Japanese) students among the 250 people testing. I had been instructed in the proper etiquette and the chosen five kata for the testing, and was to first qualify at a 1st kyu level before the final 1st dan testing.

Everything was conducted in Japanese and you were supposed to know where and when your turn was and how to proceed from start to finish. After completing the pre-test, I later was called up to do the final test and, for the first time in my life as an experienced martial artist, I truly never actually felt the sword in my hands as I completed my required kata. I was that zoned in. A short time later, there was some kind of big discussion about my performance by the judging panel. When the 60 people finished, the judging panel took a break. Sakagami Sensei was walking toward me with this very strange looking grin on his face. He stopped to talk with Tsuchiya Sensei (testing for 5th dan) from the FAJKO office and asked him to translate for me, as he spoke very good English. With this huge smile on his face, Sakagami Sensei proceeded to tell Tsuchiya Sensei what the discussion was all about after my performance. I immediately thought back to my performance and realized that, in one of my kata, I actually had started facing in the wrong direction so I quickly slid around and continued the kata as if there was nothing wrong.

As a point of interest, a few weeks before, Sadaaki Sensei had related a story to me about a person failing his 5th dan test the previous year because he got the handle of his sword caught up in the cloth number designating your performance order, which was sewn on the left side of the uniform just above your heart. That person had stopped to remove the offending cloth, then proceeded to complete his required kata. He failed because he let the small distraction throw him off and in a real draw, against another person with a sword, he would have been cut down.

Tsuchiya sensei finally had gotten the complete explanation from Sakagami Sensei and told me that some of the members of the examining panel wanted to know why, after my performance, that a 3rd dan was testing for 1st dan. They asked whose student I was and Sakagami Sensei told them I was his student and I actually did not have any dan ranking at all.

I was then told to go home to Tsurumi and wait until sensei was finished examining the rest of the candidates. When I returned to the dojo, Mrs.

# Karate Masters

Sakagami asked me how I did and I said I didn't know because sensei didn't tell me if I passed or not. Later in the evening, Sakagami Sensei returned home and finally told me I passed at the top of the 60 people testing for sho-dan. Apparently, I was a testament to the quality of Sakagami Sensei's personal instruction and teachings in the art of Muso Jikiden Eishin Ryu Iaido.

At the conclusion of my training in the Shito Ryu Itosu Kai Karate and Kobudo Association, Canada, in February 1981, I was at the level of 5th dan Shito-Ryu Karate; 3rd dan Ryukyu Kobudo, and 1st dan Muso Jikiden Eishin Ryu Iaido. From 1981 to 1991, I remained steadfastly independent of any major national or international federation by personal choice, as mentioned previously, and took every opportunity whenever it presented itself to practice with as many senior Japanese instructors as possible.

As fate would have it, during our 1991 Canadian National Black Belt Championships in Vancouver, British Columbia, I had the great fortune to meet and practice with Sensei Murayama Kunio from Monterrey, Mexico, via Japan. And I haven't looked back ever since. Since 1991, I have been a representative of the Karate-Do Shito Kai Murayama family, and directly associated with the World Shito Ryu Karate Do Federation as the official representative for Canada, and in 2006, I was appointed a director of the WSKF.

**Would you tell us some interesting stories of your early days in karate?**
I do recall vividly my very first black belt fight in a tournament in 1970. The special guest of honor at the All Canadian Karate Championships was the founder of the Wado Ryu style of karate, Grand Master Hironori Ohtsuka. I had just won second place in black belt kata and really was looking forward to the kumite competition. As fate would have it, my first match was against a very seasoned veteran black belt named George Beattie, a member of the host dojo of Sensei Basil Shintani. The match was only underway a short time when I executed a left hand low block at George's powerful side kick to my stomach and noticed, when I brought my hand back in a guard position, that my thumb had been severely dislocated and was actually facing me at a very weird angle. Needless to say, I was starting to get very worried!

The referee stopped the match but didn't know what to do next, as I was holding my left hand and asking for someone to help me. At that moment, everyone was trying to calm me down but no one knew exactly what to do. Then, from the head table area, Grandmaster Hironori Ohtsuka came into my ring and asked me in a very soothing and calm voice to show him my hand. As I did that, he took the end of my black belt and covered my thumb with it. He then started to talk to me again but, this time, in a louder, stronger voice so I would look at him and not my hand. Then he simply slapped me on the side of my head and simultaneously gave my thumb a jerk and re-set it! I must say I was greatly relieved and, after thanking Sensei Ohtsuka for putting my thumb back in place, it was starting to swell up pretty badly. I was then taken to the nearest hospital and waited for almost three hours before a doctor had a look at it. After the x-rays, he said that whoever reset my thumb did a fantastic job and he couldn't do anymore other than. He gave me a couple of aspirin and sent me home.

"My personal expression has evolved from the popular sport side as a former accomplished competitor to the more traditional Budo aspect of karate-do."

The following year I again met and thanked Sensei Ohtsuka at the Budokan in Japan. While there, I also was introduced to Nakayama Masatoshi Sensei, Yamaguchi Gogen Sensei, and Fumio Demura Sensei, by Sakagami Ryusho Sensei. I was in Japan as co-captain of the Canadian Shito-ryu Itosu-kai Karate Team training there for about a month. We competed at the East Japan Kanto district karate Championships, where I became the first non-Oriental to win the individual black belt kumite title.

The following year, as captain of Canada's National Black Belt Karate Team competing at the 3rd World Union Karate-do Organization (W.U.K.O.) World Karate Championships in Paris, France, I met Hayashi Teruo Sensei and Nishiyama Hidetaka Sensei.

As co-captain of Canada's National Karate Team, at the 3rd W.U.K.O. World Karate Championships in Long Beach, California, in 1975, I had the unique privilege of being the only non-Japanese invited to a special private meeting aboard the Queen Mary, with some of Japan's most famous karate masters to date. As a personal guest of Sakagami Sensei, I was introduced to Hiroshi Kinjo Sensei, Mabuni Ken-ei Sensei, and Iwata Manzo Sensei (JKF Shito-kai), Hayashi Teruo Sensei again, (Hayashi-ha Shito Ryu), and Uchiage Kenzo Sensei (JKF Goju-kai). I was directed by Sakagami Sensei to

# Karate Masters

"I personally believe that throughout history, kata has been the method by which the founders of various martial arts recorded and passed on their secret fighting techniques."

just keep my ears open and my mouth closed. I was to listen and learn. I remember the occasion very fondly, surrounded by these great men and watching them interact with each other!

**In karate, what does kata really represent and how important is it?**

I personally believe that throughout history, kata has been the method by which the founders of various martial arts recorded and passed on their secret fighting techniques. And by studying the kata deeply within a given system, one would be enlightened to the mysteries within the kata.

**Were you a 'natural' at karate? Did the movements come easily to you?**

I was a slow learner and it took a while for my brain to process all the intricate movements found in karate. But once I struggled my way through them, I very rarely ever forgot them because it did not come natural to me and I had to work very hard at it. My best friend Pinky, at the time of our early stages of learning karate, found it really easy to remember the kata patterns. Pinky could remember them almost instantly after being shown the pattern only once. I, on the other hand, had to constantly ask him what the next moves were. Many years later (15 years), he had virtually forgotten most of them and would come to me and ask me what the whole kata was. I had learned to be patient and persevere and never give up no matter how hard a struggle it was. It seems to have paid off.

**How has your personal expression of karate changed/developed over the years?**

My personal expression has evolved from the popular sport side as a former accomplished competitor to the more traditional Budo aspect of karate-do.

**What are the most important points in your teaching methods? And what are the most important qualities for a student to become proficient in the karate style?**

We learn through various means and I prefer to teach using the Visual Method (demonstrating it), Audible (describing it by voice), and Physical (assisting the students by physically guiding them through it). I also feel humor is an important tool for teaching. In my opinion, humor cuts the tension in the learning process the best. I also believe the student needs to have an open mind, be patient, and never give up, but persevere.

**With all the technical changes during the last years, do you think there is still 'pure' Shito Ryu karate or any style for that matter?**

History has shown us that every generation of masters has put its personal stamp on the martial arts and Shito Ryu karate is no different.

**Do you think different 'styles' are truly important in the art of karate?**

Yes, I believe that styles or personal interpretations of the original founders' training methods are important because they help us understand something of what the actual founder of that particular system felt was important to preserve at the time he created the system.

**What is your opinion of fighting events such as the UFC and Mixed Martial Arts events?**

I enjoy watching it on TV, when I get a chance.

**Karate nowadays often is referred to as a sport.... would you agree with this definition?**

I both agree and disagree. The modern form of karate was toned down a lot to gain acceptance as a viable exercise alternative in the beginning of the twentieth century. It has evolved into a world recognized sport and may well achieve official Olympic status one day. As a viable martial art today, it contains varying methodologies of self-defense that need to be investigated further within each particular system.

**Do you feel that you still have further to go in your studies?**

Most definitely! I firmly believe that I'm at the stage where I have a lot better understanding of karate than I did even ten years ago but, I am still a long way from ever mastering it. I'm still very excited about learning more and more, as it is a never ending study to reach perfection. And, as we know, no man is perfect, so the journey is what it's all about for me anyway.

I'll tell you quite honestly, when I joined the Shito-kai Murayama family in 1991, my karate knowledge exploded. I was introduced to a system of Shito-ryu karate that contained a whole new world of knowledge handed down from Mabuni Kenwa Sensei through Iwata Manzo Sensei to Murayama Kunio Sensei. Exploring the major influences from Mabuni Kenwa Sensei relating to in-depth understanding of Nage-waza and Gyaku-waza are part of this terrific system. Not to forget about the major influences of Fujita Seiko Sensei, (14th generation headmaster of Koga Ryu, Wada-ha Ninjitsu) that was passed down to Iwata Manzo Sensei and on to Murayama Sensei, and is one of the more significant developments. They include Fujita Sensei's mastery of Daienryu Jojutsu. In 1943, Iwata Sensei received his Shihan license in the short stick art, Shingetsu Ryu Shuriken Jutsu. In 1944, Iwata Sensei received his shihan license in the throwing-projectile art and Nanban Sattoryu Kenpo Jutsu. In 1948, Iwata Sensei received the honor of becoming the 4th generation Soke of Nanban Sattoryu, the art of jujutsu-like grappling combat techniques. Today, Genzo Iwata Sensei (Chief Instructor WSKF) is the 5th Soke of Nanban Sattoryu Kenpo Jutsu.

**How do you see karate in North America at the present time?**
I think it is here for the long haul, and can only improve more with the help of excellent karate-ka and researchers like Patrick McCarthy, Joe Swift, Mario McKenna, Charles Goodin, and John Sells, to name a few. By providing valuable research information about karate history and other technical aspects of karate translated into the English language, karate in North America can only get better through dedicated practitioners like them.

**Do you think it helps the karate student physically to train with weapons (Kobudo)?**
Kobudo weapons help a great deal, physically and mentally, to train and develop my traditional karate techniques. I believe the advantages are as many as there are particular weapons.

For example, the Bo could help you understand more about the need to develop a clearer understanding of the use of longer distance while the Sai may help you to apply the correct angle and direction of a technique at a closer range. The Tonfa, for instance, possibly may help in understanding better about how to generate hip torque, from the tanden or lower stomach, and transferring energy through back, chest, shoulder, arm, and wrist action. The Nunchaku also can help you to gain maximum power and speed by the use of proper hip rotation and the understanding of how to possibly overcome distance to an advantage over your opponent, while the Kama, I believe, is able to help you develop a more controlled and secure hooking and scooping action in your striking and blocking techniques.

Practicing with Kobudo weapons assists in your shifting into control of various offensive and defensive distances, to become a better martial artist. Finally, I feel all the weapons help in developing a firmer grip strength and better wrist control. Also, they aid in developing and expanding the correct breathing methods during a given encounter and improving one's physical strength, balance, and coordination.

**How does the karate style differ from other martial arts methods when applying the techniques in a self-defense situation?**

If you deeply understand your own karate system, then you'll be able to utilize the appropriate techniques required for a given self-defense situation.

**When teaching the art of karate, what is the most important element: self-defense or sport?**

Both aspects should be taught by a competent instructor for the benefit of his/her students.

"If you deeply understand your own karate system, then you'll be able to utilize the appropriate techniques."

**Forms and sparring, what's the proper ratio in training?**

I believe that in the world competition arena today, one should specialize in either forms or fighting. But as a traditional martial artist, kata principles should be trained more and not just the pattern or form of the kata or just the fancy techniques of some kata.

**Do you have any general advice you would care to pass on the practitioners in general?**

Only that if you find a particular martial art that really gets your attention, then don't give up on it. Invest in it and it will invest in you by keeping you healthier and your mind more active.

**What do you consider to be the major changes in the art since you began training?**

I've witnessed and experienced many changes, especially in the aspect of competition rules and regulations as a former international class athlete and later as an international referee.

These changes start with the kumite matches in the 1960s without the use of equipment (bare fists, no mouth guards or groin protection) to using a single point match method or two half-points, through the mirror judging system using the three-point system with six half-points and on to the present system of multiple points and superior techniques getting a higher value. In Canada, during the 3rd Canadian National Black Belt Championships in 1976, kata was first included. I had the honor of finishing in third place, behind Kim Wong in second place and Tak Samashima in first place.

A few years later, female Kumite was included and finally Junior Kumite, including the evolution of the kata performance from the mostly hard and all-powerful performances to the more aesthetic, artistic performances, with the present-day inclusion of demonstrating various theatrical self-defense aspects of the form.

And there's the fashion change in the basic karate uniform, including the use of designated competition belts and eliminating the black belt of grade. There's also the added use of specific types of uniforms for the forms competition and another for sparring competition. I also see the sporting aspect of karate evolving along the recognition lines of Tae Kwon Do if it actually becomes an Olympic event, with all the usual benefits of an officially recognized Olympic sport.

**Who would you like to have trained with that you have not?**

I'd have to say definitely Kano Jigaro Sensei, Taira Shinken Sensei, Fujita Seiko Sensei, and Bruce Lee—as well as Kinjo Hiroshi Sensei and Ishimi Yasunari Sensei from Spain.

**What would you say to someone who is interested in starting to learn karate?**

I would simply recommend they find a good dojo somewhere and start this fantastic journey, which could last their whole lifetime!

**What is it that keeps you motivated after all these years?**

I guess I'd have to say it is the thirst for knowledge in a very different art form, as well as trying to understand an ancient culture that I find fascinating. Also, to continually improve my understanding of the martial arts through constant mental and physical dedication to it.

**Do you have a particularly memorable karate experience that has remained as an inspiration for your training?**

In 1971, during my first visit to Japan, I competed in the Kanto District Karate Championships and became the first non-Asian ever to win the Black Belt Kumite title in Japan. In my mind, it proved that if I believed in myself, and my karate ability, even I could win in Japan. In 1991, at the Canadian National Black Belt Championships in Vancouver, British Columbia, I had the great experience of having one of my students become the first Canadian junior male athlete to win gold in both his kumite and kata division for his age group. And then, later in 1993, at the 1st World Shito-ryu Karate-do Championships in Tokyo, Japan, one of my female students won a bronze medal in Black Belt sparring.

"In my case, the study of karate-do has been a personal life saving experience."

**After all these years of training and experience, could you explain the meaning of the practice of karate?**

That's a very difficult question to answer. Let's just say that, in my case, the study of karate-do has been a personal life saving experience. I grew up in a small town in Ontario until my early teenage years. My late father was a very physically abusive parent who used to beat me and my brother almost daily until I was thirteen. My mother was finally forced to leave my father for fear of her life. She left the family with a broken arm and broken nose, when I was just six years old.

My brother and I grew up pretty much unsupervised and on our own, and, eventually fell in with the wrong types, which led to us getting into trouble on a regular basis. Seven years later, in 1962, when my mother finally was able to return to rescue us, we moved to Toronto. Unfortunately, in Toronto, we fell in with the same element and continued to get into trouble.

When my best friend, Pinky, suggested we investigate the JCCC, I already was a seasoned, streetwise, street-fighting teenager, with no real direction in

# Karate Masters

"My introduction to the art of karate-do was the thing that personally saved my life."

life. My introduction to the art of karate-do was the thing that personally saved my life. By beginning to learn about the power of mental discipline through a safe, organized class structure, with dedicated instructors and regular structured physical training, I was able to turn my life completely around. Karate-do has given me that, and a great way of life that I will take to my grave.

**How do you think karate practitioners can increase their understanding of the spiritual aspect of the art?**

By looking deeper within themselves and recognizing what excites them, what motivates them, what inspires them to become better persons through disciplined physical and mental training. A person who is very passionate about his/her art has an unswerving thirst for knowledge about his/her chosen field and pursues it totally, being fully committed and dedicated to the task.

**Is there anything lacking in the way martial arts are taught today compared to how they were in your beginnings?**

Perhaps a little more concentration on developing the student's character as an individual and less about promoting students quickly through the colored belt grading system in order to keep a high volume of membership.

**What advice would you give to students on the question of supplementary training?**

Basically, I feel that if you want to be good at karate, practice karate. Supplementary training can be a great help to your traditional karate training, as long as it remains just supplementary and does not become the main focus of your training.

**What do you see as the most important attributes of a student?**

Heart and the never-give-up attitude.

**Do you think that Olympics will be positive for the art of karate-do?**

No, not really; not in the traditional sense of karate-do. But I think it definitely will have a positive effect as a globally practiced sport when it is finally recognized by the IOC.

**What are your thoughts on the future of karate?**

I believe there are enough good people in karate around the world to ensure it will be around for another hundred years! O

"Supplementary training can be a great help to your traditional karate training, as long as it remains just supplementary."

# KUNIO MURAYAMA

## A SOULFUL JOURNEY

MURAYAMA SENSEI WAS BORN ON JUNE 30, 1944, IN MIYAGI, JAPAN. A DIRECT STUDENT OF MANZO IWATA SENSEI, THE YOUNG MURAYAMA MADE GREAT PROGRESS IN HIS KARATE WHILE STUDYING FOR AN ECONOMICS DEGREE. HIS HARD WORK AND DEDICATION TO THE ART OF KARATE WAS RECOGNIZED BY MASTER IWATA, WHO EVENTUALLY INVITED HIM TO BECOME HIS UCHI-DESHI (LIVE-IN DISCIPLE). THIS GREAT HONOR ALLOWED MURAYAMA SENSEI TO EXPERIENCE HIS MASTER'S GREAT WEALTH OF KNOWLEDGE, AS TAUGHT HIM DIRECTLY BY KENWA MABUNI, FOUNDER OF THE SHITO RYU STYLE. MURAYAMA CONTINUED HIS TRAINING AT TOKYO UNIVERSITY EVEN AFTER HIS GRADUATION IN 1966. HE CAPTAINED HIS UNIVERSITY KARATE TEAM FOR TWO YEARS MORE BEFORE LEAVING JAPAN IN 1970.

HAVING EARNED HIS MENKYO (TEACHING LICENSE), MURAYAMA SENSEI SOUGHT A TEACHING CAREER IN THE NOBLE ART HE HAD GROWN TO LOVE AND BEGAN HIS WORK TO PROMOTE THE SHITO-KAI ORGANIZATION, QUICKLY DEVELOPING A LARGE FOLLOWING THROUGH HIS WORK AND GROWING REPUTATION AS A WORLD-CLASS COACH, WKF OFFICIAL, KARATEKA AND TEACHER. NOW IN HIS FIFTH DECADE OF STUDY, SHIHAN MURAYAMA KUNIO IS A RESPECTED MASTER OF KARATE-DO AND A LEADER FOR THE ART OF SHITO RYU AROUND THE WORLD.

**How was the training in your beginnings in the art?**

The training during my early days was far from easy. Our sempai used to push us very hard. They knew that only by breaking our bodies would our true spirit come up so we could show how strong we were. This is part of the old traditional approach to Budo and Japanese martial arts. Karate and other Japanese arts really started to develop after World War II. The Japanese spirit was that one from the war and every activity you did was related to the development of your spirit. All Karate training then and now should be structured on the basis of the fighting spirit a warrior should have. Then karate becomes a kind of model laboratory that teaches us how to survive in the outside-budo world. And even Karate must follow the path of the laws of Universe, the same laws that dictate the movements of the body or the four seasons.

# Karate Masters

"Do not make a "decision" of what karate is or is not. You must walk the walk before you can decide what it is."

**What can you tell us about your teacher Master Manzo Iwata?**

Shihan Manzo Iwata was well known for his in-depth and comprehensive understanding of Mabuni Kenwa's Shito-Ryu system. Later, following an introduction by Kenwa Mabuni to his friend Fujita Seiko, Iwata also learned *Daien Ryu Jojustu* and *Nanban Satto Ryu Kempo*, among other disciplines for which Fujita Seiko was renowned. He was a very special man and a dedicated karateka. His ethic as a human being was outstanding and that probably is the reason why Grandmaster Kenwa Mabuni chose him as one of his top disciples. Iwata Sensei dedicated all his life to the study and development of Shito Ryu karate. He is directly responsible for the perpetuation around the world of the style developed by Kenwa Mabuni. Sensei Iwata's non-political approach to karate made people willing to exchange knowledge and techniques with him. His son Genzo Iwata Sensei is one of the technical directors of the *World Shito Kai Federation*.

**What is the first lesson that all practitioners should learn?**

Do not make a "decision" of what karate is or is not. You must walk the walk before you can decide what it is. Some people have preconceived ideas and notions of what the art is and this attitude limits their progress. Don't think that everybody has the same reason to train. Some want physical conditioning, others health, others sport, etc. ... Everyone has a different purpose. Karate offers many faces that we can use to improve ourselves as individuals.

**What do you think are the major misconceptions about the art of karate, in general terms?**

There are some but I would mention a few. Many practitioners think that in the past, the old masters had the single techniques isolated in a kihon format first, and later they were put into kata format. Actually, it is the opposite. The techniques were extracted from the kata to develop the kihon. Then, when the level of the isolated techniques (kihon) improved, the overall kata performance got better.

Another general misconception is that the karate techniques we train in kihon have to be used exactly the same in a free-style or self-defense situation. This idea is not correct. The practitioner uses the "mold" of kihon to bring a certain level of body mechanics and technical skill, but once these already are part of the karateka, the technique flows and is expressed in a natural way. One example of this is the hikite. In actual combat, we don't do "hikite." The hikite training is for other things and has its place, but not in a free-style sparring or a real self-defense situation.

### How much protection (pads, gloves, etc.) do you think should be used in karate competition?

The safety of the practitioners is always a priority, or at least it should be. I don't think competitors should look like "robocop," though. But coming from a traditional training, I think sometimes is important to spar with no gloves, pads, or protections of any kind. This bring us to the feeling of "empty hand" karate. We must be able to hit hard without hurting our hands or feet, and also think that if we are hit by a punch or a kick, no pads will prevent us from being hurt.

### Do you teach the same art that you practice?

I do. The techniques that I teach are the same techniques that I personally practice. Karate is a very complex art but its difficulty lies in the perfection of the simple techniques.

### Are there any aspects where Japanese are physically different than Causasians?

Well, the bodies are little different but I think maybe the difference was more in the old days because of the traditions. Japanese always sat on seiza a lot during the day, so hips tend to be stronger; also, ankles used to be more flexible in Japanese people because of the sandals/slippers, but these are very small differences and the mastery in karate has absolutely nothing to do with that.

### Do you think kata is a useful tool in order to perform well in kumite or self-defense?

Due to the fact that sport competition is getting more popular, the amount of techniques used in actual sparring is being reduced to those that actually can score a point in competition. Kumite is not competition sparring. Kumite allows more techniques that won't ever be permitted in a sport contest. So we should clearly differentiate between sport shiai-kumite division and karate jyu-kumite. Kata, when studied correctly, truly is a library for kumite or sparring. Kata has many fighting principles and concepts that can be used both in jyu-kumite and self-defense situations. The problem lies in the fact that many people who perform kata well and are great in kata competition never researched and analyzed the combat principles intrinsic to the kata. They never applied them in a sparring situation. Many, strategies, rhythms, and tactics in kumite come from kata principles. But not everybody recognizes them as part of kata … they just learned them as "sparring."

**What should be the main physical goal of karate training?**
The main physical goal should be to produce the maximum power with the best possible body mechanics. Try to produce the maximum output from your body. That is the key. The only way to achieve that is to dedicate yourself to constant drilling and training of the basics, to correct and intense training of the fundamental techniques of the art. Once this point is a constant in your karate fundamental techniques, then everything falls into place. Kata becomes strong and powerful and kumite seems easy and natural. Always stress the basic and simple training and don't think too much about intellectualizing things. Do it instead of spending time trying to label things and understanding the physics of your body. This will come naturally if you do enough training.

**What is your personal training schedule?**
I do a lot of teaching so I do repeat basic movements many times. I do have time for my personal training that I follow according to my physical conditions. I do emphasize more stretching and above all the natural approach to karate that Shito Ryu is based on. I would like to emphasize that what is really important is not the technique you do in your training but the thought behind it. That, and the time you invest in it, makes you better. So right thought or state-of-mind and quality training time is the key, no matter what your age may be. There is no other magic formula or secret.

**How has modern society and education changed the way karate is taught today?**
To begin with, people today have a different kind of life compared to what we had many years ago. The young generation has more commodities that we had. Their families in general are better off than previous generations, so they have to work less. The idea of "constant sacrifice" for things is simply not there as it used to be. This affects the way young people approach their karate training today. You tell them to do a gyaku-tsuki 1,000 times and they will look at you funny. These changes in the society and culture are the main reasons for the differences between our old generation and the younger ones.

### What do you think about Karate getting into the Olympics?

The development of karate as a sport may be seen as taking the art away from its roots. Competition is only one part of karate and only a few of the people who practice karate actually are involved in sport competition.

The great benefit would be a contact point with a bigger audience around the world. Only then, and through the idea of sport, can people eventually learn more about what underlies the sport technically and spiritually. Also, parents would see karate as a possibility for their children to become worldwide recognized athletes. This would bring more people to the dojos around the world and it would be a great opportunity to teach people about the true values of karate as an art and a way of life.

"Competition is only one part of karate and only a few of the people who practice karate actually are involved in sport competition."

One of the stronger criticisms of sport karate is that if we focus only on the competition aspect, only those techniques used in sport activities will be emphasized in training. All attitudes and strategies will be suited for competition and that will bring a serious deficiency in the overall balance of karate as an art. Competition is good and is healthy, but we always need to remember that karate is for one's life and not only for a few years. Do karate for yourself; always look after yourself. Don't think only in terms of the activity but in terms of "you" as an individual. The tradition of karate will be lost totally in the future if there are not instructors and students left to keep to the traditional ways.

### Some people think traditional martial arts and/or karate have very little value for street situations because the practice is not reality-based.

Whoever is saying that shows how little knowledge they have of the martial arts. That is a very narrow-minded attitude to have. But in the end, it all boils down to the individual – the way you train martial arts, and your instructor may have an important influence in that. But it is still down to "you" as an individual whether or not you can make it work in a real situation.

# Karate Masters

"The hard and soft aspects of karate are intrinsic to the style developed by Kenwa Mabuni."

**What kind of mental preparation would you recommend?**

The best mental preparation is to have confidence in what you do; and that confidence only comes from knowing that your art and training methods work.

**Do you think kata competition may push the student to focus only in the "external mold" for the form?**

Kata competition is a great challenge for any karateka, but there are things we can't forget about. You can get someone to copy the perfect technique. This technique might look great to the untrained eye, even to some trained eyes … but it's purely cosmetic. It is important to understand and maintain the essential principles of the form without losing track of its concepts. You can be a world kata champion and have a deep understanding of the essence of the kata you practice. There is no reason why not. I don't see any conflict; one is sport, the other is art and a challenging personal journey.

**Shito Ryu incorporates the naha-te and the shuri-te aspects of Okinawa, and also tomari-te. How does that translate into the physical technique?**

The hard and soft aspects of karate are intrinsic to the style developed by Kenwa Mabuni. When we think of strength, we have to remember that there are many forms of "strength" and that not all are the same. This is the case with the "soft" aspect of the art. From stances and blocks to punches and kicks, the art of Shito Ryu has many different ways of expressing the principles of hard and soft.

I don't think that any style of karate is "soft" or "hard" by nature. When we are young, we have to train hard, no matter what the style is. When we get older, we tend to use the strength and physical force in different ways, so our karate may look "softer" when actually it is not. The different breathing patterns also play a very important part of how these forces are applied in actual practice.

"Karate is what karate is, and it doesn't matter who your teacher is because it won't do any good to you if you can't pull it off individually."

**Do you think some people try to rely too much on who there is teacher to gain personal credibility in the world of Martial Arts?**

Definitely! Karate is what karate is, and it doesn't matter who your teacher is because it won't do any good to you if you can't pull it off individually. I see many like to "drop" their teacher's name in order to get respect, but that doesn't mean anything in front of a real martial artist. I like to say that karate was here before me and will be here after me, so all that I can do if train hard and use it as a tool to improve myself. My teacher can't do that for me. We simply are not our teachers' men or women. At the end, it is all up to us as individuals.

**Is there any message you would like to send to the karate practitioners or martial artist in general?**

Essentially, all martial arts are the same. The challenge and the personal journey is the same no matter what style you practice. In martial arts training, there is no ending, no completion. It is a constant and endless challenge and you always have to be questioning yourself as a karateka and martial artist and never be satisfied with your technical level and understanding of the art. Proper training is essential for progress but having the right mind is even more important. O

# TAKU NAKASAKA

## THE POWER OF KYOKUSHIN

SENSEI TAKU NAKASAKA STARTED KYOKUSHIN KARATE IN HIS HOMETOWN OF SAPPORO, JAPAN. HE RAPIDLY GAINED RECOGNITION AS A KYOKUSHIN FIGHTER, SUCCESSIVELY CLAIMING SEVERAL CHAMPIONSHIP TITLES. AFTER SERVING AS AN ASSISTANT INSTRUCTOR OF THE I.K.O. KYOKUSHINKAIKAN DOJO IN JAPAN, HIS FOCUS AND DRIVE LED HIM TO THE UNITED STATES AT THE AGE OF 23. FROM 1990, SENSEI TAKU NAKASAKA CONTINUED TRAINING UNDER SENSEI NISHIMURA. UNDER HIS VIGILANT LEADERSHIP AND GUIDANCE, SENSEI TAKU NAKASAKA WAS ABLE TO CLAIM ONE OF THE TOP POSITIONS AMONG THE NINE FIGHTERS CHOSEN TO REPRESENT THE UNITED STATES IN THE 6TH WORLD OPEN KARATE TOURNAMENT IN NOVEMBER 1995.

IN 1996, HE FULFILLED HIS CHILDHOOD DREAM OF OPENING A DOJO IN THE UNITED STATES. HIS FIRST DOJO FOLLOWED BY THREE SUBSEQUENT DOJOS, OPENED IN CALIFORNIA. SENSEI TAKU NAKASAKA, IN A JOINT EFFORT WITH I.K.O. KYOKUSHINKAIKAN, HOSTS ANNUAL KARATE CHAMPIONSHIP EVENTS IN THE U.S. HE IS INTERNATIONALLY RESPECTED AS AN EXCELLENT AND TALENTED TEACHER, AND HIS LIFE AND MANY ACCOMPLISHMENTS DEMONSTRATE THE VERY ESSENCE OF BUDO...THE NEVER ENDING PURSUIT OF PERFECTION.

**How long have you been practicing Kyokushinkai and who was your teacher?**

I started my Kyokushin Karate practice in 1982 in my hometown of Sapporo, Japan. My first teacher was Sensei Sotodate, who was one of the top world fighters at the time.

**What are the main principles intrinsic to the Kyokushin style?**

Kyokushinkaikan believes in Karate as a way of building character through rigorous training of the mind and body, so that our members can be active contributors to society. This philosophy is based on Sosai Mas Oyama's teaching and quotation, "Keep your head low (modesty), eyes high (ambition), mouth shut (serenity); base yourself on filial piety and benefit of others."

# Karate Masters

"Our greatest pursuit is to reach for the goal of international friendship and world peace."

We in Kyokushin Karate do not promote or practice discrimination or prejudice based on ethnicity, race, nationality, politics, philosophy, religion, sex, or age, and recognize that everyone has equal rights. Our greatest pursuit is to reach for the goal of international friendship and world peace.

**Would you tell us some interesting stories of your early days in Karate training in Japan?**

In 1982, my first belt testing was from white belt to blue belt (orange belt has since been added in between white and blue today); I was 15 years old. Testing itself was about three hours and it was not too hard because I was prepared. At the end of the test, there was a kumite. There were around seven to eight brown and black belts standing in single file in front of an equal number of white belts. I was sitting at the corner of the dojo floor waiting for my turn. After the taiko drum sound reverberated throughout the dojo (signifying the beginning of the kumite round), it took no more than 10 to 15 seconds before the first group of white belts were all on the dojo floor groaning and grasping their stomach or legs; some were simply knocked out from head shots via high kick. One was even having a seizure and frothing at the mouth from a concussion. The brown and black belts were all asking the white belts on the floor, "Are you okay?" while pulling them upright to spar some more. The man with the concussion was spared.

When I first witnessed this, I was shocked. I was thinking to myself, "Is it fair to do this to other humans?" After the one minute kumite round was over, although none of the white belts could complete the whole minute without going down, they had to rotate over to experience the kumite with all the brown and black belts who were there. When my turn came, all I remember is one of the senior black belts stood in front of me, and in an instant he spun and my eyesight went blank.

I don't know how long I was unconscious but when I woke up the senior black belt who knocked me out with what appeared to be a back spinning kick was looking down at me asking, "Are you okay?" This was how all the white belts were introduced to Kyokushin world back in the 70s and 80s in Kyokushin dojos all over Japan.

### How did you find the Westerners respond to traditional Kyokushinkai Karate training?

Everyone tries very hard to understand the deeper meaning and essence of Kyokushin Karate. Also, I am very humbled by the stance from Americans to try to learn the Martial Arts' stringent way of discipline. I have seen from youngsters the basic Western notion of "let me see what you got" when trying out Japanese Martial Arts, and to them I would say this: We follow Sosai Mas Oyama motto – "The heart of our karate is real fighting. There can be no proof without real fighting. Without proof there is no trust. Without trust there is no respect. This is a definition in the world of Martial Arts." Every training session is about proving and improving your ability. It is to challenge yourself. I believe that people who join Kyokushin Karate in this country will find their own individual challenge, be it physical, mental and/or spiritual.

### Why did you decide to train in Kyokushinkai and not other style?

Simply because I believe that Kyokushin Karate is the strongest Karate. My first introduction to Kyokushin Karate came via the Japanese media. One famous documentary movie from the 70s exposed me and many of the Japanese to the real Karate strength found in Kyokushin. It included real kumite fights from the world championship tournament and tameshiwari breaking demonstrations where, without tricks, a karateka would break hundreds of pounds of stacked ice. This was all authentic filming. I was in shock and awe and have been captured by Kyokushin Karate since.

### How has your personal perception of the art changed/developed over the years?

Well let me first introduce the word "osu," which is used heavily in Kyokushin dojos. It is more than just a greeting. It means "Respect, Gratitude, and Patience." That's the spirit of osu. When I first started my Kyokushin career in Japan, I was too concerned with tournament fighting. I kept asking myself, "How far can I take my fighting? How strong can I become?" That was my priority. I was too immature to understand what Kyokushin Karate actually offers its practitioners. I was too young to understand the philosophies of Karate. I was too busy playing catch up with my senpai (senior students) in terms of fighting skills. Through the process of achieving the higher belts and striving to become stronger than the prior day, I learned how to assemble my own fighting style. Mind you, this isn't just physical strength; tournament training and experience also developed me mentally and spiritually.

After I retired from competitive fighting and focused more on teaching, I found a different side of Karate. I started thinking deeper into techniques and found more essence and meaning behind our movements, whether basic or advanced. I realized that in order for me to teach one aspect of Karate, I had to learn ten. These philosophies were overlooked when I was focused purely internally.

If I didn't fight with all those opponents who faced me in tournaments, I wouldn't have learned all these techniques. If I didn't have a single student in my dojo, I wouldn't have discovered all of these deeper philosophies. Basically, I am blessed to have all these people around me; otherwise I never would have expanded my Karate acumen. So, in *Osu*, I found that Karate is a lifelong pursuit. We must always pay respect, be grateful, and be forever patient. If Budo training never ends until the day you die, as Sosai Mas Oyama prescribed, I am really looking forward to continuing down my path, learning until that day.

**What are the most important qualities for a student to become proficient in the art?**
To me, the most important point to teach is to open each individual's eyes to Karate. Everyone is at a different stage in his or her life. Their goals are going to be different. Some dream to fight in international scale tournaments. Some are not looking at competitive Karate at all. So my job is to be adaptive and pass on the Kyokushin Karate spirit and method that Sosai Mas Oyama left to us. The most important qualities for a student to become proficient in the art are not within physical ability. It is definitely the development of a strong character, right attitude and positive passion towards Martial Arts.

**Do you think there is still a "pure" style of Karate?**
Techniques can be, and should be, changed and developed. That is normal through the course of a style's evolution. The heart of Karate is not in a "technique," and thus Karate's purity will never change.

**How different from other Karate styles do you see the principles and concepts of the arts you practice?**

Kyokushin Karate is the pioneer of "Full Contact Karate" and is responsible for introducing the rigorous training regimen and competitive format found throughout the world. Today, many styles and organizations are identifying themselves as "Full Contact Karate" which is very good. As the original style of full contact Karate that Sosai Mas Oyama founded, I believe that Kyokushin always will challenge itself to evolve, to adapt to the unknown, all without losing its humbleness and authenticity. That kind of attitude is at the base of Kyokushin.

**Do you feel that there are any fundamental differences in approach or physical capabilities of the Japanese practitioners in comparison to European or American practitioners?**

By looking at tournament results at the international level, you could see that there was a definite gap in tournament success up until the 90s. The Japanese dominated the World Tournament scene. This isn't true today. Since the 90s, many outside of Japan, particularly in Europe, Russia, and Brazil, have had significant success, and their results are proof of it. Individually, there are many gifted karateka outside of Japan, but overall, there is still work ahead.

"Kyokushin Karate is the pioneer of "Full Contact Karate" and is responsible for introducing the rigorous training regimen and competitive format found throughout the world."

**How do you think the use of kicks to the legs and knee strikes change the overall perception of kumite for the fighter?**

Having more weapons at one's disposal not only allows for more variety in how one delivers damage, but also provides for different combinations at different ranges – not only for the single shot of a particular technique that usually follows, but also how one closes or creates distances with his opponent. Damaging the opponent's leg with low kicks is like flattening a vehi-

# Karate Masters

"Please believe what you practice from the bottom of your heart."

cle's tires – it destroys your opponent's mobility and puts you in an excellent position to dominate the fight.

**Do you feel that you still have further to go in your studies of the art?**

I feel that I am still at the entrance of learning and have just opened the doors to Martial Arts.

**How do you see the Kyokushin style in the world at the present time?**

There are many different Martial Arts or even styles of karate, so I would not say that Kyokushin is better than other styles within Martial Arts or among karate styles, but it is without a doubt that Kyokushin is one of the largest karate organizations in the world. We are promoting the largest full contact karate championships all across the globe and at an international level that attracts the very best fighters. I believe that through these efforts, we have established a solid reputation and have been recognized as a compelling organization.

**Do you have any general advice you would care to pass on the practitioners in general?**

Please believe what you practice from the bottom of your heart. That is the only way you achieve what you all have dreamed: the black belt. As the saying goes, "A black belt is a white belt who never gave up."

**What do you consider to be the major changes in the style since you began training?**

The style itself has not changed drastically; the real difference is that people's understanding and perception of Kyokushin has changed since I began my training, but that is due more to marketing efforts and the spread of full contact karate in general.

**What would you say to someone who is interested in starting to learn Karate?**

Definitely start training immediately, and do not quit. It doesn't matter what style.

**What is it that keeps you motivated after all these years?**

I still discover new things every time I train. It is my life's work. I can never stop this. I simply love Kyokushin Karate more than anything else.

**What is your philosophical basis for your Martial Arts training?**

Sosai Mas Oyama stated it perfectly, "Keep your head low (modesty), eyes high (ambition), mouth shut (serenity); base yourself on filial piety and benefit others."

**After all these years of training and experience, could you explain the meaning of the practice of Karate for yourself?**

Bujutsu was the ancient way of killing in feudal times. It became Budo, which is the modern variation that incorporates the martial way of life. Martial Arts training to me is the way of life. It has given me the basis to grow as a human being within society, among nature, and to be physically, mentally, and spiritually strong.

**What are your thoughts on the future of the art of karate and the Kyokushinkai?**

Kyokushinkaikan is still growing as an organization and our size in terms of membership among the youth is the largest ever. We have many tournaments specific to youngsters and so we provide an opportunity for them to develop and challenge themselves at all levels of their karate life. The majority of our top tournament fighters are in their 20s and many, if not all of them, have been fighting since before their teens. Their physical and mental development thus far has been outstanding and they all have very bright futures. However, competition is not all about Karate. It is just part of the learning process within the spirit of Osu. The practitioner who can put 100 percent into his or her tournament training can later put 100 percent into the development of his or her individual Karate practice. As far as the big picture of Karate is concerned, I am not in a position to comment. But as long as there are humans on this world, Karate will develop and keep advancing forever. O

# SHOJI NISHIMURA

## EXCELLENCE IN ACTION

ONE OF THE FIRST THING THAT STRIKES ABOUT SENSEI NISHIMURA IS HIS CONFIDENCE. HE KNOWS WHAT HE CAN DO AND HE IS SURE WITHIN HIMSELF. WHEN YOU LOOK AT HIS ROOTS AND EXPERIENCE IN THE ART OF WADO RYU KARATE, HE JUST SEEMS TO HAVE COMPLETELY DEFINED AN IMPORTANT ERA FOR THE STYLE DEVELOPED BY THE GREAT HIRONORI OHTSUKA. HIS APPROACH TO KARATE TRAINING IS REMINISCENT OF THE ATTITUDE OF THOSE WHO REACHED GREATNESS: "IN KARATE YOU HAVE TO TRAIN HARD AND RELENTLESSLY CHASE THE PERFECTION IN TECHNIQUE, KNOWING FULL WELL THAT IT DOESN'T EXIST AND YOU WILL NOT REACH IT BECAUSE NOTHING IS PERFECT. BUT YOU HAVE TO CHASE IT BECAUSE IN THE PROCESS YOU WILL REACH EXCELLENCE," HE SAYS. "YOU CAN'T SETTLE YOURSELF WITH BEING JUST GOOD."

**How many styles have you trained in and who were your teachers?**

I have been practicing karate since I was 14 years old. Also, I have been practicing Ryukyu kobudo, sai, nunchaku, and bo. In addition, I train in iaido, aiki-jujitsu. My first experience with Martial Arts was in the Saga prefecture of Karatsu, Japan. I was first introduced to karate when my friend invited me to go see the new dojo that was built in the area. This dojo practiced full contact sparring, breaking stones, bricks, and makiwara punching. Watching the punches and kicks of the black belts from the main branch dojo lit up my eyes. I started attending three times a week and built a sandbag filled with sand and stones to practice my punches and kicks.

My first experience with karate was full-contact style karate. It did not really have a name to it, but they practiced sparring with other clubs and even kick-boxers. A couple of years later, we started wearing protection similar to that worn by Nippon Kempo. However, it made almost no difference; everything still hurt really bad. I especially remember this one way of training where you held your kamae stance while other hit you from all directions. The purpose of this exercise, if you can call it that, was to improve your balance and strengthen the body. For kyu tests, we had to break stones. When I started attending Risshyo University I naturally joined the karate club. This university had many styles of karate, including Goju-

# Karate Masters

"When I first started karate, our sensei would take us to other dojos to learn other styles' techniques and skills – kumite, especially, with many different fighting styles."

ryu, Shito-ryu, and Wado-ryu. I joined the Wado-ryu club because it had the most members. All we did for the entire first year was practice kihon to remove any bad habits. Then, we slowly added kumite and shadow-training. There was no kata practice until maybe two week before the kyu or dan testing. At the time, kata was not a big priority.

**Would you tell us some interesting stories of your early days in karate?**

Suzuki Susumu was the head coach of the karate club at the university. He was incredibly strict and always made us do kihon for one hour and then kumite afterwards. If kiais were weak, you were slapped. Sensei Suzuki had very good kicks, usually targeting his opponents' shins. He also demonstrated many open-handed techniques targeting the face. Sensei Suzuki subsequently moved to Brazil where he continued to teach karate.

After Sensei Suzuki's departure, Sensei Setamatsu from the Honbu dojo came to teach. This instructor taught us concepts of parry, deflection, and efficient body movement. He was especially skilled in kumite, generally keeping very little distance from his opponent as if to lock the opponent from using their techniques. During college, it seemed all we did was practice, and quantity over quality was our motto. Suzuki Sensei always told us to get involved in street fights to strengthen ourselves mentally and physically. I tried it once but I was too excited and my punches and kicks were inaccurate and I remember tripping and falling.

When I first started karate, our sensei would take us to other dojos to learn other styles' techniques and skills – kumite, especially, with many different fighting styles. I was able to experience an array of different skills. It was very inspiring and motivating. I remember specifically the Ryu-kyu style; they hit everywhere: the shins, knees, ribs, with their toes. Today, we rarely make contact with other dojos, and we would not even think to practice with Kung Fu or Tae Kwon Do people. Dojos today are full of kids and what they teach is mostly the same: how to score points in kumite and making a kata look good in tournaments. There doesn't seem to be any diversity anymore.

**What are your thoughts about doing thousands of repetitions of one single technique in training, as in the old days?**

The act of repeating the same thing over and over, like what is done in the dojo, makes the student able to bear and tolerate the disappointments of life without resulting to negative behaviors. Especially in Martial Arts, characteristics such as focus, perseverance, etiquette, respect toward instructors and elders are important and can benefit individuals to become successful. I always was shorter than most people so I practiced harder; as a result of that, my body seemed to pick up techniques more easily than others. In Wado-ryu, similar to other Martial Arts, it is not advantageous to be bigger or smaller. The effectiveness of the techniques relies on the technique and its execution itself and the benefit of being taller or heavier is very slim.

**How has your personal expression karate developed over the years, and what is it that keeps you motivated after all these years?**

When I first started karate, the emphasis was on brute strength and being able to win fights. But nowadays, as people — including myself – get older, such ways of training are detrimental to the body. What I utilize and teach now is based on *rigitankyu*. Rigitankyu is a doctrine whereby one pursues the ultimate goal in life while searching for skills of effortless movement and freedom of body motion, which abide by Natural Law. After long years of training, researching and experimenting in Martial Arts, I feel that there is no one ultimate technique. There is no guarantee that a kumite champion will remain the champion year after year. Techniques are infinite, like the stars in the universe. Bugi (Martial Arts techniques) has no one perfect technique that can overcome any other. Techniques are not immune to change and must be able to adapt according to each situation. A block can defend against a certain punch but may be ineffective when the punch is thrown from a different angle. One should not limit him/herself to learning just a particular punch or block but having your body move reflexively to each situation, and is what I think to be the true meaning and essence of Wado-ryu. Martial Arts is not all about fighting; its foundation is *shizen no ugoki*, the natural movement of the body. Rather than opposing or resisting an opponent's attack, one should evade, parry, or ride the attack. It is vital that you do not go against the force.

# Karate Masters

**What are the most important points in your teaching methods?**

Knowing how to use your body effectively is what I believe to be the most important trait one can acquire. Without relying solely on strength, you must use your body as a whole, not in parts. With that, the mind must be able to focus at a moment's notice. Techniques are useless unless you can execute them when they are necessary. These things and more will be attained gradually through practice and training. The ability to see what the opponent will do before he/she actually makes a move, and being able to move accordingly, is the ultimate goal. Also, congregating with other styles will expand your own knowledge of the art. In addition to learning various training styles, new techniques will start to develop. The specific emphasis points from each style will become useful information. Absorbing these different, yet very similar, techniques will help develop and advance your comprehension of the art.

**Karate nowadays often is referred to as a sport; would you agree with this definition or is a Martial Art?**

Karate has evolved over the years into a sport in which safety is the top priority. In regard to that, techniques, which are coined dangerous, are disappearing. As for Wado-ryu, we still practice what is considered original, kihon-kumite and the supplementary kumite ura, jujitsu kempo no kumite-kata, idori, tachi-ai, tantoutori, goshinjutsu, and shira-hadori. Everything else has moved toward competition style techniques. As long as karate is considered a Martial Art, the utmost importance is respect. Everything starts with a bow and ends with a bow. People who want to be a good karate-ka must always honor their sensei, and the instructor will reciprocate by looking at each student's personality, strengths, and weaknesses and appropriately choose the right teaching method. Humans are not solitary creatures; people cannot live solely by themselves. The one who learns must aspire to become better. Bowing before everything and after everything, that is the spirit of Budo.

**What is your opinion of fighting events such as the UFC and Mixed Martial Arts events?**

I like it. I have done kickboxing, judo, and various styles of jujitsu and I think it is very interesting to watch.

**Why is it, in your opinion, that a lot of students start falling away after two or three years of training?**

Nowadays, the majority of karate dojos are directed towards kid. And for this reason, the aspect of safety is a priority. Even the adults who join karate – their main reason for training is not to become better at karate but to become healthier. The Budo spirit and contemporary sportsmanship have very similar values: respecting others, observance of the rules, and graciousness in losing. Therefore, in this respect, I do not believe either label is more fitting; it is both a sport and an art. Since the majority of students now are kids, the shift has been made to make it more sport-like, with emphasis on training styles geared toward tournaments and body conditioning. As for the adult students, the number of older people who are joining to learn discipline and improving their mental strength and physical fitness has increased. And a majority of these adult students want to continue training for a longer period of time, compared to kids who want to quit as soon as they become a black belt. I think that there currently are some very good instructors in America and Europe. However, there also are many slapdash, shoddy instructors. Europeans seek more of a traditional karate while Americans seems to be geared toward sport karate.

"The road of Budo has no end. I am always training myself, feeling and developing and researching what s effective and efficient."

**Do you feel that you still have further to go in your studies?**

Of course. The road of Budo has no end. I am always training myself, feeling and developing and researching what is effective and efficient. When you become 50, 60, or 70 years old, you have to filter your vast knowledge of the art and decide what is an effective skill against an opponent. The fundamental nature of Wado-ryu is *nagasu, inashi, noru*, roughly translated as "flow, dodge, and ride." Nagasu is being able to manipulate the opponents' attacks with a combination of body movement and sweeping technique. Inashi is the concept of blocking and attacking at the same time. Noru, overly simplified into "ride," is a counter technique that utilizes the trajectory of the opponent's attack to neutralize his/her assault.

**What are your views on kata and kata bunkai?**
Kata is the physical representation of the specific movements and techniques of a particular style. Therefore, just because you know a lot of different katas, I dont think it would make much difference compared to someone else who knows 10 forms. Rather than doing a bunch of different katas, I think it would be more efficient and effective to focus on a small, set amount. Also, even if you are able to master all the katas, that does not make you any better in kumite.

Bunkai is an important part of karate training. Each movement in a kata, even if it is the same movement, can have more than one application. Bunkai also has to take into account the physique of the tori and uke (the attacker and defender), and the techniques, as well as the angle they are executed. Transporting these ideas of bunkai into a live situation like kumite is important. *Tai no shinshuku*, *chikara no kyoujaku*, *waza no kankyu*, *jyushin no antei*, and *zanshin* are the most important aspects when training kata. Ma-ai (combat distance), aite wo yomu (reading the opponent), and how quickly you can execute your attack is important in kumite. The things learned in kata should transition to kumite and one should experiment which moves are usable and effective.

**What can karate offer to the individual in these troubled times?**
Many Martial Arts have roots that are traced back to Japan. Aikido, iaido, karate, and other Martial Arts have morals and values interwoven into them. In this day and age, I think that morals in our generation are starting to diminish and I do not think that is good. This generation is always looking for instant gratification, like the joy you feel when you win a tournament or pass a kyu test. There is, however, another gratification of doing Budo; looking back at your journey to see where you are today, a distinguished, capable karate-ka, is another fulfilling affair. For kids and young adults, sport style karate is safer and more easily understandable than its self-defense counterpart. However, self-defense also is a very important aspect when teaching karate. I think the more cultural and historical aspects of the art are more appreciated by the older generation. Karate's foundation is based on self-defense so I believe incorporating it into practice is vital.

### What advice would you give to an instructor who is struggling with his or her won development?

The very first thing is training. Research and experiment what works for you. Each person is different. Observe other styles and ask questions if you do not understand. Look for the best and try to mimic that. You have to train your eyes to differentiate the good from the bad. In Japan, there is a proverb called "Suhari." This is very important for karate practitioners. "Su" means to obey, observe and follow. The teachings, both spiritual and technical, should be followed faithfully. "Ha" means to break; after mastering these teachings thoroughly, one needs to develop them even further. "Ri" means to separate from, or part from – to create something superior apart from the two precious stages "Su" and "Ha." This, however, is not possible to achieve in five or even ten years. You need inherent ability. Even then, you need devoted training for many years. Endurance, the will to go further, courage, and harmony are the traits one develops over years of karate training. Especially in Wado-ryu, wasted techniques and movement are the two major hindrances that will halt your progress so you must strive with all your might to purge them through training.

### What is your opinion of the direction that Wado Ryu took after the dead of Othsuka Sensei?

Firstly, I would have liked to learn in depth about nagasu, inasu, and noru; how the first grand master Hironori Ohtsuka, the founder of Wado-ryu karate, came up with them and how to use them properly. Second is Daitoryu aiki-jujitsu Yukiyoshi Sagawa Sensei. This sensei is the master of hand-to-hand combat. His techniques are discrete and look as if they would not work, but nevertheless they did, and it looked amazing. He could throw an opponent with the slightest movement, utilizing his momentum against him. However, his dojo was highly exclusive. Even if you were a high-ranking martial artist, you most likely would have been refused entry. He thought the dojo as a place to polish and advance one's techniques, not for beginners to start learning fresh. Even till the end, he kept refining and researching his techniques. His unique training style is what piqued my interest.

### After so many years of training in Wado Ryu, what is so appealing for you in this style of karate, and why?

Karate is not only about kicks and punches; it is about mental strength, as well as physical strength, effort, and creating the right mentality. Once people start karate, I would want them to continue until they become a black belt. And within the journey to become a black belt, I would hope that one creates friendships and bonds with the instructors that will last a lifetime. It always is important to have a target or goal. Things like "I want to be like that" or "I want learn how he does that" are what are always on my mind. What is left is to just train and follow the path that leads me to my goal. And when I reach my destination, I look for another goal to attain. Being able to surpass my sensei is my ultimate goal. I believe that continuous practice or training will make anyone good at virtually anything. This is what my sensei always preached to me. At one point in our lives, I am sure we all have had the feeling to stop and quit, to give up, whether it is karate, work, school, etc. But the point is to not give up and overcome this. If you do give up, everything up until that point would have been in vain. It is important to always step up and challenge yourself, and to never give up.

**What advice would you give to students on the question of supplementary training?**

If one were interested in karate as a sport, I would recommend exercises to increase endurance. To effectively strengthen your kicks and punches, I believe some weight training will add positive results. Punching a makiwara or kicking a sandbag also will be effective as well. However, if your only goal is to polish your techniques, these things are not necessary.

**Have there been times when you felt fear in your training?**

During my years in college in the karate club, I was brutally kicked and punched by my seniors. Especially, when sparring with the sempais, the sparring sessions would go on for 10, 20, and 30 minutes, and they would not stop for breaks. When training, if you moved back even a little bit, you were struck by a large stick. And during these days when we didn't wear mouth guards or much protection anywhere, a lot of the sempais had missing teeth. My gi was always soaked in blood and washing it usually didn't get the bloodstains out. This continued for two years. It was a painful and agonizing two years. Back in the day when we had free sparring, we frequently used to kick the opponent's shins. When the opponent was stunned, we then would use our kicks and punches. I remember when I was still young, I was kicked in the shins by a sempai and could barely move for a whole week. And during that time, there were a few occasions where my kicks and punches came out freely, almost reflexively, and that that made me feel good. It was what I have been practicing for many years.

**Do you think that Olympics will be positive for the art of karate-do?**

I think it is a major step for karate to be recognized as a sport. Whether it is a good thing or a bad thing is still up for debate. Once karate becomes an Olympic sport, it would unite all the karate groups and styles. Techniques will become "Olympic style" and I believe some traditional aspects of the art will be lost. Traditional karate dojos probably will see a decrease in membership as a result. The various styles of karate also most likely will disappear. The requirements for a black belt will certainly change. The need for different styles will die out. I think it will inevitably follow the path judo has – practicing only techniques that are suited for competition – and the number and variety of techniques will unavoidably dwindle. This would bring about many changes to how we currently teach karate, and in the end may be detrimental to karate as a whole.

**Finally, what advice would you like to give to all Karate practitioners?**

You may first start karate with feelings similar to what I had; "I want to get stronger" or "I want to be able to do that kick," evolves over the years into something more complicated. The aspirations you may have had in the beginning of your training will evolve into respect, camaraderie, friendship, and your personality and behaviors start to change as you keep training. The will to never give up, good sportsmanship, and respect: these things become more important. The strictness of karate allows practitioners to become disciplined, being able to overcome obstacles and challenges in ones life.

There are many types of karate and I believe there will not be much change in the coming years. There are a handful of masters today and it is up to their students to continue. It is up to the next generation to keep training so it will not die out. The survival of karate will be dependent on the number of students who can surpass their sensei. O

"The aspirations you may have had in the beginning of your training will evolve into respect, camaraderie, friendship, and your personality and behaviors start to change as you keep training."

# HIROYOSHI OKAZAKI

## *DELIVERING VALUES*

CARRYING HIS LAST NAME IT WOULD BE A BIG CHALLENGE TO ANY KARATE PRACTITIONER BUT FOR HIROYOSHI OKAZAKI IT SIMPLY IS "ANOTHER PIECE OF THE PUZZLE." FULLY AWARE OF HIS RESPONSIBILITY AND DESTINY, SENSEI HIRO OKAZAKI, 7TH DAN, IS IMMERSED IN A LIFE OF CONSTANT DEDICATION TO PRESERVE NOT ONLY THE ART AND TEACHINGS HE HAS RECEIVED FROM HIS INSTRUCTORS BUT TO MAINTAIN THE ETHICS AND MORALS OF GRANDMASTER GICHIN FUNAKOSHI'S PRECEPTS.

ALTHOUGH HIROYOSHI OKAZAKI, SHICHIDAN, IS HUMBLE REGARDING HIS COMPETITION RECORD, HE WAS U.S. NATIONAL KATA CHAMPION 16 TIMES. THIS IS A RECORD THAT TO THIS DAY HAS NOT BEEN BROKEN. WITH A DEEP UNDERSTANDING OF WHAT THE "BALANCE" SHOULD BE BETWEEN THE DIFFERENT "SLICES" OF WHAT KARATE IS AND REPRESENTS, SENSEI HIRO OKAZAKI CONTINUES HIS PERSONAL JOURNEY TRAVELING AROUND THE WORLD AS ONE OF THE MAIN DIRECTORS OF THE TECHNICAL COMMITTEE FOR THE INTERNATIONAL SHOTOKAN KARATE FEDERATION. "AS INSTRUCTORS, WE DELIVER INFORMATION BY TEACHING. I TRY TO MAKE SURE THAT I NOT ONLY AM PASSING A WONDERFUL ART BUT ALSO DELIVERING VALUES TO THE STUDENTS," HE SAYS. "AND THAT IS A VERY IMPORTANT PART OF WHO I AM."

**How long have you been practicing Karate and who is your teacher?**

I have been training for 30 years and my first instructors were the instructors and instructor trainees at JKA Headquarters in Japan back in the late 70s. Each class had at least two instructors, sometimes three, plus assistant instructor trainees, so you had no choice, but try your hardest. My instructors in the U.S. were Master Okazaki, Mr. Ronald Johnson, Mr. Gerald Evans, and Mr. Eugene McKnight. Also, my seniors like Mr. Nihei, Mr. Yokota, and others who tossed me around the dojo floor.

My father (older brother to Master Okazaki, and I believe they took the 3rd degree black belt test under Master Funakoshi together) trains, so since I was little I saw him train and he taught at Waseda University, and when he went to teach and train I went with him and trained. At that time, I did not have a deep interest in karate yet. When I decided to come to the U.S. to go to school, my uncle, Master Teruyuki Okazaki, told me if I was to come to

# Karate Masters

"It is important to remember that there always should be tradition, whether you are training in a dojo or a tournament."

the U.S. to go to school I would have to practice karate. So, before I came to the U.S., he told me I had to go to the JKA headquarters and join. It was either the end of the year or beginning of the year because when I first went there they were having a ceremony and demonstration. When I watched that, I was impressed. The demonstration was given by the instructors and trainees. It was a great benefit to go at that time to see that demonstration – it really motivated me to join.

**Have your training methods changed since you moved to the U.S. to train directly under your Uncle Sensei T. Okazaki?**

No, the training here is exactly the same as in Japan.

**How important do you think the supplementary training – running, weight lifting, etc. – for a practitioner of Karate?**

Doing them is good and have a lot of benefit, but you shouldn't spend too much time on them. You should be spending more time working on your makiwara, basics, kata, and your karate in general.

**How do you see the level of the art in America compared to Japan?**

I think it is more challenging for Americans and/or Europeans. Japanese people's physique is better suited for certain techniques. This makes it somewhat easier for the Japanese, which may help them to develop faster than Americans or Europeans because it is a little more difficult for them. Also, in Japan, good karate practice begins at an early age, such as 5, 6, or 7, and more time is spent on the martial arts in schools there.

**Self-defense, sport or tradition: what is karate for you?**

All of them. It is important to remember that there always should be tradition, whether you are training in a dojo or a tournament. When I was competing, sport was a part of my martial arts training. In competition, there is winning and losing, which makes it sport. My competition career was long, so when I retired from competition, it was a natural transition for me to train more for tradition/self-defense. Kata competition always is tradition, whereas kumite competition is more sports because it is a points system. When I was competing in kumite, I always strived for the traditional method of finishing with one blow. I always strived to win the match with a full point, but I never was able to achieve that. I would win by half point plus half point. So, even in kumite competition, which can be sports, I strived for the traditional finishing blow – ikken hisatsu! When I was competing in kumite, my goal was not to win by Shobu Ippon. I wanted to finish with one blow.

"Kata competition always is tradition, whereas kumite competition is more sports because it is a points system."

### What are the main differences in structuring Karate training for children and for adults?

When teaching children, you have to make it more interesting for them and keep their focus on their training. There is a fine line between training and trying to make it like a game, but you still have to keep discipline. You have to encourage kids more and explain to them more logically in a shorter amount of time how it is done. Each person is different and their feelings toward their practice will be different.

### You have an important position within ISKF; do you feel the pressure of working under a legendary Karate master like T. Okazaki Sensei?

No. Master Okazaki has developed the ISKF into a united family. He says we are all family, so we help each other. I know that in the future if I have a certain position and have a difficult time with something, I know I will have all the help I need in this organization. Tradition, etiquette, and the principles of karate are very important to us.

# Karate Masters

"As you get older, some parts of your body won't move as they used to, so you must alter some of the movements to fit your ability."

**Have you altered your own personal training in any way, say in the last ten years?**

I haven't changed much; I just stretch and warm up more before going to full speed.

**You travel all over the world; do you see much differences with the students' standards, and which countries are closest to Japan technically?**

They are all the same. As my uncle, Master Okazaki, says, we may speak different languages and have different cultures, but in Shotokan karate, we are all the same and do things the same way.

**Do you think that the approach to Karate changes when the practitioner gets older?**

Technically, yes. As you get older, some parts of your body won't move as they used to, so you must alter some of the movements to fit your ability. But we always should continue to strive for the same philosophy of Master Funakoshi, to keep growing. As you get older, you gain more knowledge and wisdom. Because of philosophy, people continue to practice. Physically, you cannot get stronger like younger people. You cannot move like young people, but technically, like timing and the quality of training, you can continue to develop. As you get older, you have to train smarter. Everything balances out; when you are younger, you train hard physically and don't think too much about philosophy. But when you get older, your body won't move like a younger person so you think more about the philosophy. When you acquire that balance, you have reached the desired stage of your training.

**Do you think sport Karate can be practiced and Budo principles can be maintained at the same time?**

That is what we train to do. That is what we try to show the public.

"When you do not want to train, force yourself to train, and during the course of that training you will find out something special."

**Do you think it would be positive or negative for Karate to be in the Olympic Games?**

If we can keep and maintain the strict set of rules and regulations that will allows us to preserve the important values and ethics of the art of Karate, it would be positive, but if we have simply sport-oriented Olympic rules, that would be negative in the long run. In the ISKF, we do not think of competition as sport. It is just another part of training.

**What advice would you give to those who wish to start training and to those who already have been training for many years?**

You must keep training. When you do not want to train, force yourself to train, and during the course of that training you will find out something special.

**Finally, could you tell us your feelings on the future development of Shotokan Karate?**

I am not trying to see the future right now. If you just follow the principles of Master Funakoshi's philosophy day by day and try hard, then I think something will happen in a positive way. O

# RICHARD RABAGO

## A HIGHER STANDARD

*Sensei Richard Rabago has the experience, training credentials, and budo skill to have earned the right to be called "master" several times over. If you call him that, however, you'll most likely get a roll of the eyes, a slightly embarrassed laugh, and the words, "Just call me 'sensei' - that is enough." A throwback to the age of budo and honor, where a karateka earned respect through skill and dedication, not by self-given titles, Sensei Rabago measures himself against a higher standard than commonly is used in martial arts today. Trained by two of karate's most famous masters, Hidetaka Nishiyama and Tsuomu Ohshima, he learned his most important lesson from them - the basics are everything. It wasn't until he met Tadashi Yamashita, though, and saw how the Shorin-Ryu master generated tremendous power from flexibility and speed, that Sensei Rabago truly found his martial arts path in life.*

*Still training and teaching, Sensei Rabago insists that the most important lessons he can teach his students are not the physical ones, but the mental. "I teach my students never to say the words, 'I can't do it,' because this will help them for their entire life. If you have a positive attitude from a young age, and then become an adult, your positive thinking will push you to whatever goals you might have."*

### How did you get involved in the martial arts?

I started in about 1955 when my uncle, who was in the Air Force, took the martial arts from Professor Chow. So when he would come home on furloughs I would see him practice the art and this got me interested in the Kenpo area, which led me to karate. I was already taking judo back in Hawaii at the time. From there, I started to think that the art of Kenpo was very useful and practical. It was similar to boxing, yet they were using their feet and hands to fight. I was only about 12 then, but I still was very impressed by it.

When I was growing up on the Hawaiian island of Kauai, karate was not as popular a martial art as it was Oahu. Boxing, Judo, and Aikido were

# Karate Masters

"The training was more difficult than team sports because of its focus on individual achievement. There were no teammates to help you in the dojo."

more popular martial styles in Kauai during that era. It was not so much a commercial enterprise as it is today. We learned from those who were knowledgeable, and were willing to teach us what they knew. We picked up bits and pieces of different martial arts styles, and we were always looking to apply them in our communities. I always liked sports, so taking up karate was not a difficult transition. The training was more difficult than team sports because of its focus on individual achievement. There were no teammates to help you in the dojo.

**How long did you do judo before finding Kenpo and Karate?**

Judo was basically done from around 8 years old on. All the kids in the area were doing it, so I kind of followed in their footsteps. This was on Kuai, so there wasn't a lot to do besides judo, because it is a sleepy place. I was born in Honolulu but raised on Kuai. I told myself that when I found someone who had a really strong teaching foundation in karate that I really would apply myself to it.

**What did you like about karate as opposed to judo that would motivate you to make the vow?**

Because of my size, basically. I didn't really want to hold onto people who were bigger than myself and try to throw them, or wrestle them to the ground. I wanted to hit and run in a fight, and use my speed to my advantage with my feet and hands. But I always wanted the art of karate. I always really like sports. And being a boy and having friends who played sports and did martial arts, I said to myself: why not and go ahead and find an art you really like and then stick with it? So that is why I'm where I'm at today; I found an art that I really liked. I'm past 50 now, and still doing it. I started training shotokan with Sensei Nishiyama and then with Sensei Ohshima - both great masters. Then, after a while, I switched to shorin-ryu, where I still am today.

**Was there a big difference between training with Nishiyama and Ohshima?**

Not really. They both leaned toward teaching the basics - punching and kicking - hundreds of each. There were no fancy punches or kicks, just the basics. That's where I think the martial arts have gotten a little lost today - they've forgotten the basics. People are not getting the basics. They're more into the real acrobatic techniques such as the high spinning kicks because they want to do things that they see on television. So they both just did the total basics. I don't think that people would like that kind of training today. To me, because of the early training, I like focusing on the basics.

**So you trained in shotokan but then switched to shorin-ryu...**

I did it when I saw my sensei, Tadashi Yamashita, do a couple of kicks and punches with my kid brother. Sensei was no bigger or heavier than I, but he would throw his punches with the force of a 250-pound person and with the speed of lightning. The same was true with his kicks - they were very crisp and powerful. So this showed me what the human body could do with very good training and proper technique. The shorin-ryu, to me, was not as hard as the shotokan that I learned. It was based on relaxation, which I felt developed more power from the techniques. Also, because of my personality, I think that being looser fit me better. But, both styles had the same type of training mentality with the emphasis on the basics. The basics will work for you 99 percent of the time.

**You don't spend a lot of time talking about your belt ranking. Why?**

To me, a ranking is something that should be kept within. But today, I see a lot of people walking around with high ranking belts, calling themselves masters. I really hate that, for myself. I don't want to be called master. I'm just myself. Respect me as a sensei and I will be honored enough. But to be called master is something that should be reserved for the legends. Actions are a lot stronger than words and I see a lot of people with very high rankings who do kata, kumite, or bu-kai that I would be ashamed to see a first degree black belt do. A true master doesn't think of himself as one. They don't seek to draw attention to themselves. They just want to be themselves.

**Do you feel weapons training is important to karate?**

Yes, because it forces you to use the basics. The most important aspect of weapons training is first learning the basics of empty-hand karate. If you don't have the basics, then you won't be able to control the weapon - any weapon. Because of my training in shorin-ryu under Sensei Yamashita, who is know for his weaponry, I have gotten some knowledge of his weapons expertise. So I instill that same quality in my studio. My favorite weapon is the bo, or stick, because of the weapon control - you have both hands on the weapon so you get more control. I also like sai, tonfa, and kama. Sensei Yamashita is one of the best weapons masters around; he brought the kama to California and today, I think every studio is using the kama, especially the version that has the rope tied around the end and swings free. He is most famous for that. But the weapons that he uses are not dull or fake - they are real. That is why one needs to work with the basics to control the weapon. If you can't control the kama, you're going to have cuts all over your body because the kama is razor sharp. Of course, today, because of tournament competition, the real weapons are not used. I always start beginners with the bo because of the control factor.

**What are the most common questions you get from beginners?**

Most people come into the dojo and first ask how long it takes to become a black belt - that's the number one question. Then they ask if we fight a lot. Then they ask what weapons we teach. I tell them that we do, but that it takes time to get to where they can handle the training. So, once they learn the truth about the martial arts - that it takes a lot of work - they usually shy off. I tell them they can come in and train and see if they like it.

**What advice would you give to students on the question of supplementary training?**

Martial arts always has included supplementary training. Training for the war requires conditioning. The science of physical conditioning has improved tremendously over the past. One always should seek to adapt training methods for the best end result. What is most important is that the karate-ka engages in supplementary training that only enhances his martial studies. Conversely, one should stay from activities that diminish one's abilities.

**Do you feel that the physical or mental part of karate helped you the most to get parts like this?**

Everything in the martial arts is beneficial to everything you do. You really can't separate the physical and the mental. But, most of the martial arts that I've really tried to teach my students about is the mental area before the physical area, because if your mind is not strong, your physical skills will never follow. No matter how strong you are, if you get hurt, what does you mind tell you? "I'm hurt - I don't want to do it anymore." But if your mind is strong enough to overcome that negative thought, then the physical will follow. So, you will never be weak in any of the areas: spiritual, mental, physical. That is why I tell my students to work on their mental area. And by doing strong workouts, you will gather the mental areas. If your mind says, "The training is so hard that I can't do it; I can't do 50 punches, I can only do ten," then you have negative thinking and will stop at that point. So, even in school, if your teacher gives you a mountain of homework to do, your mind might say, "I can't do this. It's too much work." But, by training your mind, you'll be able to overcome those negative thoughts. So, this mental aspect of karate applies to life as well as the martial arts. That is why I say you cannot separate the aspects. They all work together and are part of each other.

"If you don't push your body to the limit, then you will have the negative part of human nature in control."

**So, is the mental training just a part of doing the exercises?**

Very much so; I'd say about 90 percent of the time. If you push your body to the limit, you've already gone a long way toward conquering the mental side of the art. But, if you don't push your body to the limit, then you will have the negative part of human nature in control. You always will stop at the point that things get hard - in everything you do. So, by helping the person to push themselves, you have to be strict with them. You might tell them to do ten push-ups at first; but in your mind, you know that you're going to ask them to do five more after the ten are finished. By asking them to do five more than ten, this is where the training becomes stronger and their mind becomes stronger. Then, from 15 you go to 20; and from 20 to 50 - and they will never know the difference between 10 and 50. So, now their minds become stronger and more positive. And they get stronger physically, spiritually, and physically. It all comes from going beyond yourself - pushing yourself into unknown territory, not getting caught in a comfort zone where you never challenge what you know you can do. They never say, about anything, "I can't do it." They automatically assume that they can. And this is what helps everyone in life. Because if you start from a young age, and then become an adult, your positive thinking will push you to whatever goals you might have.

# Karate Masters

"Education and becoming a better person is the number one goal I have for my students."

**Do you encourage your students to further their education? Do you focus on them winning a tournament to make you look good, or to practice hard to make them better people?**

Education and becoming a better person is the number one goal I have for my students. Martial arts is second. Martial arts helps you to develop a winning attitude about yourself. Then, I want them to take that attitude and move forward into life with it. Once you can focus, then you can focus on anything. I design integrated circuits, for example. Sometimes I will get to a layout or a problem area that requires me to set it aside for awhile, so I can come back and approach it from a different angle or a different perspective. It is the same thing with martial arts. If you're in a tournament and you get hit, you might say to yourself, "Man, I don't want to get hit anymore." Then, you say to yourself, "That's my mistake. I need to analyze what happened and adjust accordingly, to make sure it doesn't happen again." So, then, you'll be able to defend it the next time. Life, as well as martial arts, is all about focus, attitude, and taking responsibility for your actions and for yourself. In order to increase one's understanding of the spiritual aspects of martial arts, one should put one's whole soul into the practice. Over time, the mental, physical, and spiritual aspects of our nature are strengthened and merge. This development grows and is witnessed in all aspects of a martial artist's life.

**What is your favorite part of karate?**

I don't really have a specialty. Every kata that I do is a favorite of mine. The most basic kata, actually, are my favorites. I want to use something that is natural and is second nature. You don't want to use something that you have to think about in your movement. If you think too much about the kata, you'll forget what the kata is about. So the simplest kata that you do every day becomes the one that does you the most good. It will become a natural movement. The most important thing about karate technique is making it reflexive, so you don't have to think about it. You don't want to be thinking, "Okay, this guy is doing a straight punch so I'll do a fancy block." You'll get hit. But if you react without thinking, then you'll always be able to defend yourself because there is no lag time.

I think that once you have a strong relationship with karate, you will have a strong relationship with the right way to live your life. That is why the traditional values of karate are so important to pass along. What you're trying to do with the training is to have total positive thoughts, not negative thoughts. I think, to a point, that the fighting part of the martial arts has become overemphasized today because of the entertainment factor. People who are not martial artists like to see blood and guts in events like the UFC, or other no-holds-barred shows. I don't think that there is a lot of respect for traditional values shown there because you're taking away the mental and spiritual part of the martial arts and emphasizing only one part - the fighting. But, over the long run, I think you'll see that the traditional arts will flourish and grow. Traditional martial arts have survived for thousands of years because there is much more to offer than just fighting.

Competition is not very important to the karate practitioner. Much of what we learn in the karate dojo cannot be applied in competition due to safety and insurance considerations. For example, strikes to the groin, eyes, and back of the neck are not used in competition, but they are paramount in self-defense. Martial Karate by its very nature is different from Sport Karate.

**What would you tell a prospective karate student?**

You'll get out of it what you put into it. What students get out of martial arts depends on what attitude they have going into it. If they focus on fighting, then all they'll get out of it is the ability to fight. But, if they include other things, then they'll get other things out of it. Basically, when you take karate, you know what you could do to someone who has no knowledge of the martial arts. If he comes up to you and says, "I'm going to kick your butt," that guy already has lost because he doesn't know what you know. You could have punched him right away but you have more self-control than that. So you try to avoid the conflict of a fight. By doing that, you have learned something from martial arts - walking away from trouble. But, if you're cornered, you can defend yourself because you have the knowledge of martial arts. You have the distance and the timing and you have the whole body to work with, whereas the person who's trying to start trouble is just limited to trying to punch you. He doesn't know you have defenses with your feet, legs, elbows, palm, et cetera. Karate in its true essence is, first and foremost, a martial art. It is a way to defend yourself, and your loved ones. The karate that the general public sees is mostly the sport and entertainment aspects of karate. The two are very different in both quality and application.

**How has your personal expression changed/developed over the years and what is it that keeps you motivated over the years?**

My personal expression has not changed significantly over the years. Traditional karate speaks for itself. I am motivated by the challenge to keep my students motivated to stay in the system and not quit. It takes a significant effort to teach them to access and utilize their inner strengths.

**What is your opinion of fighting events such as the UFC and Mixed Martial Arts?**

Events such as the UFC and Mixed Martial Arts are somewhat realistic and make for good entertainment. They both focus on lots of fighting action, which is what the audience likes to see. It is unfortunate that the competitors endure significant physical trauma as compared to their financial remuneration. The biggest winners are the fight promoters who control this billion-dollar industry.

**Is there anything lacking in the way martial arts are taught today compared to how they were when you started training?**

There are many teaching aspects of martial arts that are lacking as compared to the traditional methods of instruction. In general, there is not sufficient emphasis and training today on the basics, focus, balance, and other crucial fundamentals. There is too much focus on fighting before a student is proven to be fundamentally strong. Belts are frequently awarded before actual martial proficiency is achieved. Students today need a clearer understanding of true martial skills. Their lives one day may depend upon it.

**Do you think that the Olympics will be positive for the art of karate-do?**

The Olympics will be positive for karate-do in that it will introduce the art to a worldwide audience that previously may not have had real exposure to it. This international marketing will be of significant benefit to the retail business of karate. Sport karate is a niche aspect of the art that had a value to the whole of bushido. I support it.

"Karate is an anchor that keeps you from getting swept away by the tide of life."

### What can karate offer to the individual in today's troubled times?

Karate training is, at a minimum, a healthy distraction from the negative societal impacts. At its best, a martial artist is better at internally responding to and successfully navigating the socioeconomic bumps and bruises that currently confront us.

### So do you think of yourself as an actor, an engineer, or a martial artist?

I think of myself as an everyday person. I don't think of myself in any one sense. I try to be myself; I don't try to be what others think I am or what others want me to be. I believe in keeping everything in balance and that includes yourself. Never forget who you are and never lose your sense of self. People always will try to influence you to go their way. I don't want people to see me or think of me as anything other than who I am - which is myself. Karate is an anchor that keeps you from getting swept away by the tide of life. My final and most heartfelt advice to Karate practitioners is to "Never Give Up." There is no end to learning. Embrace your training and seek to incorporate every day in all aspects of your life. O

# TED RABINO

## IN THE SPIRIT OF SHITO KAI

*Sensei Ted Rabino began his Judo training in 1966 under Watanabe Sensei and his karate training under both his brothers Sam (Shorinji Kempo) and Pete Rabino (Shuri-Ryu). Pete Rabino was one of Robert Trias's first Chief Instructors in the USKA. Ted Rabino received his 1st Dan in Karate in 1972. On the recommendation of Mr. Trias, Sensei Rabino started his training in the Shito Ryu style of karate. From that point on, he trained in Motobu-Ha Shito-Ryu with Shihan Bayani Adlawan, and Mateo Mangosing. Mr. Rabino received his 1st and 2nd Dans in Shito-Ryu and continued training with Adlawan Sensei until his untimely death. Then, he continued training in Motobu-Ha Shito-Ryu under the personal guidance of Soke Shogo Kuniba, from whom he received his 3rd and 4th Dans. After that, Sensei Rabino began his training in the Shito Kai method of the style founded by the late Kenwa Mabuni. Presently Sensei Rabino is the U.S.A. Shibucho under the direction of Shihan Kunio Murayama and the World Shito Kai Federation of Japan.*

**How long have you been practicing the martial arts?**

In the early years of my life, the early 1960s, while residing in farm labor camps throughout California and Arizona, I had observed various martial arts. The different origins of these arts were Chinese, Filipino, Japanese, and possibly Malaysian. The young fighters always would train by sparring and teaching each other on Sunday afternoons at the labor camps. Since a lot of the migrant workers did not have much money to spend, they would entertain each other by training, playing musical instruments, and holding chicken fighting events on Sundays. Each summer, while working in the grapes, we would spend time on the weekends mingling and trying to get information from these practitioners. Some would share, but quite a few would not. It was different than the regular street fighting that you would normally learn in the barrios (neighborhoods) of the rougher inner city South Phoenix, where we resided.

# Karate Masters

"The variety of kata, kumite, and bunkai techniques always encourages me to look further into the arts."

I have been training in various Japanese/Okinawan and Filipino martial arts since 1966, initially in Judo under Watanabe, K. Sensei here in Arizona. Watanabe, K. Sensei would teach us ukemi (falling), over and over. The art was taught in the backyard in both Peoria and South Phoenix and my father would take me to these training sessions. I always was curious but never asked questions. The Watenabe family had vegetable and flower harvest fields and my father, who was a seasonal migrant Filipino farm laborer, worked for them during the season. But we would spend off-season at home in South Phoenix.

Mr. Watanabe was my best man in our wedding; it was a pleasure to know he was instrumental in my martial art career. And giving me life advice to help me stay happily married to my wife Sara Rabino, who I have been married to since 1976. She was instrumental in my contining my training. Without good support of your spouse, many a marriage has taken its toll on a martial arts career.

I also trained under my older brothers Samuel and Pedro (Pete) in my early years. My brother Sam was stationed in Misawa, Japan, while in the U.S. Air Force. During the late 60s, he continued his martial arts training, learning traditional Japanese arts such Iado, Judo, and Karate in Japan. My brother Pete began training under both Sam Rabino and Robert Trias (U.S.K.A. founder), since Sam was Pete's first instructor as well as mine. Sam had his orders to depart to Japan, leaving Pete to continue his training under someone who could further his martial arts training. Sam took Pete to fight in almost every dojo in Phoenix, attempting to find him a dojo where he could continue his martial training. Mr. Trias's dojo was where Pete stayed. With Pete's newly-found instructor, he furthered my knowledge in martial arts training by instructing me in this art that he was learning under Mr. Trias. It was Mr. Trias who advised me to seek a Japanese-based karate style; he suggested one of the four major styles: Goju-ryu, Shito-ryu,

Shotokan, or Wado-ryu. I picked Shito-ryu karate and have not changed styles since. The variety of kata, kumite, and bunkai techniques always encourages me to look further into the arts. Murayama Sensei has been a living treasure with a source of information on this subject, and very loyal to the Iwata family.

But my true mentor to the martial arts was my father. My father (Cayetano Rabino), an immigrant from Santa Catalina, Ilocos Sur – Philippines. Dad introduced my brothers and me to boxing and basic stick arts (Eskrima/Knife). Later, Lonnie and Leto Acosta taught me a more regimented art of eskrima while working as a farm laborer in my early years. Felix Carbahal (Guji) taught Kajukenbo to us and to most of the Filipino community. Guji's cojo was located a block down from the Filipino Center and the Luzon Pool Hall, which was a part of the Phoenix's historical downtown Chinatown. This is where the Filipino men and women (Manongs and Manangs) could go to and meet their friends and acquaintances. Today, I am under the guidance of Shihan Kunio Murayama, a kind but stern man from Miyagi, Japan. He is my present mentor and master instructor, and a classical warrior in today's society and Shihan Genzo Iwata. These men are guiding me through a Budo experience of true karate and jujitsu that it like no other. I am blessed to have such instructors to teach a non-political martial art, whereas today Budo is being set back due to political organizations.

**How many styles of karate or other methods have you trained in?**

During my lifetime, I have trained in various Shorin-ryu factions (Kobayashi-ryu, Matsubayashi-ryu), Shito-ryu (Motobu-Ha Shito-ryu, Tani-Ha Shito-ryu, and Shito-ryu of Kenei Mabuni and Manzo Iwata), Goju-ryu, Wado-ryu, and Kodokan Judo Shuri-ryu. I also have trained in different views and methods of Filipino Martial Arts. Because of previous training of different arts, I always believed in having an open mind. But if you teach Shito-ryu, or whatever art that you instruct, that is what you should teach, not a blend.

**Who are your teachers?**

I presently am under the direction of Shihan Kunio Murayama (Shito-ryu) and plan to be under him until I learn everything there is to learn, which means a lifetime. He is a great and very technical master instructor.

Mr. Murayama was the Uchi Deshi to Sensei Manzo Iwata. Mr. Iwata taught him both Nanban Sato-ryu Kenpo (grappling art) and Shito-ryu Karate-do. Murayama Sensei is a kind but a no-nonsense instructor with classical methods of teaching. He has introduced me to bunkai as I have never seen or felt. At one training seminar in Phoenix, which our U.S.A. club sponsored, he literally knocked me out with a takedown utilizing technique from one of the intermediate katas. Practitioners take kata for granted; that is because they were not taught the techniques hidden in each kata. Sensei always makes me a believer in the classical arts of Jujutsu (Nanban Sato-ryu Kenpo) and Shito-ryu Karate. I always wonder what people are missing when they are not taught the movements of kata and their style's specific techniques. Murayama Sensei introduced me to Sensei Genzo Iwata (Shito-ryu) during a training seminar at the Copa Murayama, an annual karate tournament held in Monterrey, Mexico. Sensei Iwata is very precise in his training methods; his kata and kumite teachings are accurate and authentic Shito-ryu methods as taught by his father, master instructor Sensei Manzo Iwata. Mr. Genzo's instruction this year was Tomari Bassai kata; it always is amazing to train under such master instructors. It was a memorable event to be with this great company and to learn these inside secrets in the presence of Mr. Kanazawa and Sam Moledzki. Other instructors in the past that I have trained under were Soke Shogo Kuniba (Motobu-Ha Shito-ryu), Sensei Shogen Oyakawa (Kobayashi-ryu), Sensei Toshihiro Oshiro (Matsubayashi-ryu), Sensei Bayani Adlawan (Motobu-Ha Shito-ryu), and Watanabe, K. Sensei (Kodokan Judo).

**Would you tell us some interesting stories of your early days in karate?**

There are a few, but most memorable were with Oyakawa Sensei. He was a karate instructor by night; by day, he was a shiatsu therapist at a chiropractor business in Los Angeles. He was visiting for an annual Karate/Kobudo clinic that he taught four to six times a year, and afterward, we always would have a picnic, and he always was the umpire. The kids loved him, but one of my students, Sempai Doug Gill, who still trains and teaches for me, asked Sensei: "Can you teach the striking bunkai to the White Crane (Hakutsuru) kata" that he taught earlier. Sensei was about 5-foot-6 and Doug, who was a muscular 5-foot-9, threw a punch at sensei's request. Doug responsively held onto his chest after being struck by sensei. Visually, it looked as if Doug was having a heart attack, but sensei mentioned these are the secrets that are in the applications of the empty hand. These are the secrets that are not taught and are dying out with the old masters. Yes, they hurt when the answer is revealed, but the Eastern way is not to ask these questions. You, as students, need to ask these questions; if not you will not have the answers. This changed my martial arts frame of thought, thanks to Doug's hurtful encounter.

## Which kata best represents you, and how important is it?

Kata *Seipai* is my favorite, due to its fluid technique and rhythmic tempo. The kata is internally energy driven, but that doesn't mean that all katas are not like this, just that Seipai is very powerful and very fluid-influenced. I really appreciate the bunkai; it is very physical and quick. It actually lets your mind wander while your body is in lethal cruise control.

## Were you a 'natural' at karate; did the movements come easily to you?

I felt that I was, but this was due to my early experiences with Judo and Gung-fu. This helped with my relaxation and my ability to learn at an easier pace. Karate is an art that helps one to understand oneself. If the beginner karate-ka could refrain from battling his left side if he is right side dominant, that is half of the fight from training in a natural state. Sensei would call that the "wild horse"; he would say a wild horse would always do the opposite of the direction of the rider. If the reins are pulled to the right, the wild horse would go to the left. Understand your wild horse before your natural side can come out.

"Teach the traditions but open your mind; know your art very well before you start thinking about adding an adaptation to your rendition of your art."

## How has your personal expression of karate developed over the years?

Just as fads of martial arts change, so should your defenses and offenses. In my earlier years, I found myself moving more telegraphically, with a slight tension in my movement. In the dojo, our kata and bunkai stay the same, as traditional karate should. If one changes the movement, it is not considered traditional, but that doesn't mean that your classes should not include streetwise techniques. Yes, karate has every set of defenses available. But as famous military figures have said repeatedly, "to know your opponent is to know how they fight." Teach the traditions but open your mind; know your art very well before you start thinking about adding an adaptation to your rendition of your art. Sensei Murayama's teachings of Jujitsu have open doors to a more clear and complete art of Shito-ryu Karate-do.

**What are the most important points in your teaching methods? And what are the most important qualities for a student to become proficient in the karate style?**

I never can overstate the teaching of the basics. I think that in some of today's dojos, they go around the teachings of the kihon because the youth get bored easily and do not like repetitious movement. This is a part of our teachings – basics, basics, and more basics. What we also express is where to hit, not just throwing a punch or kick and wherever it lands is good. More important is what will stop your opponent and what the effects of a precise technique are.

**With all the technical changes during the last years, do you think there still is 'pure' Shito Ryu karate?**

Yes, because of the line of teachers—starting with Kenwa Mabuni (founder of Shito-ryu), and Mabuni's protégé Sensei Manzo Iwata, and Mr. Iwata's protégé Sensei Kunio Murayama. Karate-do Shito-kai Murayama U.S.A. teaches the Shito-ryu of Kenwa Mabuni. But how pure was Shito-ryu when Mr. Iwata was being taught? Most Karate styles have changed, depending on when the recipient learned from the master. At an older age, there were body movement limitations that altered the kata and techniques.

**Do you think different 'styles' are truly important in the art of karate?**

Yes, if there were not other styles, the argument of my style is better than yours would not exist (jokingly). Each style has its own flavor. Without different styles, there would not have been the various challenges in the development of these arts. It's like having only one football team; where would the competition be? This competition promotes improvements within; in turn, other styles will improve.

**What is your opinion of fighting events such as the UFC and Mixed Martial Arts events?**

I always have believed any martial art is good, but when events like these become more spectator sports, they become cloned in the streets. This makes today's martial arts evolve, which means instructors should not become complacent in their dojo. Quite a few karate dojo do not include ground fighting; this is an Achilles heel to their art. If they do not teach it now, they should start to prepare their students better for that rough battleground—the streets.

**Karate nowadays often is referred to as a sport. Would you agree with this definition or is it a martial art?**

No, I do not consider Karate a sport. But the sport aspect has kept karate alive, in many ways. Sport karate (kumite and kata) has done well by giving youth a better out than street activity. Just like baseball, basketball, and of course soccer, karate has done a lot of good for today's youth. But martial arts still has to be taught along with sports, so they can understand the difference, such as where to strike and to truly understand timing.

**Do you feel that you still have further to go in your studies?**

Yes, we have 50 plus kata in our style of Shito-ryu. This is a very long path of trying to learn the kata, including their bunkai (applications). It is fascinating to learn the history, kata, and their bunkai; this is a true life endeavor as written in most Karate rank certificates—especially learning these studies from Sensei Kunio Murayama. He is very knowledgeable in the art of Shito-ryu; he is a wealth of knowledge.

**How do you see Shito-ryu karate in North America at the present time?**

This art has sprouted, thanks to Sensei Fumio Demura and his kindness as a true karate-do master. We also can thank Masters Shogo Kuniba (Motobu-Ha Shito-ryu), Teruo Hayashi (Hayashi-ha Shito-ryu), and Chuzo Kotaka for their contributions to the growth of Shito-ryu in the USA. We also have Sensei Kunio Murayama, who visits our dojo conducting seminars in Phoenix, Arizona, and Texas.

**Do you think it helps the karate student physically to train with weapons (Kobudo)?**

Yes, I have believed that ever since the first time I picked up as pair of sai. The coordination that comes with weapons training is very rewarding for each student, especially two-man drills (Yakusoku kumite). Short/long weapons provide either weight or wind restrictions, making the resistance with weapons training very strenuous. It also makes the martial artist a very versatile karate practitioner.

**How does the Shito-ryu karate style differ from other methods and styles of karate?**

Shito-ryu karate is a unique style, due to the founder Kenwa Mabuni combining the kata and theories of the Tode (Chinese hand) styles of all three

Okinawan villages (Naha, Tomari, and Shuri) where Okinawan Empty hand arts originated. Most styles are combinations; for example, Goju-ryu has Naha, Okinawa origins, plus the Gung-fu influence of Pa Qua Chuan of Fukien, China. Shotokan has Shuri, Okinawan influence from Itosu and Azato. By Mr. Mabuni (Shito-ryu founder) incorporating these origins to its style, we differ by including these Okinawan methods.

**When teaching the art of karate, what is the most important element: self-defense or sport?**

Of course, self-defense is the most important aspect of karate. But with a ratio of 60 percent more of today's youth training and filling our dojo, we have to teach sport karate, without the martial art included.

**Forms and sparring, what's the proper ratio in training?**

The ratio we go by is 60 percent kata and 40 percent kumite. Kata (form) teaches movement and versatility, but jyu-kumite (free sparring) improves timing and builds reflexive reactions. Kata teaches you good attacks and defenses, and kumite tweaks your confidence, spirit, and of course timing/speed.

**Do you have any general advice you would care to pass on to practitioners in general?**

As most practitioners would say, keep training your basics. But I'd like to add something different, and that is to not just train in the basics but also try to understand your movements. Listen well, and respect your instructor and senior classmates. Conduct yourself in a professional manner, especially in front of the younger classmates. You may be tomorrow's mentors, and how you act will be mimicked by your peers.

**What do you consider to be the major changes in the art of Shito-ryu since you began training?**

Some Shito-ryu practitioners have modified the kata to look more flowery for competition purposes. Shito-ryu forms are beautiful just as they are, without any modifications. I also have noticed that there are more 7th and 8th Dan now then there were in the 80s or 90s, and quite a few red/white belt bearers.

**Who would you like to have trained with that you have not?**

I would like to have trained with Kenwa Mabuni; the stories of his training methods are historic. I also would like to have trained with Manzo Iwata. I always have been fascinated at how Shito-ryu karate might have looked in the early years. I always ask Sensei Murayama this question: "Can you teach me the way that Mr. Iwata taught you?" He always says, "These are my present methods of teaching. Nothing has changed but my age and my hair. I have less."

**What would you say to someone who is interested in starting to learn karate?**

Why do you want to train in martial arts? Is this something that you want to do; will you be able to make a commitment to your training? Make sure you do your research on schools in your area before you commit. Write questions down and take them with you to the school that you have an interest in; spend time to ask the instructor what you might expect. Do your research and let yourself know you are going to get hit.

"Make sure you do your research on schools in your area before you commit."

**What is it that keeps you motivated after all these years?**

I always have been motivated since I have trained with some very good mentor instructors. I never have had one karate or kobudo instructor swear or curse in class or around students; I have kept the same tradition. Since they have been great mentors, I am trying to keep the tradition of these great master instructors. This goal keeps me learning and teaching year to year. The most important factor is seeing the face of some of the young students testing for their first belt ranking; their smiles are so pure and truthful. This is my highlight and motivation, that I have changed someone's life for the better—hopefully by setting a good example by teaching the culture/customs and respect of these martial arts.

**What is the philosophical basis for your karate training?**

To continuously train and teach the tradition of an art that was taught to me, so the next generation can benefit from yesterday's martial arts discoveries. I find this to be a lifelong commitment, which motivates me to con-

# Karate Masters

"True master instructors are instructors who truly teach instructors."

tinue to learn more and hopefully to fulfill my goal as an instructor. Part of the base is to abide by the meaningful principles of Shito-ryu fighting philosophy. For instance, *Rakka*, in which the principle is to powerfully parry the attack; *Ryu Sui* (Water Flow), in which the principle is to evade the opponent's attacks without parrying them; *Kusshin* (Body Bending), in which the principle is to parry the adversary's attacks by bending your body; *Ten-i* (Position Change), in which the principle is to parry the purpose of the adversary's attack by displacement; *Hantsuki* (Reflection of the Attack), in which the principle is to reflect the attack by matching the adversary's move. These examples of Shito-ryu's martial philosophies are only a few of the highlights in our art.

**Do you have a particularly memorable karate experience that has remained as an inspiration for your training?**

I was invited to a training seminar for instructors taught by Sensei Kunio Murayama (Shito-Kai), and the class was on basics. But it wasn't the subject that fascinated me; it was the method of how he taught, and the overall classical Eastern way of doing things. Sensei was not rude, but he was stern, and he taught the courtesy and the martial ways of the Japanese. He kept going over how to teach strikes, kicks, and blocks—the fundamentals. I looked around the room and not one participant looked bored; it was the basics and everyone enjoyed it. Sensei sat everyone down with the command of "Seiza." He began to teach us the rules of the dojo and how to treat students. This was very memorable, because how many instructors teach their students how to teach students? True master instructors are instructors who truly teach instructors. How many really do that—not just advanced kata or kumite, but what martial arts really are about? This is what Sensei Murayama and Sensei Genzo Iwata have done for my true martial experience, and have kept the light burning in my martial career.

**After all these years of training and experience, could you explain the meaning of the practice of karate?**

To practice in karate is to follow all Japanese and Okinawan Dojo Kun (The Place of the Way Rules) and follow the true traditions of respect. Leave all of your thoughts and emotions outside, and let your body demonstrate mental expressions by executing kata with kime (spirit).

### How do you think a practitioner can increase his understanding of the spiritual aspect of the art?

Martial art teaches the practitioner how to look deeper into his/her inner self by learning about the body's limitations. By preparing for their periodical evaluations / testing period, the students ready themselves mentally and physically. By this preparation, they learn to minimize errors, to push and strive for a better character, not to earn another level belt but to gain an accomplishment that improves inner spiritual confidence.

### Is anything lacking in the way martial arts are taught today compared to how they were in your beginnings?

I think manners and respect are lacking in today's dojo. I alwaysthought martial arts were all about respect, but instructors are lacking in teaching these methods and conveying these rules to their students. If these rules are not conveyed, the idea of respect will be lost. Otherwise, the domino effect occurs—if they never were taught, how can they teach the next generation of black belts? This is one concern; the other is the teaching of yesterday's methods of martial arts.

I find that when I travel to Monterrey, Mexico, and Japan for training, the teachings are the same as yesterday's. One fear here is that in the USA, today's teachers are refraining from past methods due to possible lawsuits. You hear in the past of shinai being used to correct improper moves; also shime (body testing) methods for proper body tension. Some of the Naha-te schools still use these practices of yesterday.

### Could I ask what you consider to be the most important qualities of a successful karate practitioner?

I believe they have to know what their goals are or should be, such as life. If their success is just acquiring a black belt, they only are on a partial path to their martial progression. Learn your Budo (warrior way) history/customs, where/how to strike, and find your true self.

### What advice would you give to students on the question of supplementary training?

Today's athletes have improved their performance by far. This did not happen because they were the plain Joe/Jane. They have learned "how," "when," and "what" nutrients to consume and how to push their limits in

# Karate Masters

"Karate is moving forward and growing as an art and as a sport. But a few of the qualities of yesterday's traditions are drifting slightly."

isometric and weight training. Jyukumite (free sparring) training drills are, in many ways, better than most machines or free weights; they can offer as much as gym equipment. But the karate-ka may need to get a physical checkup to know one's limits. Knowing these facts may prevent possible injuries.

**What do you see as the most important attributes of a student?**

The will to learn, and to have patience. I know that when learning a technique or kata, one always wants to learn what is next, just like a movie. Learn and practice what you have at home. Patience and practice are two attributes that students need to have a little more of. They may have one or the other, but not both attributes.

**Why is it, in your opinion, that a lot of students start falling away after two-three years of training?**

I think that in three years they may have attained their black belt and, after acquiring this, they believe mentally that they have reached their goal. We know this is where one really starts to learn, but to the majority, this is a completion. Another reason is that if they did not acquire their black belt, they wonder why not? So they may go to another dojo that might give them an easy way out, by accepting a black belt from another teacher. The last is they may have been burned out on the same old routine. Again, this relates to my comment on patience. In today's world, where everything is fast paced, they may believe why not martial arts?

**Have been times when you felt fear in your training?**

Actually, yes, during a training session in which Sensei K. Murayama was teaching the finer points of both Nanban Sato-ryu Kenpo (Jujitsu) and Shito-ryu kata. This was the first year we brought Sensei to visit this first USA and Hombu dojo. Thanks to my Sempai Sam Moledzki, my sponsor in the *Japan Karate-do Shito-kai*, Sensei asked me if I knew ukemi (how to fall/roll). I replied, "Hai Sensei (yes)." Mind you, I had just picked him up at the airport from an international flight, with no practice and not knowing what he was going to do. At the seminar, he asked me to grab his lape. He commenced to throw me around like I have never been thrown. But in Nanban Satoh-ryu Kenpo, the positioning is to place your opponent in a bind where they cannot preventively roll out of the attack. Let me tell you, I wasn't as fearful as I was astonished at what he did. I remained on the ground with my students viewing this technique that Sensei just did to me. I was down for maybe 20 seconds, but it felt more like 20 minutes. After the session, my students were impressed to see what Sensei did to me—but not as impressed as I was.

**Do you think the Olympics will be positive for the art of karate-do?**

Yes, the exposure of karate in the event will be great. I know a lot of traditionalists are against this move and there are karate organizations that are working hard to see this happen. And, do you know what? They are doing a fantastic job. But the question that always is asked is: what are the rules this year? Do we have to get certified again, how much will this cost? Cost is a big question, because when money is involved, a lot of funny things happen. We hope for the sake of the competitors that they are not the ones paying for political gains.

**What are your thoughts on the future of karate?**

Karate is moving forward and growing as an art and as a sport. But a few of the qualities of yesterday's traditions are drifting slightly. I have observed that respect and loyalty, which are great humane qualities, need to be reinforced in today's dojo. Quite a few young black belts are leaving their Sensei and opening their own dojo, for one reason or other. Some of the finer points of karate are taught when acceptance of black belt rank merit has been achieved. Leaving their dojo is a growing issue. We talk as senior instructors and wonder what will become of tomorrow karate-ka generation. We only can pray for the best, and just train and sweat and practice our kata and kumite as our styles' originators would have wished it to be. O

# AVI ROKAH

## IN THE NAME OF THE MASTER

AVI ROKAH IS ONE OF THOSE FEW SELECTED INDIVIDUALS WHO HAD THE PRIVILEGE OF BEING A STUDENT AND ASSISTANT TO THE LEGENDARY KARATE MASTER HIDETAKA NISHIYAMA. HE STARTED TRAINING AT AGE 15, AND HASN'T STOPPED EVER SINCE. RIGHT AFTER COMPLETING MILITARY SERVICE IN ISRAEL, HE MOVED TO THE UNITED STATES TO TRAIN UNDER THE SUPERVISION OF NISHIYAMA SENSEI UNTIL HIS MASTER'S PASSING IN 2009. HE REMEMBERS THE BEGINNINGS: "TWENTY YEARS AGO IT WAS KARATE WITHOUT PRINCIPLES; KARATE THAT WAS BASED ON ATHLETICISM. NOW, IT IS MORE PROFOUND IN TECHNIQUE, STRATEGY, TIMING, AND THE STATE OF MIND NECESSARY FOR THE APPLICATION," HE SAYS. THE ART OF KARATE CHANGED HIS LIFE AND GAVE HIM DIRECTION WHEN HE NEEDED IT THE MOST.

SENSEI AVI ROKAH IS THE FOUNDER AND CHIEF INSTRUCTOR OF THE TRADITIONAL KARATE ACADEMY, AND THE 1994 WORLD CHAMPION, FIVE-TIME U.S. NATIONAL CHAMPION (1990, 1991, 1992, 1994, AND 2001) AND 2001 PRE-WORLD CUP CHAMPION. MANY KARATE EXPERTS CONSIDER HIM THE FINEST AND MOST KNOWLEDGEABLE KARATEKA AFTER HIS MASTER TEACHER, NISHIYAMA. A GIFTED, DEVOTED AND PATIENT INSTRUCTOR WHO SPENDS ALL HIS WAKING HOURS FINDING BETTER WAYS TO TEACH HIS MANY DEDICATED STUDENTS, SENSEI ROKAH'S GOAL IS TO PRESERVE THE PRECIOUS LEGACY THAT HE RECEIVED FROM MASTER HIDETAKA NISHIYAMA.

**How long have you been practicing the martial arts and many styles have you trained in?**

I practice since I was 14. I always focused on karate and everything else was to enrich my karate, to see different perspectives, and to understand total movement and self-defense better. I studied Muay Thai, Tai Chi, Brazilian jiu Jitsu, and wrestling for the past 15 years.

I also like to look at other sound karate styles that bring different perspectives and angles of the same principles. We always have to keep open and learning without losing our base. Other styles might do things differently for different reasons; I remember that when I took Muay Thai, Sensei Nishiyama commented to me about my kamae and that the way I hold my arms had changed. I did not notice it until he commented about it. In Muay Thai, the

# Karate Masters

"I trained with a dislocated shoulder, broken bones, with fever; there was never a question of missing a class."

kamae is different because of different distance preferences, and it is good for them; but for us, we use distance differently and our kamae is different. So, when we look at other styles we have to be careful not to be influenced in the wrong way.

I did train under Sensei for 28 years; it was not just like going to school, but that was the purpose of my life. It was like being in military basic training for 27 years; that is all I did and all I was thinking about. Everything I did, even out of karate, was to improve my karate. For the first 12 years I train with Sensei at least 5 hours a day, 12–2, and then in the evening, 6:30–9:30, and then more on my own. Every day was a fight, but I loved every moment. And than Sensei got older and was teaching only two to three hours a day, but I was discipline and trained on my own at least two more hours. I was finished at the end of every day.

On top of this, I was teaching at my own small dojo and at some elementary schools, so I rode my bike for few hours a day for teaching. In the first few years, I also took the bus twice a day to Sensei's dojo, and that meant almost four hours a day in buses. The only times I missed Sensei's classes was if I was teaching in different country, and even then I felt worried that I might lose something very important. I trained with a dislocated shoulder, broken bones, with fever; there was never a question of missing a class.

**I remember Sensei passing by me about once a month and saying, "need haircut."**

My friend Toru and I use to have a dojo together, and we slept in our dojo. We used to take showers on the roof of the dojo with a hose, and sometimes we even had spectators from the nearby apartments. Well, it might have been a little too much; it got to a point that even Sensei told me that I should take a vacation, go to the mountains. I was surprised; Sensei himself never took vacations, but he realized that some balance is necessary.

When I look back, now that I know more from the point of view of sport science, for optimal performance, it would have been better to take some time off, and to periodize the training. I cannot say that it was not good for forging budo spirit.

**Were you a 'natural' at karate; did the movements come easily to you?**
No, I had to work hard to get the technique and the timing and the feel of it. I was a good athlete in elementary and high school, I did the long jump and shot put, but karate required hard work from me because there are many details that have to be digested so they can become reflexive. Pure athleticism is not enough. When I started karate, I just imitated the movement; I had no idea of the mechanics and timing; it was primitive karate. When I came to Sensei Nishiyama I started to understand the mechanics, the principles that the kata is there to teach us. I started to understand that karate is about proper timing and being smart and skillful, not fighting by power and resistance. With the years under Sensei, the subtleties became clearer, how all the different components of movement, and also the mental and physical affect each other and link to each other. It become clearer how to make more power with less action, and how to spend less energy and move less when facing an opponent, and to be more effective.

**What are the most important points in your teaching methods?**
Basic principles, good posture, maximizing ground reaction forces (stance), sequencing (all action is chain reaction from the ground up), the role of the body center in initiating the action and producing force, proper body dynamics, maximizing muscle action (the rate of contraction and expansion), using the breath to effectively apply all of the above. The main point of technique is making maximum shocking power and initiating without back motion. Then comes ways to apply the technique, understanding chance, understanding distance and timing, making strategy, developing reaction and action without the interference of consciousness so all of this can be applied.

**What is your opinion of fighting events such as the UFC and Mixed Martial Arts events?**
I like the fighting when it is at a good level and you can see skillful use of timing and distance and strategy, or even when you see the great skill of wrestling and grappling. I don't like it when they are brawling and there is clashing of powers.

# Karate Masters

**Karate nowadays often is referred to as a sport . . . would you agree with this definition or is a martial art?**

It is what you make out of it. If you let go of the principles transmitted to us through generations and focus on pretty kata and scoring points, then it is a sport. If you persist on the principles of good technique and application, and apply them to competition, and competition becomes just a means of testing ourselves for future development, than we can keep it a budo. It is what you like it to be, but doing it as a sport is the easy way, and unfortunately most people do karate as sport. This is why Sensei Nishiyama insisted on keeping all the details that make karate as budo from being lost. I believe that we never can compromise and we must keep karate as budo. I believe that many people never had the chance to be exposed to karate as budo, and if they did, they definitely will want to do it that way, which is a deeper way.

**When teaching the art of karate, what is the most important element: self-defense or sport?**

There are many important elements in karate, but it first of all is budo. It depends on who I teach. If it is middle-age people, I will emphasize proper sequencing, moving from the center out, developing good, balanced posture so they can be healthy and functional for many years. I also will stress the mental side, developing the intuition, making quick decisions without brain interference. Those are good things for life, but they are essential for karate as budo, since only with good posture, movement timing, and an intuitive mind can we have good martial art. If I teach younger guys, I might stress the martial arts aspect. But whenever someone is interested in competing, I make sure that they are not going to lose the budo aspect because of competition. Budo defines competition and not the other way around. Competition is only a stepping stone in one's budo life; the goal is much bigger. It is good to be put under pressure and under the magnifying glass of competition, if you take the lessons from it and don't think of it as a goal. It is not essential; not everyone has to compete. Competition is important especially for the mental side.

**You have spent more than two decades training under the supervision of Sensei Nishiyama; would you tell us how you saw his karate evolution and his approach to kata and kumite teaching?**

Sensei Nishiyama used to say, "You can imitate Picasso a thousand times, but this is a copy, not art, and you are not Picasso. It is the same with karate. You imitate and repeat until the point that you are able to digest the principles of karate into your own body – then it is your own karate and becomes art."

For instance, with Sensei Nishiyama's guidance, I learned how to create energy – how to coordinate the body to one single line of energy. My technique now is dependent on skill, not mere strength. In sparring, I don't fight my opponent; I get in tune with him, set him up, and then use his technique to my advantage. I feel that my training is much more efficient because I know what I'm looking for. The main principles never changed but the teaching without doubt was much more in-depth. His teaching always was detailed and logical.

**It is interesting how you are describing the sparring element...**

Under his guide, the aspect of kumite became deeper with more detailed explanations of correct reactions, timing, set-up, and strategy. A lot of people rely too much on speed. Speed is good when used with proper timing, but it is not going to help against a skillful opponert. He empha-

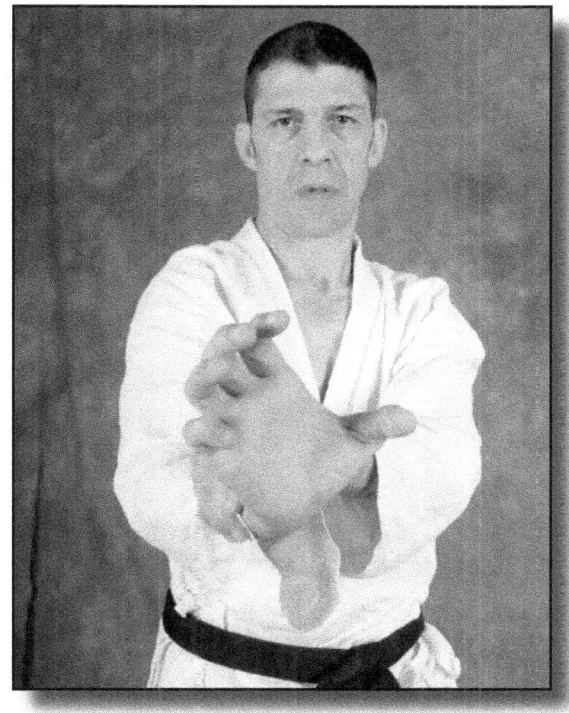

"My technique now is dependent on skill, not mere strength."

sized how to develop the right state of mind that allows techniques to be applied. Kumite became like a chess game, not a game of strength. Sensei Nishiyama used to scold me when I was too aggressive: "Don't use your power and speed against a lesser opponent. Imagine that he has a knife – would you charge at him then? Use the right moment when he cannot react," he used to say.

**How important is kata training?**

Very important. From kata, we learn principles of body movement and combat. For example, we learn to move the body from the center out as a unit, rather than moving the arms and legs independently. It is impossible to seize a split-second opening if there is extraneous energy or unnecessary movement in our technique. Kata teaches us to synchronize mental energy, breath, muscles expansion/contraction, and sequence of joint movement: ki first, breathe next, then follow with muscle movement and technique. It

# Karate Masters

"There is no need to block when moving away from an opponent's attack because we use space to avoid the attack."

teaches us continuity between techniques; if there is space between techniques, there is a chance for the opponent to counterattack and we will miss many chances for attack combinations. An example of a combat principle from kata is that with few exceptions we always move in when blocking. There is no need to block when moving away from an opponent's attack because we use space to avoid the attack - amashi waza. We also learn that block and counterattack are one action; block is not a technique by itself unless the block is used as attack, such as against a joint. From things like this, we understand how important kata is for kumite. Even if you favor kumite make sure that you always come back to kata and improve your kumite weak points. Now, kata training by itself will not make you a good fighter. Only through timing and distance training can you bring the techniques in kata to life.

**Kihon, Kata, and Kumite; what's the proper ratio in training?**

It changes, depending on what I feel that I need at the time. In general, I would say 30 percent kihon, 30 percent kata, and 40 percent kumite, but also bag training. And also, most people should work on keeping the body in balance, so some stretching, spinal stabilization, and some strength is necessary. If I do not do enough kata, I feel that my kumite deteriorates and is not as sharp and precise.

**Who would you like to have trained with that you have not?**

I would like to see what training with Master Funakoshi was like, and some of the older Okinawan masters from his time. Also, maybe Sensei Nishiyama's first sword teacher, whom he talks about a lot in his teachings.

**How do you think a practitioner can increase his/her understanding of the spiritual aspect of the art?**

When you train long enough and face many people, you should realize that without stable emotions, no skill can be fulfilled; without being able to be there in each action wholly, mentally, spiritually, and physically, one cannot maximize his/her technique, no matter how correct the mechanics are.

Without giving yourself up, you cannot become the opponent, tune to him, and you will fight him by speed and physical ability alone; it is limited and is not a complete budo.

Karate is moving meditation and, as budo, the goals are beyond fighting, being a better more fulfilled person and making a better more harmonized society. First, transform yourself and then you will affect those around you and society in general. Always be open-minded; always seek, be patient, work hard, but smartly, and don't be afraid of making a mistake. You always have to discover; don't try to get it.

**Is there anything lacking in the way martial arts are taught today compared to how they were when you started training?**

It depends on the teacher. There always are good, true teachers, with passion, and those who are not. If a teacher keeps learning and seeking, he will be a good teacher, and will be able to give to his students. Yes, training was rougher years ago, and there was more repetition. This is not always good. Repetitions are good to instill proper movement patterns and sequences into the nervous system, if done with the right direction, but in many cases, repetitions will strengthen bad habits that will be hard to change. Also, one does not run a marathon to improve his short sprint; likewise, if the purpose is to improve speed, repetition is not proper. So, a good teacher should know how to periodize training and what he wants to achieve in a class or over time. I feel that karate training is an endless search; there always is more to find out, and that is the beauty of karate. Sensei Nishiyama told me, "When you think, you know you are finished." I agree; I think that we are not looking for conclusions but are looking to find out.

**What advice would you give to students on the question of supplementary training?**

I would do some weights training, but not machines, since machines isolate muscles and are for body builders. They confuse the nervous system, because you isolate in the gym and in karate you will ask the nervous system to work the muscles as chains in integration. The brain does not know individual muscles; the brain knows movement patterns and that is how we should strength train.

We also must improve spine and joint stability in order to improve performance and prevent injuries, so I would recommend certain Swiss ball exercises and some spinal and core stability exercises to improve the recruitment sequence of the inner unit muscles, so we can deliver force from a stable platform, which is our body center.

I also would recommend stretching at the end of each class to improve range of motion and to balance the body. Certain muscles in the body tend to get tighter and shorter than others, such as the hip flexors, the lumbar erectors (low back), hamstrings (back thighs) if those are tight there will be compensation in movement. And, before class stretch dynamically, not statically.

**Why do you think that a lot of students start falling away after two-three years of practice?**
Sometimes, we do a lot of basics and no application, and it is boring for students. I think that from the beginning, kumite and basic timing should be incorporated, so students can see the relationships between basics and applications, how basic principles are applied, and that will make their basics better, because they will understand why it is done that way. Of course, everything worthwhile needs patience and hard work and not everyone has this, especially in our fast society.

**Have been times when you felt fear in your training?**
Sure, there was time that going to Sensei Nishiyama's class was like going to a war. There was a lot of tension but, truthfully, I loved the challenge.

**Do you think that Olympics will be positive for the art of karate-do?**
Yes and no. It will be a great exposure and recognition, a great support for karate, and it can draw a lot of younger people. But, it can carry karate in the wrong direction, and the depth can be lost if we are not careful how we handle it. We must protect the purity of karate and not let it become merely athletics.

**What are your views on kata bunkai?**
I think it is important to understand bunkai, so the techniques have life and are not just decoration. But, at the same time, we have to acknowledge that we did lose some of the original meaning of some katas. The kata still has great value in teaching us principles of movement and combat and instilling proper movement patterns and sequences into our nervous systems. We must have a clear picture of each technique line of energy.

"Kata is an example and a code. Through the practice of kata we search to understand the code, to understand the underlying principles that kata symbolizes."

The outer form of the kata is a vehicle for us to understand, not just intellectually but with our whole body, the principles that are contracted into the kata. Let's not forget that kata originated from real fighting experience, not theory. Kata is an example and a code. Through the practice of kata we search to understand the code, to understand the underlying principles that kata symbolizes. Of course, kata is limited – it is a form. We cannot apply kata in a real fight. Principles, on the other hand, are not limited. They are formless and they can be adapted to any circumstances. When we internalize the principles of kata, we can apply karate techniques to any self-defense circumstances. I believe that the understanding of body movement is on a higher level and that kata is still the best means to help us improve and bring our technique to new levels.

**Could you explain the technical points of contraction and expansion in Karate?**

We have two sources of power in karate: body dynamics and inside muscles action (contraction and expansion; expansion is relaxation or reaction of contraction). Those two methods are used together, but as the movement

# Karate Masters

"Breathing affects everything in the technique."

space becomes smaller, and the force we can produce by external movement becomes more limited, muscle action becomes more important. In Shotokan, a beginner starts by learning big action and proper dynamics, and gradually learns to produce great force in smaller action by using muscle action. We use contraction as internal wind up, loading without external back motion, and then expansion to release, drive the technique, and then contraction, to allow maximum shocking power. At impact, we want total body contraction from the ground up and from the spine outward to the technique line, so the total force is delivered in the shortest amount of time. Of course, this is general; different techniques require different types of contraction and different types of energy. The result of all this is not only a more powerful technique, but also no mental or physical gaps between techniques, which means no chance for the opponent to attack.

**How does breathing affect the technique in general?**

Breathing affects everything in the technique, to the point that I can say that ultimately there are no details of technique in your mind, only intention and breathing, and you must develop such a body system or reflexive movement patterns that the rest happens by itself. So, all the basic points we learn have to be "forgotten," and when we have intention and the breath is initiated, the necessary technique will just "happen."

For example, we say "breathing from floor," which is not true, but it is an important feeling, since then the breath activates the muscles from the feet up to maximize ground reaction forces and the use of the stance. The breath makes kime (focus) by applying pressure to the floor at impact to produce force, and maximizes muscle contraction to make maximum impact and shocking power. Breath controls all phases of the technique; if the breath rises, then one cannot maximize ground reaction and the use of the legs and abdomen, and the tendency will be to overuse the shoulder and make a top heavy technique.

# Rokah

The breath also is important for continuation between techniques, making no gaps or spaces, and keeping potential energy at any instant. If posture is distorted, optimal breathing and muscle control is impossible; if one is floating and has a weak stance, the breath will tend to rise. I used to have a voice teacher who put me in the karate stance with the feet firmly connected to floor because he claimed, that only there do I use the lower abdominal. When I was floating, I used the throat and facial muscles in excess.

The breath is important for interaction with the opponent, tuning to the rhythm, mixing up the rhythm. Setting up the opponent and reacting to the opponent has to be done with the breath, to achieve perfect timing without gaps. The breath is important in keeping stable emotions, which is most important for the application of any skill under pressure.

We say that your breath and the opponent's breath should become one, and in the more advanced levels, your breath will conduct the opponent's breath and movement. You are the commander and he is your soldier. Through connecting to the opponent's breath we connect to his intentions, since the breath is the connections between the mental and physical. We also react to the opponent's action with our breath rather than with the eyes. Light reaction is too late since you have to look, analyze, decide and than act. We bypass the conscious brain by reacting with the breath, which means reacting directly at the spinal level, and at the same time the breath also activates the body center. The breath initiates reaction and action, so reaction and action become one, without space.

**What is the correct way to use the eyes during combat?**

In karate, we understand that the eyes affect the brain. If we look at the opponent too hard, we will judge, confirm, and be behind rhythm and out of tune with him, and we easily will become overly excited and emotionally unstable. When we rely on the eyes, we become hesitant and have doubts. There are many ways of describing the use of the eyes, depending on the level, with the highest level being "you don't, see yet you see." In other words, you don't try to look, yet you see inside your opponent without trying. There are three main principles we must remember at all times:

1) Enzen No Metzke – eyes back as if looking at a mountain from a long distance. This is one of the most basic and important methods of using the eyes. When looking from close, you can see a house or a tree, and you get stuck in details. When looking from afar, you can see the whole without getting stuck in one place. The feeling should be as if the eyes are monitor-

# Karate Masters

"What Sensei Nishiyama was teaching was different than anyone else. His ideas were beyond the external form."

ing the situation, observing, looking softly, and not trying too hard.

2) Looking at the shining star – looking to the opponent's eye as if looking at a star. When the eye shine changes, you know the opponent's intention changes and he is about to move.

3) Tani no Metzke – looking through a canyon, or looking through the opponent' eyes to his heart or feeling. You are looking to the opponent's eye level, not staring at the eyes but rather through and down to his heart.

At the end you don't look in any special way; you just see inside your opponent.

**What are the most important principles of karate you have learned from Nishiyama Sensei?**

That is hard to summarize, but I will try. There is so much and everything seems most important; every line that came out of him is like a jewel. I used to sit down after he passed and write eight pages of one-line sentences that Sensei used to say regularly – and each has huge meaning and importance.

What Sensei Nishiyama was teaching was different than anyone else. His ideas were beyond the external form: What does the form symbolize? What principles are contracted in the form that allow us to transform the form from a copy to a lively, individual karate? He also showed us how all the principles interlink, and that the principles of technique have to do not only with movements but with real and practical application – things like posture and its effect on the quality of movement and the mental/emotional state necessary in a fight; maximize ground reaction forces and not use a "decoration" stance, which is a stance that looks good but has no function; using the breath to control all phases of technique and interaction with the opponent; and that every technique must have the following order: intention, breathing, muscles, and technique. He always emphasized initiating tech-

" Sensei Nishiyama himself still was searching and improving until the last days of his life. He was a true example of what a Karate practitioner should be."

rique without back motion, by using the muscle around the spine (small diameter), and using internal loading and muscle reaction, by means of intention and breath, etc.

But the main thing is that understanding all the structure never will work without the subtle points that one cannot discover even in a lifetime without the oral transmission and proper guidance. Sensei Nishiyama himself still was searching and improving until the last days of his life. He was a true example of what a Karate practitioner should be. O

# LES SAFAR

## A WEALTH OF KNOWLEDGE

Leslie Safar is co-founder, International Technical Director, and Chief Instructor for Europe of the AJKA-I (American JKA Karate Association – International). He has practiced Shotokan karate since 1959, and received his go-dan ranking from the JKA in 1980. He has a strong following on both sides of the Atlantic for his mastery as an instructor, his deep understanding of the core technical and philosophical principles of Shotokan Karate, and the development of an unparalleled, internationally accredited instructor training program. He is absolutely dedicated to building total and complete instructors, and paying attention to how the AJKA-I can create something positive for its individual members, instructors, and clubs.

Before establishing the AJKA in 1984 (then a revolutionary concept, but now something that is recognized as inevitable and as natural as any other type of human development), Safar Sensei was Okazaki Sensei's most senior student. Safar Sensei tours the United States on a regular basis, but spends the majority of his time teaching, directing, and developing AJKA-I karate in Hungary, Germany, and throughout Europe.

**How long have you been practicing the martial arts?**

I came to the US from Hungary when I was a very young man and I've practiced karate since 1959. At that time, there really was no karate around. In California, there was Bruce Tegner and Oshima, but on the East Coast there was nothing. We had found a Japanese exchange student at Pennsylvania University, Toshio Siguria. He was a nidan from JKA and he agreed to teach us, so we started a club in Philadelphia. In 1961, he had to go back to Japan, and he made the recommendation that someone go back with him. He would introduce that person to Sensei Nakayama, who headed the JKA, and he would help us get another instructor. The only guy who had any money was Bob Schwartz. He went, sponsored Sensei Okazaki, and this is the way karate started on the East Coast. We rented a big, vacant, supermarket, fixed it up ourselves, and made it into a dojo. I trained with him after that for most of my karate career.

# Karate Masters

"I have seen many different styles of karate over the years, but I have never seen anything that was better than Shotokan—especially JKA Shotokan."

**How many styles of karate or other martial arts methods have you trained in?**

I have seen many different styles of karate over the years, but I have never seen anything that was better than Shotokan—especially JKA Shotokan. I liked the way it was organized. I liked the discipline that the Japanese instructors expected. I liked how intense the training was. So I never got interested in any other style. I think you need to use all your time and effort to learn something really well, so I did not feel like I could do more, or get more, from anything else.

**Who were your teachers?**

Okazaki Sensei was my main instructor. But I was very fortunate; at the time all the good instructors and JKA champions came through Philadelphia on their way to Europe, and they stayed and trained and taught for a while. This way I had a chance to work and study with all of them, such as Kanazawa, Shirai, Enoeda, Kase, and Mori. Also, from time to time, Sensei Nakayama visited us and I had several chances to work with him personally.

**Would you tell us some interesting stories of your early days in karate?**

There are a million stories I remember, but there are a few that directly relate to karate that I would like to share with you. One has to do with when I got my first dan. This was so important at the time because there where no other American black belts. We were the first group. When I passed the test, I walked around everywhere with my black belt on for two days, even to the supermarket. The following Monday, I went to training and Sensei Okazaki said, "Give me your black belt." I thought he was going to write something on it, so I quickly took it off and gave it to him. With that, he pulled a white belt out of his desk, gave it to me and said, "now your karate training begins." I tell you, I was a young man at this time and did not understand what was happening; I almost cried. Well, for six months, I wore that white belt and just trained. I was not even thinking about it any more, and then one day Sensei came to me and gave me a nice embroidered JKA black belt and said, "Now you are ready for your black belt." That's when I first understood the point he was making. I understood that the color of the belt did not matter, and that the belt does not make you special, but rather, you make the belt special by continuing to train hard, and to show pride, and by living your life according to the principles of karate-do.

**In karate, what does kata really represent and how important is it?**
Kata exists to improve karate techniques and our ability to apply them. Usually, we practice the techniques that are in the katas by moving in straight lines, or standing in one position. In a kata, we must move in different directions, and rotate and change positions quickly. So, in part, they teach us to be able to shift our bodies and move effectively in any direction. The timing and rhythm that kata teaches also is very important. That is why you will see that all good kata men and woman are good kumite people.

**Were you a 'natural' at karate; did the movements come easily to you?**
I was training in boxing and playing soccer when I left Europe, so it was not too hard, but it wasn't easy either.

**How has your personal view of karate developed over the years?**
One of the most unfortunate things is the way karate has changed over the last several years. But there are a lot of good changes, also. One of the biggest problems is that a lot people are trying to learn karate by reading about it or viewing DVDs, and no one knows better then me that this it is impossible.

**What are the most important points in your teaching methods? And what are the most important qualities for a student to become proficient in the karate style?**
One of the most important things I stress to my students and instructors is how important it is to learn very well the things that are at hand. Don't try to jump ahead too fast. In other words, if you do not learn the body shifting and body rotation in *Heian Shodan*, you will have a very hard time learning it in *Bassai-dai*.

**With all the technical changes during the last years, do you think there is still a "pure" Shotokan karate?**
Well, I work hard to teach nothing but pure shotokan karate from the low-

# Karate Masters

"Good instructors equal a good style. I think the JKA style is the best due to the discipline of the training."

est to the highest level. I always say, "Once I cannot teach and do pure karate, I will not do it any more."

**Do you think different "styles" are truly important in the art of karate? And how is JKA Shotokan different from other styles of Karate?**

The styles do not really matter. All styles are good. The difference comes in where the instructors are concerned. Good instructors equal a good style. I think the JKA style is the best due to the discipline of the training, the methods, and the organization of teaching. This is when I see the relationship of karate and karate-do.

**What is your opinion of fighting events such as the UFC and Mixed Martial Arts events?**

It has nothing to do with traditional martial arts.

**Karate nowadays often is referred to as a sport. Would you agree with this definition or is it a martial art?**

Sport karate is a very important part of karate. Sports karate is what made karate popular and allowed it to be introduced all over the world. But we have to remember that only about 5 to 8 per cent of all the people practice sport karate; it's the rest of the people who pay the bills, and also give it its true value.

**Do you feel that you still have further to go in your studies?**

Let me answer this with another story. One time, Sensei Nakayama was in Philadelphia and I missed a class. So the next day when I go to the dojo, I see Sensei, and I say, "Sensei, I am sorry I missed class," and as I start to say why, he stops me and says, "It does not matter why. The important thing is that you were not here, so you missed out on what was to be learned." He pointed to the sky and asked me, "You see the sun?" I said, "Yes, I see it." Then he said, "When the sun goes down, you are one day closer to death. You cannot make that up. So, remember any day you spend without learning something, that day was wasted in your life." I never made excuses again.

**How do you see Shotokan karate in the world at the present time?**

I still think Shotokan karate is the best and most organized system. But due to the fact that the old Japanese masters are dying and changing, it is evening out somewhat.

**Do you think it helps the karate student physically to train with weapons?**

One time, we did a demonstration and someone asked Sensei Okazaki, "Do you study or teach weapons?" He replied that, "Karate means empty hand. If you want to learn to use a weapon, learn how to use the most modern ones, such as a gun. Those weapons are things of the past. Also, I have been practicing karate for more than 50 years and I am still trying to learn karate. I really don't have time for anything else."

**How does the karate style differ from other martial arts methods when applying the techniques in a self-defense situation?**

Basically, I don't think there is much difference. A punch is a punch, a kick is a kick, and the strike is a strike.

**When teaching the art of karate, what is the most important element: self-defense or sport?**

Traditional karate has four elements that all are equally important and combine to create the art: budo, self-defense, physical education, and sport. So by practicing good karate, one will have useful knowledge of all.

**Forms and sparring: what's the proper ratio in training?**

Sensei Okazaki often has said that 70 percent of karate is kata/kihon and 30 percent is Kumite, and that is the way his classes were conducted. It worked. We always had good results in competition in both Kumite and Kata.

**What do you consider to be the major changes in the art since you began training?**

Science. Today we understand how the brain and body work, and why we need to do a single technique thousands of times in order for us know it, and to be able to do it naturally.

**Who would you like to have trained with that you have not?**

I would have loved to have spent more time with Sensei Nakayama. I think he was the best, not only in his technique, but as a human being.

**What would you say to someone who is interested in starting to learn karate?**

Go and learn what karate is all about. Look closely at different instructors and different clubs. Look for the discipline and knowledge. Remember one thing: it is your time and your money. Don't waste it. Train as much as you can. Do not compare yourself to anyone. And be the best you can be.

**What is it that keeps you motivated after all these years?**

The students that I have worked with over the last 50 years, and the letters I get from them on exams, my birthday, and some other occasions. It is so gratifying to hear that they feel that their association with me as a karate instructor has changed their lives for the better.

**What is the philosophical basis for your karate training?**

I have had a wonderful life and I believe that everything good that has happened to me in my life I can relate to my karate training and to the understanding of karate-do. We can only understand the spiritual aspect of karate-do through hard training.

**Do you have a particularly memorable karate experience that has remained as an inspiration for your training?**

I really I don't know if there is any one thing that stands out; there have been so many. I've always felt that karate was the most challenging thing I've ever done. Everything about it inspired me to go on and try to be better in everything else I did.

**After all these years of training and experience, could you explain the meaning of the practice of karate?**

I find the meaning of life itself in karate-do. It is so deep, and relates to so many different things. If someone truly can apply karate practice to his or her everyday life, and not look at it as a hobby, or something to do in one's free time, it can be one of the most meaningful undertakings of all.

**Is there anything lacking in the way martial arts is taught today compared to how it was in your beginnings?**

For many, in many places, hard and disciplined training. One time we stood in deep kiba-dachi stance for an hour and 45 minutes. I thought we were crazy, but now I know that nothing is impossible if you apply yourself.

"I find the meaning of life itself in karate-do. It is so deep, and relates to so many different things."

**What do you consider to be the most important qualities of a successful karate practitioner?**

Endurance and discipline.

**What advice would you give to students on the question of supplementary training?**

Supplementary training, like running, weights, etc., is OK, but I feel that we can develop strong legs by doing kata and staying low, working on the makiwara for the upper body. So this way, as you are getting stronger, you're getting better at karate as well. You technique improves as your physical condition does, too.

# Karate Masters

"I always say, give me a student who truly wants to learn karate, and I can teach him."

**What do you see as the most important attributes of a student?**
Heart. I always say, give me a student who truly wants to learn karate, and I can teach him.

**Why is it, in your opinion, that a lot of students start falling away after two-three years of training?**
I think it is the instructor's fault most of the time. Many have no more karate to teach. They stop being interesting, so the students get bored and stop training.

**Have there been times when you felt fear in your training?**
No, not really. I was so interested in all we were doing that I didn't have time to be afraid.

**Do you think that the Olympics will be positive for the art of karate-do in case that happens one day?**
I think that if karate ever gets into the Olympics; it will have a great and positive general affect. But, really, it is very doubtful that this will ever happen. The people cannot get together to decide which karate should be in the Olympics.

# Safar

"Karate is too great a tool for human development."

**What are your thoughts on the future of karate?**

At times, I am afraid as to the future of karate. Sometimes, I feel that I am a dinosaur as far as karate is concerned, but yet, we cannot give it up. Karate is too great a tool for human development. As long as the tradition goes on, we have to try. It is gratifying that I see through my teaching, and our Instructor Training Program, that I am developing some students and instructors who understand this, and are taking it to the next level. As modern life gets better and easier, it has becomes more important that true karate somehow survives and become a more important part of our life. That is the essence of our International Instructor Training Program, that Karate is truly a tool for human development. The five words that I still try to live by—character, sincerity, effort, self-control, and courtesy—are the essence of life. O

# DEL SAITO

## A JOURNEY OF WISDOM

HE IS ONE OF THE MOST HIGHLY RESPECTED KARATE-DO INSTRUCTORS AND OFFICIALS IN THE WORLD. HIS EXPERTISE IN THE ART OF KARATE HAS MADE A GREAT IMPACT NOT ONLY IN THE UNITED STATES BUT ALSO BEYOND THE AMERICAN FRONTIER. BORN AND RAISED IN HAWAII, HANSHI DEL SAITO BEGAN HIS MARTIAL ARTS TRAINING AT THE AGE OF 11. HE RECEIVED HIS KARATE TRAINING FROM TWO OF THE MOST OUTSTANDING INSTRUCTORS IN THE SHITO RYU STYLE, CHUZO KOTAKA SENSEI AND SOKE MABUNI KENZO, SON AND HEIR OF THE GREAT MABUNI KENWA.

MORE THAN THREE DECADES OF TEACHING KARATE HAS LED TO A STRONG TRADITIONAL APPROACH, COMBINED WITH AN OPENNESS TO NEW IDEAS AND CONCEPTS FOR GROWTH. TEACHING KARATE FOR MORE THAN TECHNIQUE, HE ATTEMPTS TO HELP PEOPLE TO FIND THEMSELVES, TO DISCOVER THEIR CREATIVITY AND THEIR CAPACITY FOR OVERALL GROWTH THROUGH THE ARTS OF BUDO. HIS GOAL NEVER HAS BEEN TO GLORIFY HIMSELF, BUT RATHER TO PRESERVE ALL THE KNOWLEDGE PASSED DOWN TO HIM BY HIS TEACHERS IN ORDER TO PERPETUATE THE ART OF KARATE.

AS THE NATIONAL EXECUTIVE DIRECTOR FOR THE AAU KARATE, HANSHI DEL SAITO BELIEVES THAT A MORAL AND ETHICAL BASE SHOULD BE TAUGHT IN ALL THE DOJOS: "KARATE IS A SYSTEM WITH DEEP TRADITIONAL ROOTS. OUR SPIRITUAL NEEDS, OUR MORALITY, AND OUR BELIEFS HAVE SLIPPED INTO AN ABYSS," HE SAYS. "IT IS IMPORTANT TO ACT TO INVOLVE OURSELVES WITH PROPER ATTITUDES AND TO FIND OUT MORE ABOUT THE ABSOLUTE TRUTH. THIS IS THE TRUE BASIS OF THE ART OF KARATE-DO."

**How long have you been practicing the martial arts and why did you start karate training?**

Back in my childhood, I watched a lot of Chambara (samurai) movies, but karate and other martial arts were still mysterious to me. I knew more about sword fighting than any other martial art. My introduction to martial arts as a practitioner came when I was eleven years old, in 1961. I had convinced my parents to sign me up for Judo in Kahuku, a nearby sugar plantation town, and I can still remember the vigorous formal exercises that we were put through, as the sound and smell of the sugar mill also were a part of the dojo. I was just a skinny kid and many of my partners were on the chubby

# Karate Masters

"Our knuckles would get all callused and that was our trademark for karate excellence."

side and had a few pounds advantage over me. I hadn't yet figured out the throwing techniques and depended a lot on strength, which I also lacked. Needless to say, I cleaned the mat on many occasions and would go home frustrated. I wouldn't dare complain, however, because I knew my dad would lecture me on commitment and not feel sorry for me one bit. After a year of that "abuse," I was fortunate to meet Sensei Al Kahalekulu. He introduced himself to several of us kids during our summer break and asked if we were interested in karate. I jumped at that opportunity and managed to talk my parents into letting me sign up for his classes. As I recall, I told my parents that tuition was only five dollars per month and that the dojo was only a couple of miles away from home, in Sunset Beach. They agreed and a happy kid emerged from a shaky start in Judo to a more tolerable art of Chito-ryu karate-do.

**What was most interesting or challenging to you as a youngster?**

In karate, I would have to say that it was how to break boards and cinder blocks. My friends and I would meet after school or on the weekends to challenge each other on who could break the most boards or bricks. We would constantly be toughening our hands and feet by striking hard rubber targets or jury-rigged makiwara pads. Our knuckles would get all callused and that was our trademark for karate excellence. No one would mess with you if you had those calluses. Fortunately for me, that period did not last for more than a few months. The pain we suffered when the board or brick proved harder gave us a lot of laughs as well as tears.

Aside from karate, sand surfing had a great appeal to me. As the waves would swipe the sand and leave a slick surface, I would run, throw my flat smooth board in front of me, and jump on it for a thrilling ride into the oncoming surf. If my timing was less than perfect, the board would stick in the sand or would be enjoying the ride without a rider.

For lessons in life, the most interesting as well as challenging thing would have to be the Christian education I was exposed to since I was five years old. My parents were leaning towards the Buddhist religion back then, but never hesitated in placing me in a Christian School. We were taught strict principles and our teachers and pastor would even frown upon dancing. Yet the biblical stories and lessons were interesting and made a lot of sense. A lot of positive seeds were planted in my mind in those early years and it was always a challenge to stay on the straight and narrow path. I can say, though, that a sound spiritual base has been vital in steering me through much stormy weather and many of life's challenges.

**How many styles of karate or other martial arts methods have you trained in?**

Kodokan Judo, Chito-ryu Karate-do, shito-ryu Karate-do, and Muso Jikiden Eishin-ryu Iaijutsu.

**Who were your teachers during all these years?**

I had several. When I met Sensei Palimo (Judo), I was only eleven and don't remember too much about him, other than his emphasis on mat work, proper methods of grappling, footwork, throwing, and submission techniques. Later he allowed randori (sparring) and I certainly had my share of cleaning the mat.

Al Kahalekulu Sensei was a gentle yet tough sensei and he was the saving grace for me to exit from judo training. He introduced karate to me, and for that I will always be grateful. His training was tough and he always reminded us to polish our character. He made his monthly home visits to check how we were behaving and was a big asset for our parents, as they could keep us in check when we would get a bit testy. His Chito-ryu instructions helped me develop confidence.

Chuzo Kotaka Sensei was my first shito-ryu instructor. He emphasized the kihons and that in itself solidified my overall karate foundation. His vision was directed more into competition, and many of us did quite well in that arena. He still maintains that focus and his students continue to be very successful, winning at all levels of competition.

Kenzo Mabuni Soke was my second shito-ryu instructor and I came to know him as a sincere and good man, a friend, and a sensei who wanted to pass on his father's legacy as best he could. He had a clear vision as to what he wanted to accomplish. He wasn't interested in subjecting me to doing things exactly as he had his students do in Japan. Rather, while instructing me in kihon, kata, and kumite, he would point out things that seito shito-ryu emphasized. One of the major difference from his ryu-ha and my last shito-ryu experience was keeping all the preparatory positions closer and less exaggerated. Once I accomplished this, he was very pleased.

Masayuki Shimabukuro Sensei is my iaijutsu teacher. I am always fascinated with his stories of the samurai, their strict code, and their ability to use the sword. Sensei Shimabukuro has helped me understand how to make the sword come alive through perfection of technique and spirit.

**What was you first impression of Al Kahalekulu?**
A very powerful man who you did not want to mess with. Yet, you could sense compassion and kindness that kept you from avoiding him. Sensei Kahalekulu was a big Hawaiian man whose arms were larger than both of my thighs, and yet he could move very quickly and gracefully, which really impressed me. He taught me many lessons on life and his encouragement made it possible for me to improve my leadership skills. In the dojo, he would bark out commands, and because he gained our utmost respect, we poured everything we had in every class. In those days, we could not even scratch an itch or look around while we were in training. If you did anything that was unacceptable, a quick sting of the shinai reminded you to maintain total awareness on the task at hand. Our dojo was in an old house that someone had let us use, and the screenless windows invited many mosquitoes that we used as our excuse for getting swatted by the shinai. After each class, our dogi would be soaked from the workout, and walking home afterward in the cool offshore breeze made everything worthwhile.

**Have there been times when you felt fear in your training?**
I never felt fear in my training but needed lots of encouragement in teaching classes. I was very shy and had difficulty getting in front of people. The karate environment changed all that, as no one teased or commented negatively when I first began assisting in class. Unlike giving a book report in school, everyone in the dojo was respectful and understanding.

**What did your father do for a living?**
My dad was a carpenter and worked for my uncle Fred Shimote for many years. He then joined the union and began to work on some larger projects like the Del Webb Kuilima Hotel, now the Turtle Bay Hilton, on the North Shore of Oahu. My parents were born on Maui and were second-generation Japanese. During summers of my younger years, my dad would take me to work with him and would teach me how not to hit my thumbs with a hammer. I learned how a finish carpenter had to have lots of patience and car-

pentry skills to produce a finished product with excellence.

## Who were some of the karate notables when you first began karate training?

Well, there were quite a few names that I kept hearing back then, the first being Dr. Tsuyoshi Chitose, the Grandmaster and founder of the Chito-ryu karate-do group, who had his headquarters in Kumamoto City, Japan. Then there was Sensei Tommy Morita, who was the chief instructor of that style in Hawaii. I also would hear about other instructors, whom I eventually met later, such as Sensei Bobby Lowe of the Kyokushinkai group, Walter Nishioka from the Statewide Karate League, James Miyaji from the Butokukai, Kenneth Funakoshi from the Shotokan group, and Chuzo Kotaka from the IKF, whom I eventually trained with. There also were other instructors in other disciplines that were heading strong organizations in Hawaii as well as on the mainland, such as Professor Okazaki, a massage therapist and Jujitsu expert, Professor William Chow from the Kempo group, and Sonny and Adrian Emperado of the Kajukenbo group. As there were many ethnic groups in Hawaii, so were there diverse karate styles. This led to a strong martial arts base that eventually would make a great impact for the growth of karate in the United States as well as abroad.

"In the late sixties and early seventies, I was fortunate to meet several influential instructors who helped expose karate to many people throughout the country, if not throughout the world."

In the late sixties and early seventies, I was fortunate to meet several influential instructors who helped expose karate to many people throughout the country, if not throughout the world. One of them was Ray Dalke Sensei. He was one of the top JKA American instructors who trained directly under Hidetaka Nishiyama. I came to know Ray as a friend and respected him for his courage to accept me, a non-JKA (shotokan) practitioner, as his peer, rather than his adversary. We would practice together and help each other with the tournaments we held.

# Karate Masters

"I was introduced to Sensei Dan Ivan. I remember him as a considerate, kind, and very knowledgeable martial artist."

About that same period, I was introduced to Sensei Dan Ivan. I remember him as a considerate, kind, and very knowledgeable martial artist. He shared his interesting stories while he lived in Japan. He always helped me arrange demonstrations for my tournaments with his popular Japanese Village demonstration team. He reminded me of David Krieger, who helped Kotaka Sensei establish the *International Karate Federation*. Dan did the same for Sensei Fumio Demura, as they established the Japan Karate Federation in this country.

It was about 1971 that I met Sensei Chuzo Kotaka, and after several meetings, he accepted me into his organization. He impressed me with his strong techniques and beautiful form. He appointed me National Director for the IKF and I carried that position until 1999, when I decided to establish my own organization.

It was also in the 1970s that I met Sensei David Krieger. He was an exceptional man with a gentle heart. His karate was good and we had lots of great times together, both in Hawaii and in Santa Barbara, where he presently resides.

**Why do you think you and your friends were able to keep out of trouble?**
Many of us were poor compared to those who lived in the city. Parents lived paycheck to paycheck, and that taught us to share, to be creative, and to enjoy the outdoors. We all had gardens to manage and from that came many of our meals. We learned to work together and oftentimes we would all congregate at one of our buddies' homes to help him finish his chores in order for him to play with us. Most of the moms were at home, and they all made sure we behaved. Whenever anyone of us failed to measure up to what was expected of us, our parents were informed and the belts didn't feel so good when our dads came home. Parents also took the time to teach

us skills and lessons in life. They made sure we addressed the adults as Mr., Mrs., Miss, and Sir or name. Whenever we made a promise, they made sure we followed through. We also had supper together and I think that kept a tight family. We would never want to do anything that would shame our families or let our parents down.

**How long did it take you to really "get" karate?**

Not until many years of study of not only its technical aspect but also the challenges that solidified my understanding of character. The mental training was very trying and difficult to accept at times, but after hours of repetition, things started to connect and made sense. The clarity of the philosophy at times would become very cloudy, but that was because the underlying agendas of the karate leaders made it almost impossible to grasp the full concept of this art. Interestingly, the politics, personal goals, and organizational strategies of the leaders had a great deal of influence on the standards of karate. Some organizations were like fraternities, and if you endured their initiation and oftentimes humiliation, then you were considered one of the boys. Many traditional instructors prohibited their students from learning from other instructors and would ostracize those who did. It was all of those kinds of things that caused me to understand karate-do, and it was from then on that I felt it was my mission to help maintain karate-do in the spirit it was meant to be.

**What was your biggest frustration in training?**

From the technical point of view, at first the movements were very foreign and it took many months of training for them to sink in. In my early days of training, I was unable to reference books, video, or television. Everything was totally new and many aspects of karate were missing. It was like putting a puzzle together with many of the pieces missing. However, through time, I began to understand the principles that allowed me to execute the movements properly without being too stiff or overly zealous to be the best in my class.

The dojos of yesteryear usually were at community centers, churches, or classrooms shared by other groups, and supervised training was limited to only a few days per week. I wanted more direct instructions from the sensei, especially in the beginning stages, and I was frustrated when formal training was limited to only a few hours per week. My biggest frustration, however, was due to instructors who thought that their style was the only one that had any merit. Their tunnel vision caused many students to eventually abandon the traditional styles and to form their own open or "eclectic"

# Karate Masters

"Even my students now have surpassed me in many areas, and I am grateful that I was able to teach them."

styles. Perhaps that trend would have occurred anyway, but I would argue that it was because of these earlier instructor's attitudes that karate was revolutionized in this country.

Another frustration is how many instructors still hang onto the coattails of past martial artists who seem to have no one equal or better. If all that they still advocate and teach holds true, why is it that no one has yet achieved such a level of excellence. I know that in my style of karate, we have many outstanding teachers, students, and athletes. Even my students now have surpassed me in many areas, and I am grateful that I was able to teach them.

**Are any of the students you grew up with still active in karate?**

I don't think so, not from the original group of guys and gals that started with me. However, a good friend, John Isabelo, who began training with me a few years later, still works out with Sensei Walter Nishioka in Honolulu. He earned a "Medal of Valor" while serving with the Honolulu Police Department and was one of their outstanding homicide detectives. He now works as an investigator for the Attorney General's office for the State of Hawaii.

**Who were your biggest role models?**

Definitely my mom and dad. They both were loving and kind and always taught me life skills that I have learned and accepted. Mom was a housewife and always was home to care for me and my five brothers. She was always washing clothes, sewing, or cooking, and kept everyone of us in line. We had to learn how to wash, cook, iron, and clean house. My dad was a carpenter and worked constantly. Even after returning from his job, he would be working in the garden or doing something that he managed to involve us in. We would do everything the old-fashioned way, which was never easy, and he made sure that we did it right. He would even make his own bows and arrows and I would be the one to turn the handle for his makeshift lathe. I sure did my share of grumbling but little did I realize at that time that dad was teaching us how not to be afraid of work, which would have positive results both outwardly as well as inwardly. My parents never used profanity and always seemed to make ends meet.

My dad was interned right after the attack on Pearl Harbor. He was placed in a camp at Tule Lake, California, for about four years. Eventually, I began to ask my dad all kinds of questions about his ordeal, which I thought was totally unfair. He never once had anything negative to say about our country, even though he had to endure those troubling times. He would remind me however, that in order to prove that we (the Japanese people in Hawaii) are good citizens, we needed to move on to become productive and hard workers. I always remembered those words of wisdom and respected him even more.

Aside from my parents, my first instructor had a lot of influence on me. His concern on my well being also helped me at home. Sensei Kahalekulu would make periodic visits to my home and would check to see if I was practicing my karate, by-laws, and resolutions. My parents also would remind me whenever I became too testy, that their report to sensei would not be taken favorably. I would immediately straighten up, as even the slightest thought of upsetting him was too embarrassing.

I attended Sunset Beach Christian School on the North Shore of Oahu from Kindergarten to eighth grade. One of my favorite teachers was Miss Aileen Miller. She was a sweet educator who had lots of patience, and her love for her students was very apparent. Her close relationship to the Lord, total commitment to her mission work and daily instructions, provided me with an abundance of hope in the years of challenges that would come my way.

David Krieger was another great man whom I admired, and was in many ways a role model for me. He was well-educated and the person responsible for getting the IKF started with Kotaka Sensei. He held a Ph.D. in Political Science and headed the Peace Now Foundation (a nuclear disarmament program) based out of Santa Barbara, California. Since then, he has also completed law school and obtained his real estate broker's license. He also is a very accomplished Shito-ryu sensei and founded the Pacific Karate-do Institute. David Krieger was a gentle man who would find good in people and did not dwell on the negative. Although very intellectual, he would not even remotely talk down to anyone, even if they were quite ignorant. I admired all he stood for.

# Karate Masters

Another role model was my late friend, Mr. Henry Takaki. He was the local postman, and would take time on the weekends to gather a few of us kids to treat us to a movie. He would teach us how to communicate and think, and would do so by cleverly asking us things that would spark our interest. He always was involved with community organizations, and spent countless hours in keeping the North Shore community alive and educated. He was instrumental in guiding me to be involved with community projects and taught me about volunteerism.

**Did you prefer kata or kumite?**

I preferred kumite at first because we were not allowed to spar until several months after signing up for classes. We would watch the adults spar and then, on the way home from the dojo, stop at Ehukai Park at the Bansai Pipeline and mimic the moves. We made sparring very dramatic as we would announce to our opponents what technique we were about to do. As I recall, the "Shooting Star" was one of our favorites; it was a glorified jump kick that was prepped by Kung Fu-like hand gestures. We had a blast and thought that was the ultimate in karate. It was not until my senior year in high school that I became more interested in kata. I guess I came to realize that the kata held more information and learning tools that I could gather with more acceptance and seriousness of its practice. That realization came from my personal development and maturing. As I'm getting older, I enjoy kata more than ever. The bunkai-oyo, or practical application, and kakushite (hidden techniques) are fascinating, and the wealth of information kata holds always amazes me. I still enjoy kumite as well, as it pushes me to maintain my agility and stamina while maintaining my distance and timing practice. It also is more enjoyable sparring with my friends as we have come to learn how to train with it rather than to prove our strength by hurting each other.

**Did you compete a lot in Hawaii?**

Not a lot. When I first started training, my instructor was not into competition. It was not until the late 60s that I began to compete in Hawaii, and I competed in only a handful of events there. By the seventies, I had already moved to Southern California and was more interested in preparing my students for competition. The last tournament that I competed in was in Hawaii in the early 80s, where I was fortunate to win first in all my events.

Most of the tournaments I competed in were in California. Kumite in those days were all shobu-ippon or one-point matches. You could be preparing for a tournament for months only to be beaten in a couple of seconds. There were only a few round-robin or double elimination tournaments. And repechage was not even heard of. Athletes back then did not want to win by contact penalties, either. If your nose was broken, you would hold the bleeding with toilet paper and be ready to fight on. We were tough then but perhaps our young impressionable age made us a bit foolish. But how much fun it was just to survive. I just hope that the abuse we put our bodies through doesn't come back to haunt us.

The most enjoyable and memorable competitions and events were those at the Japanese Village and Deer Park presented by Senseis Fumio Demura and Dan Ivan. Not only was the Japanese Park setting ideal, but there were always players from Japan who kept the competition interesting. One year, after winning the Black Belt Kata division, I met a stocky Japanese in the finals. After several exchanges, I landed a front kick to his stomach that nearly tore my toes off. The pain was excruciating but the win made it bearable. Until this day, I am reminded of that match every time I look at my crooked toe.

"The most enjoyable and memorable competitions and events were those at the Japanese Village and Deer Park presented by Senseis Fumio Demura and Dan Ivan."

### Who were your greatest rivals and what were they like?

I guess I would have to say the players from Japan. In those days, all you heard about in competition was how tough the Japanese Nationals were. They were the ones that ruled. So whenever I had the opportunity to face one of them, I was very prepared. Fortunately I was able to beat every one of them. Aside from competition, our greatest rivals were students and instructors from other dojos. Oftentimes, they would appear unannounced to challenge you to a kumite match just to test your worthiness. Some of those fights would get pretty rough, but if you emerged victorious, you would be left alone. Those that didn't fare well eventually closed their dojos.

# Karate Masters

"One of the positive changes I see is that more traditionalists are allowing their students to mingle and to train with other instructors in the form of clinics."

**What are your favorite techniques?**

I have managed very well with keeping my arsenal simple. I rely on foot sweeps, thrusts and front kicks for success. The magic is in the timing, distancing, and confident execution of the techniques; and of course, strategy has an important role in packaging my delivery. Some have said that I have a mean look about me when I'm in the ring which causes my opponents to be intimidated. If that works, I guess I won't be needing the services of a plastic surgeon.

**How has your personal expression karate developed over the years?**

One of the positive changes I see is that more traditionalists are allowing their students to mingle and to train with other instructors in the form of clinics. It would seem a given that an instructor would see to it that his students have accomplished instructors. As an example, parents who think they can teach their children everything, and not allow them to be exposed to others to be taught or mentored, are surely stunting their potential to grow. As for development of the karateka, I believe today's students are stronger, have more technical savvy and develop quicker than those when I first began training. The understanding of nutrition, stretching, muscle development, psychology, plyometrics, et cetera, plus easy access to information, gives the modern karate warrior access to many more pieces of this fascinating puzzle. Of course the old timers who are still active also have progressed and can hold their own. They still possess courage and confidence that equal or oftentimes surpass the younger martial artists.

We definitely were tougher back in the old days. We never wore any protective gear, and if you got hurt, other than very severe injuries, you kept on going. Much of the kumite training was to survive. It was that kind of dojo climate we all endured, and you had to be prepared for outsiders who would come to your dojo to basically challenge you (dojo yaburi).

The important point of my teaching is to utilize karate-do as a vehicle to develop good character, healthy minds and bodies, and assist in directing those who I serve to learn to be of service to others. Students, on the other hand need, to understand and practice commitment. Students who are committed to learning correctly and training for the long haul provide me with the opportunity to expose them to all the necessary tools to build a solid foundation. From strong roots and with healthy spirits, students will be able to keep a healthy attitude to preserve the style for others to learn and enjoy.

I don't think that it is healthy or even reasonable to cling to things that have no room for improvement. Changes and adjustments are necessary as long as they don't wander too far from the original source. Can you imagine where medicine would be today if we kept it "pure" as of yesteryear?

**Do you think different 'styles' are truly important in the art of karate?**

I think it is good to maintain the various styles, as each has many unique qualities and flavor. Styles offer healthy choices for students. Once they have come to understand their style, they can better appreciate other styles while maintaining their unique characteristics and integrity.

**What is your opinion of fighting events such as the UFC and Mixed Martial Arts?**

I imagine there is a following for that type of fighting. Perhaps there is even a need for those who feel that they have to constantly prove that they can whip others into submission. It should be kept away from the impressionable eyes of our youngsters.

**Karate nowadays often is referred to as a sport . . . would you agree with this definition, or is a martial art?**

There is definitely "sport karate." In fact, many athletes only practice kumite if they wish to excel in sparring, or practice only kata if they wish to perform well in that arena. True karatekas learn how to defend themselves internally and externally. The delicate balance to practice correctly is definitely a part of the martial aspect of karate. Senseis need to sculpt a landscape that all students, young and old, can appreciate. Too often, I see older students retire and put to pasture because the interests of their teachers have waned. A healthy dojo would have many seniors practicing eagerly for the love of the art, nothing more.

# Karate Masters

"Without the proper discipline and respect, teaching becomes almost a chore rather than a blessing."

**How do you think karate has most influenced you?**
By teaching me from a young age to be disciplined, focused, and balanced. By doing so, I became confident and overcame my shyness. What the public schools lacked in fulfilling my shortcomings, my karate school provided. Throughout the years, karate has opened the door to many opportunities to serve in a leadership capacity. Karate also has led me to meet many outstanding practitioners of the martial arts, and has provided me the opportunity to help others overcome their obstacles. Karate has become a part of my life and, as life unfolds countless lessons, so does karate. I am always searching for ways to keep students healthy and active, in order to provide me with enough time to teach them adequately. As the new-age approach of teaching has invaded many circles, I want to maintain the disciplined dojo atmosphere without negative reactions from students or parents. Without the proper discipline and respect, teaching becomes almost a chore rather than a blessing.

**When did you get involved with the AAU Karate?**

In the mid 80s, I met Sensei Joe Mirza, another Shotokan practitioner, at one of Dalke sensei's tournaments in Riverside, California. He was a man of good character and his love for karate became very apparent to me. Soon after that first meeting, Joe Mirza convinced me that I should become active in the AAU National Karate Program, which he was chairman of. I guess he sensed that I was looking for an organization that I could really sink my teeth into, to make a difference in strengthening classical Karate-do in the U.S. My hat goes off to him as he has accomplished so many things that our earlier pioneers pursued but came up short on. His passion and dream to take Karate-do to greater heights of excellence also has made me partner with him to make that a reality.

**How do you see karate in the U.S.A. at the present time?**

Confused. Instructors who have used martial arts as a business are winging the approaches of successful operators who make a hefty income from their dojos. I say more power to those who have been financially successful. I'm sure they are not losing any sleep at night, despite the fact that their students look rather sloppy in their techniques. Then you have those instructors who keep their students in one rank for a long time and boast how difficult it is to obtain a black belt at their school. Their classes are small and, even if their students look impressive, their growth potential is almost nil. How then can we keep karate-do growing in a wholesome way without damaging the integrity of our precious treasure? All true senseis need to be finding a sane and wholesome solution.

**How does the karate style differ from other martial arts methods when applying the techniques in a self-defense situation?**

I would hope that karatekas would defend themselves wisely, quickly and effectively. By utilizing self-defense techniques of awareness, confidence, and positive body language, karate students will be able to defend themselves before actually being attacked. Some of the other martial arts provoke one to attack just to test his or her abilities. I recall a martial art school in Hawaii that did just that. The instructor taught his students how to fight, and after training they would go to the local bar and stir up trouble with the GIs so they could test their techniques. Technically, karate incorporates grappling, throwing, submission maneuvers, and non-tournament applications that are very effective. Regardless of the techniques applied, karatekas understand the need for control and not abuse their right to defend themselves.

# Karate Masters

Self-defense is a very important element in the art of karate-do. And self-defense is not only physical but mental and emotional as well. Sport karate also should be urged as a learning tool for competition. Life is competitive in many ways and, despite all the necessary preparations, there are winners and those that have to wait for other opportunities.

**Forms and sparring: what's the proper ratio in training?**

In the beginning the ratio should be 90 percent kata. After the kihon is solid, sparring and forms should then be equal. Then, for those who reach the autumn of their lives, I feel the ratio to be 70–80 percent kata and a slower pace of sparring. Kata is very important in the budo aspect of karate-do. By practicing kata, one can fulfill physical and mental training and learn how to become victorious over oneself; that is, to destroy the enemy within. So many times, students, especially adults, are hesitant in performing kata in front of an audience due to their insecurities. Yet, by practice and encouragement, they learn to push that aside and come to enjoy the opportunity to share the movement of their body with the proper components with others. Kata also is a very ingenious way of transmitting information from teacher to student in order to preserve the style and self-defense techniques.

**Do you have any general advice you would care to pass on to the practitioners?**

Seek out the right sensei. One of the most important phases of training is the beginning. Correct application of techniques, healthy attitude, wholesome philosophy, and a clean and safe environment are important considerations to hold in your quest for karate excellence.

Train regularly. Hold yourselves accountable to your trusted dojo mates and keep karate a healthy attitude that nourishes your mind, body and spirit.

For senseis, learn to communicate effectively. It is an ongoing process that needs to be understood in depth in order for positive learning to take place. Instructors and students alike have a built-in basis, such as culture, religion, politics, and age. For example in many circles, physical contact is taught to be kept within the immediate family. As a result, when a teacher corrects a student's technique by touching him or her, it may not be taken as the teacher intended, but rather cause a negative reaction because it may be in direct violation of the parent's rules. Religions that advocate that one should not bow to anyone but God bring questions of bowing to others in the dojo. And then there are those who teach their children to always question authority because many who are placed in superior positions have abused their power and taken advantage of those in their care. These are some of the filters that need to be addressed to maintain an open line of communication. Compared to the World War I veterans, who were totally committed to honor, respect, duty, and sacrifice, the Baby Boomers believe that honor is based on their personal ideals, duty is formulated with teamwork and not independent hard work, respect may come after authority is questioned, and respect is embraced only if it encompasses diversity.

**What do you consider to be the major changes in the art since you began training?**

More networking with other instructors and students is tolerated. The earlier pioneers were myopic and hard-headed in many ways, and considered themselves to be the authorities of karate-do, when in reality, they were young, adjusting to a different culture, and building a reputation for themselves. They frowned upon mingling with practitioners of other styles not their own, and made those who came from Japan achieve higher status no matter if they were juniors to those who were their sen-pai here in the States. This resulted in a major meltdown and the beginning of the American revolution of the martial arts. I don't know if we can bring the extreme right wing martial artist to some happy medium with the left, but those of us who understand karate-do must work together to preserve what we have.

"Those of us who understand karate-do must work together to preserve what we have."

**Who would you like to have trained with that you have not?**

Chojun Miyagi and Kenwa Mabuni. Miyamoto Musashi for Iaijutsu. Miyagi Sensei knew that many trappings, such as belt color and titles, would allow karate teachers to be judged by their belt and rank, rather than their character.

# Karate Masters

**What can you tell us about the late Soke Mabuni Kenzo?**

I came to know him as a dear friend and I respected him greatly. He supported me when many of his own instructors first had doubts about me, especially when they were unclear as to my real motives in karate-do. Soke Mabuni also recognized my TKO organization and the AAU as important organizations of Karate-do. He made it possible for me to run my organization without having to interrupt our day-to-day operations by joining another organization. He provided me with a direct line to him. He trusted me with making wise decisions that would enhance the betterment of Shito-ryu in this country as well as abroad. When he stayed in my home, it was a treat to hear his stories of his dad and of what karate meant to him. It was also a joy to go outside with him to practice kata. I was also very honored when Soke allowed me to direct the 4th International Shito Cup in Grants Pass. I admired him for being able to be a great leader, orchestrating as well as challenging all the leaders in his organization. I also saw the special joy he had seeing children performing kata. The smiles and twinkle in his eyes clearly told me what karate is about. The autumn of his life began to wear on him; yet, although very frail, he managed to be a part of our AAU Nationals. He loved karate for the right reasons and I will always remember that.

**What keeps you motivated after all these years?**

Students who have grown to be outstanding citizens and continue to be of service to others. Students who have overcome adversities thanks to their karate training. My good friends and colleagues who continue to strive to maintain a sane and useful art.

**What is the philosophical basis for your karate training?**

Train with what you are able to accomplish without injuring yourself. Always try your best but don't beat yourself down in the trying.

**After all these years of training and experience, could you explain the meaning of the practice of karate?**

If you are talking about keiko and not renshu (training), I believe it goes hand-in-hand with shu-ha-ri (the stages of learning and mastery). Drawing from the past to identify the core of karate-do is important. Once a level of mastery is present, the journey then requires improvement to better the path of those who preceded us. Incorporate the infinite wisdom of old with modern concepts. This kind of understanding will keep the art improving with each generation. That is and should be the practice of karate-do.

**How do you think karate practitioners can increase their understanding of the spiritual aspect of the art?**

I believe that as one becomes more in harmony with oneself and with others, a deep spirited manifestation to seek truth becomes apparent. God has planted seeds in each one of us to grow and to seek Him. He has provided an internal compass to find Him. Through practice, one needs to understand what is God's will as opposed to man's will. In the dojo, we are constantly appraised to determine our self-worth. Unlike buying a car or property, where the worth is based on the blue book or appraiser, our worth should not be left to the sole appraisal of the sensei. We need a higher source to keep our character value high. For example, there are instructors who keep students who make them look good on a pedestal and allow their shortcomings to be overlooked. Then, there are those who will keep promoting students, not keeping them at a high standard, fearful that they may quit and reduce their financial bottom line. That self-interest equates to selfishness and ultimately results in disappointments. Senseis and students need to look for the interests of others. This will result in humility. Spiritually, then, we should all keep God as the captain of our ship and allow Him to direct us in our karate mission in order that we may all stay the course.

"In the dojo we are constantly appraised to determine our self-worth."

**Is anything lacking in the way martial arts are taught today compared to how they were you began?**

I would have to say seriousness. We worked hard and learned karate to experience the unexpected. It was survival. If you were not serious, you paid for it. For many these days, karate is just another seasonal extracurricular activity.

# Karate Masters

"Instructors need to reevaluate their teaching methods in order to maintain a good student enrollment."

**Could I ask you what you consider the most important qualities of a successful karate practitioner?**

Trustworthiness, humility, and sincerity, augmented with the willingness to train hard on a regular basis. Learning karate-do to improve one's well-being and applying it in one's daily life in order to be a productive and outstanding citizen. To apply karate lessons which have been rooted in one's moral values and overall conduct that defends one from negative peer pressures.

**What advice would you give to students on the question of supplementary training (running, weights, et cetera)?**

I recommend wind sprints, correct weight training, stretching, (cross-training), plyometrics, and balancing it with healthy reading, fishing, and golf.

**Why do you think that a lot of students start falling away after two or three years of training?**

I blame lack of enthusiasm, too many extracurricular activities that fog the vision, classes that become boring and lack motivation, and phases of their lives that need more tending to. Also, lack of commitment; disciplined environment (the dojo) not readily accepted by today's youths; other activities such as soccer; computer games; parents who don't take the time to teach their children commitment; and the relaxed overall attitude that becomes a conflict with a structured and disciplined dojo.

And the old methods of instructing need to be modified in order to keep students long enough to be able to teach them the true benefits of karate-do. With all the extra fun curricular activities available, instructors need to reevaluate their teaching methods in order to maintain a good student enrollment. The fact is that many technically unqualified karate instructors, as judged by the traditional masters, pack their schools with hundreds of students. Their modern methods of teaching fits in perfectly with the times, and their marketing and business savvy puts many of these masters to shame in that department.

For other disciplines, one marketing strategy is to make the black belt easily attainable, much easier than at the classical dojos. Once achieved, this new black belt will always elevate their status and spread the greatness of their style, school and instructor. Traditional instructors, on the other hand, relish how hard it is for their students to achieve the black belt. It becomes a no-brainer when a parent asks how many students have achieved their black belt this year and you say five, compared to 100 in a non-traditional school. I'm not advocating that we all begin teaching that way or begin handing out black belts, but we certainly need to re-think how we can preserve our art.

### What led you to become the Director for the Traditional Karate-Do Organization?

I would have to say that all the interesting chapters of my life led to my present position with the TKO. In the late 60s, Sensei Al Kahelekulu retired completely from karate. He gave me the authority to continue teaching Chitose-ryu and promoted me to Godan. I then formed the Goshinjutsu Organization and was unattached to any other organization at that time. My dad had heard the name Goshinjutsu and said that it was a good name so I agreed. I had Sensei Kahalekulu sign each certificate and operated the independent organization until the early 70s, when I joined Kotaka sensei's IKF. In 1998, Sensei Jo Mirza, who had already established the TKO, invited me to head the Shito-Ryu Division. I told him that I would perhaps consider it one day, not knowing that I would accept the offer the very next year. Sensei Kotaka had made a few changes in his organizational operations, which led to my resignation from the IKF. I informed all of my branch instructors of my decision and gave them my blessing if they wished to remain attached with the IKF. Fortunately for me, they all decided to trailblaze with me, and as they say, the rest is history.

### What would be your ideal for karate?

That karate would be incorporated into every junior and high school. I think there is a definite need in the school system for this kind of training, which could benefit everyone involved. I believe that ingredients of discipline, respect, honor, awareness, motivation, accountability, and responsibility provided in a dojo atmosphere would definitely extend into the classroom. I see so many good kids who have too much unsupervised time that gets them in trouble. If we could only figure out a way to minimize that

# Karate Masters

"Those who understand what our service provides for them will stay and become a vital force in keeping the positive training spirit alive."

problem and get them involved in a wholesome yearly activity, the lessons they would reap will keep them from learning the hard way.

**To what do you attribute the success of your program?**

Honesty, fairness, and my autocratic methods of running my program have been the keys to the success of our schools and organization. Karate sensei, students, and parents need to be assured that what we provide is a sound program that will be of benefit to them. I always make sure that each person has ample time to research our program before admitting him or her to our school or organization. I go over what is expected of them and what they can expect from me. My leadership in the dojo is not democratic because, throughout all the years of teaching, I have found it to be ineffectual, that it leads to wasted time, confusion, and at times even corruption. Those who understand what our service provides for them will stay and become a vital force in keeping the positive training spirit alive. Those who choose not to embrace our philosophy will fade away and not harm the prestige or integrity of our program. As for training, I still demand the utmost respect and discipline from every student. They do not leave the mat as they wish, and I expect them to give their best effort. Their achievements are based on their own hard work and diligence, and once they figure that out, they have learned the formula for success. I also end each class with a brief discussion on lessons of life, which include nutrition, behavior, dating, community service, and drugs, to name a few.

**Do you think that Olympics will be positive for the art of karate-do in case that happens one day?**

I don't know about the art of karate, but it may be for the sport if it main-

"Seize every opportunity to keep karate-do from eroding, and to maintain its integrity for future generations to enjoy."

tains many of the classical principles that we now embrace. If the international sports leaders constantly change the composition of karate just to satisfy the sport aspect, then the UFC type of fighting may seem to be more appropriate for the IOC. It would certainly be clearer who the winners are.

**What are your thoughts on the future of karate?**

I am very optimistic. Although many of the pioneers of karate in this country had their shortcomings, those who made a sincere attempt to teach and preserve what they knew with passion and conviction can be appreciated and respected for their efforts. Likewise, today's instructors must teach wholesomely and seize every opportunity to keep karate-do from eroding, and to maintain its integrity for future generations to enjoy. O

# FRANK SMITH

## A HEART FULL OF FIRE

FRANK SMITH HOLDS A VERY SPECIAL PLACE IN THE HISTORY OF KARATE IN AMERICA. A PIONEER IN FIGHTING FOR WHAT HE BELIEVED – REGARDLESS OF THE CONSEQUENCES – SMITH BECAME A "POWERHOUSE" NAME IN THE COUNTRY DURING THE 1960S. HE WAS LARGELY RESPONSIBLE FOR TRANSFORMING THE KARATE COMPETITION ARENA INTO A TEST OF STRENGTH AND COURAGE. HIS GOOD LOOKS, POLISHED MANNERS, AND IMMACULATE TECHNIQUE EARNED FRANK SMITH A REPUTATION THAT CROSSED FRONTIERS, REACHING TO THE VERY SAME JKA HEADQUARTERS IN JAPAN. HIS DETERMINATION, SELF-CONFIDENCE, AND DRIVE MADE HIM ENEMIES AS EASILY AS HE CHARMED OTHERS. HE ALWAYS WANTED TO BE A KARATE-KA AND NOTHING ELSE. HE LOVED THE ART AND THE CHALLENGE, THE TRAINING AND THE SWEAT. HIS TALENT, BACKED BY UNSHAKABLE SELF-BELIEF, PROVED HE HAD MADE THE RIGHT CHOICE. "HE HAD THE KEENEST AND MOST ANALYTICAL BRAIN THAT EVER GRACED THE ART OF KARATE IN AMERICA," SAID ONE OF THE GREATEST JKA INSTRUCTORS OF ALL TIME WHEN DESCRIBING SMITH'S TECHNICAL SKILLS.

HE DECIDED TO RETIRE IN 1990, BUT NOT BEFORE SAYING WHAT HE HAD TO SAY TO THOSE WHO HAD TO HEAR IT. HE NEVER PULLED ANY PUNCHES AND EVEN TODAY, HE WILL SPEAK HIS MIND WITH A PAINFUL HONESTY MIXED WITH A DELIGHTFUL CHARISMA... AND SAYS THAT IF YOU ARE NOT TOUGH ENOUGH TO TAKE IT, GET UP AND LEAVE.

**When and why did you start practicing the art of karate?**

I was 13 years old when my school friend wanted to take Judo. He was my best friend, so I went along. We started training in Judo. The instructor told us that in Judo you must first learn to break your fall when you're thrown. All we did was fall backwards and slap the mat over and over. Then, we would flip to the left and then to right side, slapping the mat. Then, they threw us all over the dojo. All the time, I was complaining: when do I get to throw someone around. This was not fun. I was a 13-year-old with chronic back pain. I didn't know at the time how valuably learning to fall would serve me in karate.

# Karate Masters

"When I saw the JKA/ Shotokan instructors do their demonstrations. I was hooked. I had never seen that level of karate before."

One day we went to the dojo to train, but the dojo was closed. The judo instructor had quit; there were not enough students. We were told: you will have a new instructor soon. The call came two weeks later: come and train.

My friend said he was quitting. So I went alone to train with the new judo instructor. I was determined to get my turn to throw someone around the dojo—a young boy, wanting the pound of flesh that was due to him. The new instructor's name was Bill Babich. He was a Ni-Dan. There were about 25 people in the class. Some students were wearing purple and green belts. Two had brown belts.

We lined up for class, and the brown belts walked around assisting the instructor. The instructor demonstrated an upward block and a reverse punch. I called one of the 16-year-old brown belts and asked him: "What are we doing? I had never done this with my other judo instructor." The brown belt looked at me and said, "This is not judo; this is Shorin-Ryu Karate." That was in 1958 and the rest is history. I had trained for 32 years, at the time I resigned in April 1990.

**How many styles of karate or other methods have you trained in?**

I trained in judo for six months; I do not recall the instructor's name. I then trained four years in Shorin-Ryu Karate. I obtained my Sho-Dan, at age 16 years. In 1961, I went to the first AAKF Karate Tournament held at the Olympic Auditorium in Los Angeles. It was my first time to see organized competition. When I saw the JKA/ Shotokan instructors do their demonstrations. I was hooked. I had never seen that level of karate before. I started training one year later with Sensei Nishiyama, in November 1962.

**Please tell us some interesting stories of your early days in karate and your experience training under Hidetaka Nishiyama.**

Sensei Nishiyama had the extraordinary ability to motivate and get every ounce of sweat out of you. He could push you to the limits of your mental and physical endurance.

I remember my first Team Summer Camp in Oxnard, California, in August 1964. We rented a house on the beach for one week. The dojo was at a Buddhist Church in the city of Oxnard. Our instructors were Senseis Nishiyama and Mori from New York. This was the time before summer camps were popular.

The L.A. Central Dojo Team at that time was approximately 12 people total. I was the youngest in age and rank, a Sho-Dan of one month. So I had to sleep in the garage where everyone hung their smelly gis, with five other low on the pole guys like myself. We were up at 5:00 a.m., on the beach by 5:30. We trained for one hour, stretching, doing basics, and ran three miles. We had to be at the dojo, ready to train at 8:00 a.m. The morning training was two hours in basics and kata. The afternoon class was from 1:00 to 4:00 p.m., a total of three hours. This was the hardest training I can ever remember doing. We trained one and a half hours, then we were given a five-minute rest. Everyone ran for a drink of water. Then, we started the second one and a half hours. This was every day for six days.

The only way I could make it through the training was by knowing that we were going to get a five-minute break. If had to train straight through the total three hours without stopping, I don't think I could have made it through the training. When I think back to that time, Sensei Nishiyama was the best instructor I ever trained with. He could push you past your limits, limits that you didn't know you had.

**Were you a natural at karate? Did the movements come easily to you?**

When I was starting, I was big for my age. At 13 years old, my body was starting to develop muscles. The movements or actions in karate at that young age became normal quickly, or natural to me, and I was self-motivated. I also was fortunate to have a mother who understood the value a proper diet and balanced meals. We ate all the food groups. We also ate at the same time every day, at 5 p.m.. When I was young, I never ate what is now called fast food. My classes started at 7:00 p.m., so I had enough time to digest my food and have energy. I also never ate after training. This was very important.

**Do you think karate has changed/developed over the years? How do you see the evolution of the art?**

Karate is very popular throughout the world today. People are people and karate is karate. What has changed is society as a whole, but this is inevitable. What has changed from my early years in the 60s? I don't remember seeing any children and only a few women in the dojo. Today, this has changed, for the best. Karate is art for the people—men, woman, and children, young and old. It's not just for the athlete who wants to compete in tournaments.

**Do you think different styles are truly important in the art of karate? Why or why not?**

We are very fortunate in this country to have such a wide variety of martial arts to choose from. I think all styles or methods of karate have something to offer. We have styles that teach hard /soft, passive/aggressive, and weapons/non-weapons. Most styles offer self-defense or competitive sport karate. People training in karate must be careful. If you want to train in more than one style, do it one at a time. You may find a conflict in styles, including your instructors. I trained in one style four years, and JKA/Shotokan 28 years. My advice: find one style and perfect it. My training in Shotokan style will last me for a lifetime. Remember the old adage, "Jack of all trades, master of none."

**After wining several major national championships, you were "told" not to compete anymore. Why was that and how do you think that affected you personal progression in the art and also the level of the competition in the U.S.?**

After I won my fifth National Tournament in 1969, Sensei Nishiyama summoned me to his office. He said: "You will no longer be competing in any of the local or national tournaments. You may only complete at the international level." My first thought was that this did not make any sense. I was 25 years old, with the rank of San-Dan. In karate, one doesn't reach maturity until age 34. The U.S. National Tournament was the stepping-stone to test and hone your skills for international competition. It was the method of selecting the strongest competitors. How would I maintain the level to compete internationally? His decision would reverse the direction of the dojo, and was part of the internal politics in the school.

I stopped training with the Central Dojo Team in protest in early 1970. Soon after that, only three or four people would show up for team training. Sensei Nishiyama refused to teach, so the team dissolved. All of the senior people I trained with had left...all due to politics. To my knowledge, he has never produced a team as strong again. It was the end of an era for the United States to have an opportunity to reach a higher level of karate.

I did not leave or quit the dojo. I self-trained in the dojo, three days a week. I also trained with Sensei Yutaka Yaguchi. He was Nishiyama's assistant instructor, a Go-Dan at that time and JKA Instructor. He was also third place Kumite Champion 1965.

Sensei Yaguchi taught on Tuesday and Thursday at the Central Dojo. I would meet him at the dojo, after he finished teaching class. We would get everyone out of the dojo around 9:30 p.m. and lock the door. We would free spar for 1 or 2 hours, two nights a week. We did this for about two years, until he was sent to Denver, Colorado, to open a dojo. Sensei Yaguchi was a friend and my best man at my wedding. We always maintained an instructor/student relationship in the dojo. He was fast and capable of hitting you with any technique. We would spar and he would try different techniques. At first, I was taking a lot hits from him. That was okay; I was learning. We were keeping in shape and were both benefiting from the opportunity.

Most of the people I trained with did not have Yaguchi's speed or skill level. We would spar, and he would tell me, "you are to close" or "your face is open." He would warn me two or three times. If I did not adjust, he would attack me, holding nothing back. I learned really fast. This training elevated my level in strategy. When I sparred with other people, they all seemed to be slow in comparison to Sensei Yaguchi's speed and power.

Sparring with Sensei Yaguchi, as the student, I always had to take what he gave and never show any pain. One day, I saw Mrs. Yaguchi at the dojo. She said, "Frank, I want to talk you." I replied, "Yes, what can I do for you?" In broken English, she said, "you too strong now, Frank; take it easy on my husband. He always comes home and complains about pain...you hit him." I told her that I was very sorry and I thanked her. She had no idea how much that meant to me—that pain was being inflicted both ways and neither one of us would show it to each other!

**Karate nowadays is often referred to as a sport. Would you agree with this definition?**

No, I would not agree. Karate's origins were formed and taught with specific applications to defend oneself. Self-defense is the spirit to survive—to save one's life, maybe your own, against a hostile person who tries to do harm to you. Karate should first be a martial art. Then, sport is used to test your level and skills. Karate is a martial art. Its origins are from Okinawa.

# Karate Masters

"Karate will survive as a martial art. Karate will not survive if taught only as a sport."

Karate was a means of self-defense for the peasant people: men, women, both young and old. Sport karate is okay, but it must be reinforced by the roots and foundation as a martial art.

Sport karate, however, is the spirit to win at competition, to test or measure one's ability against another opponent, who also is trying to win. It's a contest to enjoy and have fun, win or lose. But, of course, the goal is to win decisively.

If an instructor only teaches sport karate, because that is all he knows, or it's how he was taught, he will flounder like a ship lost at sea because he is limited. Karate will survive as a martial art. It has for 300 years. Karate will not survive if taught only as a sport, without its martial arts foundation. This could be one of the reasons there is so much division and politics in karate.

To explain this, in sport karate, the goal is to score and gain points without making hard contact to win a trophy. If you make contact, you lose the match. Self-defense is to drive your elbow as far as you can into the base of your attacker's neck, three times before stopping. I know that sounds brutal and violent—a trophy vs. the possibility of serious injury or losing your life... two different approaches. I don't mean to be dramatic, but I hope readers understand my point. I know the UFC- type fighters understand what I am talking about.

**Many people recall the incident with Keinosuke Enoeda, when he was visiting the U.S. What can you tell us about it?**

I have heard many different stories over the years. One I remember is that Enoeda and I were in a tournament, when he kicked me in the head with full contact. If that were true, I would have won, because he would have been disqualified for contact. That would have been big news at the time!

This is what happened: Sensei Enoeda was on a world tour after he had won the All Japan/World Championships in Tokyo. It was April 1963. His final destination was England. His second stop was Hawaii, then Los Angeles. Senseis Kase, Enoeda, Shirai, and Kanazawa arrived in Los Angeles on June 4, 1963. The LA Team met them at the airport to greet them with a big "oss" and carry their bags. It was a big deal... they were celebrities! Especially Enoeda; he was the World Champion. The only words I spoke to Enoeda that day were, "May I have your autograph?" which he gave me by the way.

I was told they would be training and practicing their demos at the Central Dojo the next day at noon. I remember it was a Friday. I took off work to see them train. I would not have missed it. That morning when I arrived, the dojo was very crowded, and the people were standing only; nobody was sitting to allow more room. The four JKA instructors were warming up on the floor. Senseis Nishiyama and Okazaki walked on the floor to start the training.

Sensei Nishiyama saw me standing in the crowd. He walked over to me and asked if I had my gi. I said "yes." He said, "Good. you train now!" With the speed of a rabbit, I went for my gi, changed, and was on the dojo floor ready to train. Sensei Nishiyama was in charge of the training. After warming up with basics, we lined up for free sparring. I first sparred with Shirai. He was very strong and fast. Nishiyama told me to attack him as hard as I could. I knew if I didn't, it would be disrespectful. Shirai escaped with ease; he was very soft and smooth. There was not much body contact between us, just moving around the floor sparring.

We rotated sparring partners. I was now standing before the great World Champion, Keinosuke Enoeda. I thought: what a great honor to train with him. Sensei Nishiyama again told me to attack as hard and show good spirit. He escaped easily, as Shirai had. After a few minutes of attacking with no success, Nishiyama told Enoeda something in Japanese.

The next thing I knew, I took a roundhouse kick to the head with full power. It dropped me to my knees. A lot of blood was coming out of my mouth. I knew my jaw was broken because I couldn't close my mouth.

I read somewhere, "Smith deserved what he got because he showed no mercy to anyone." Before people judge me, they need to back up a few years. This was no contest of equal opponents. We were sparring in the dojo with what I though was no contact, much less "full contact". I was an 18- year-old Sho-Dan. I had not won my first U.S. National Tournament. That was in November 1964. I had been a Sho-Dan for a period of nine months. I was not a professional. I was employed, working 48 hours a week as a toolmaker apprentice, and I trained three times a week.

Enoeda was 32 years old, Go-dan, a professional JKA instructor and World Champion. He was going to be the new head instructor in England. Enoeda could have beaten me ten out of ten. My level was not even close to his technical skill by any stretch of the imagination. It was no "duel in the sun," as some people have reported and would like to believe.

Before I complete this answer, let me say that I learned a valuable, and hard, lesson that day. I would not recommend it for others. That day, I turned from being a boy who was naive and trusting to a man with a mission. I decided to train and become as technically strong as I could. No one ever since has kicked me in the head. I became a different karateka because of that.

In a bittersweet way, I would like to thank Sensei Enoeda, who has since passed away, for the lesson I was taught that day, "Never trust anyone who stands in front of you as an opponent, and protect yourself at all times."

I have never told this story before. As fate has it—or was it God's will?—the broken jaw put me in the hospital for one week. I had been drafted by the U.S. Army. My induction notice was to report June 19, 1964, for basic training. Because of my injury, I received a three-month exemption from reporting for duty. One month later, I joined the California Army National Guard for six years. This was the time of the Vietnam War.

**How do you see karate in America at the present time?**
There are many styles of karate in the United States today. This was not the case when I started. I think karate is more popular today than ever. When I was competing in the 60s, there were only about 50 black belts, total, who participated in the national tournament from all over the United States. We never had to pay an entrance fee to compete. That was unheard of; all tournament expenses were covered by the spectators at the gate. The total tournaments would take three or four hours to complete.

Today, we see fewer spectators and a lot more competitors. The spectators are usually family members, who come to support their children or spouses throughout the day. Some tournaments can take as long as two or three days to complete. The problem with this is that it requires a large number of judges and referees. Having to judge all day for 10 hours causes the judges to burn out. It is of utmost importance to maintain quality judges and referees. Today, tournaments have evolved into a sport for the participants, rather than for the spectators' entertainment.

### Who were your most difficult opponents at that time?

I remember Ken Funakoshi, George Sasano, and Eugene Watanabe from Hawaii. They were formidable opponents. I knew they wanted too win as much as I did. I won the U.S. Nationals five times. Two times I fought Ken Funakoshi, and one time with George Sasano for the championship. Hawaii always had strong competitors back then.

Tony Tulleners comes to mind. We competed against each other in 1965. We were on the United States Team together that went to Paris, France, in 1972. I was the team captain. I did not see Tony as an opponent. I wanted him to win, and you could always count on Tony to do just that.

"I have always believed that the style is only as effective as the person doing it."

### How do karate styles differ from other martial arts methods when applying the techniques in a self-defense situation? Do you think that karate is superior to other arts when it comes to a real self-defense situation?

I think all martial arts have some aspect of effectiveness. or it would not be called a martial art. Karate is most effective as self-defense. I have always believed that the style is only as effective as the person doing it.

### Kata and Sparring: What was the ratio in training under Nishiyama?

Kata and Kumite were encouraged equally. It was mandatory to compete in both events. My training schedule, was three days a week:

Mondays were Kata. I trained in the intermediate class one hour, advanced class one and a half hours, and team training one and a half hours.

Wednesdays were Basics. I trained in the Intermediate class one hour, advanced class one hour. and team training—basics, sparring, and kata—two hours.

Fridays were Free Sparring. We warmed up with basics, thirty minutes, free sparring one hour, and always kata when we were the most tired, thirty minutes. At the end of class was conditioning: push-ups, sit-ups, carrying one of your teammates while moving forward front kicking. What I remember most was what we called squatting hops. After doing squatting hops, you couldn't stand up or walk. So we did push-ups and sit-ups. What I also remember is Sensei Nishiyama saying, "One more time!" and everyone would say, "Oss!" If one person failed to complete the exercise, we all had to do it over again. The class was schedule for two hours, from 8 to 10:00 p.m., but I never remember finishing until after 11 p.m.

**Do you have any general advice you would care to pass on to the practitioners in general and to someone who is interested in starting to learn karate?**

I would recommend first that one select two or three dojos and do a comparison. You can narrow it down if you already know what style you would like to practice. You should watch all the classes, from beginners through advanced. Compare the differences between the two levels. Inquire how long the dojo has been there. This shows establishment. Is the dojo clean and neat? This shows pride. Has the instructor invested in the dojo? A good quality wood floor or mats are imperative. Never train on a concrete floor, due to possible knee or impact injuries. Don't be pressured to buy a gi (uniform) right away; wait three months. Gis are expensive. Don't be pressured to compete before you're ready.

Making rank is good to challenge yourself. Building confidence is part of your training. Don't be pressured to join a national organization right away. I have seen too many people quit because they are pushed too fast in some of these areas. Karate is a business, and businesses need to make money to keep the dojo door open. Most important of all, what are the qualifications of the instructors? If the instructor is 24 years old, and he or she is a ninth degree black belt, my advice would be to find another dojo.

**Who would you like to have trained with that you have not?**

I would like to have trained with Sensei Nakayama. The last time I saw him, I was at a banquet. Sensei Nakayama was sitting at the head table by himself, and I was sitting at a table in the main hall. He smiled and motioned for me to come over to his table. He asked me to sit down and join him. We were talking about karate. He asked me about my condition and my training.

Then he asked me if I liked tequila. I was surprised by his question. I said "yes" and took the hint. I asked him if he would like some; he nodded affirmatively. He said, "I like to drink it Mexican style!" After three shots, chased down with lemon and salt, we continued talking about karate. He was laughing and enjoying himself.

His face was now glowing red like a beam shining brightly. One of the JKA instructors saw us and came over to us. He looked at me and said, "What are you doing? Sensei has a heart condition. He's not to drink." I also had three shots and felt very good. I didn't like his scolding tone. I stood up and said, "Maybe you should tell him that." He asked me who was I to refuse him or tell him no. I thanked Sensei Nakayama, excused myself, and left the table. That was the last time I saw Sensei Nakayama. He passed away two years later, on April 15, 1987. His death was a great loss to karate, and it was the start of the JKA fragmenting and dividing into multiple organizations.

### What differences do you see between the competitors of your time and the modern athletes in karate today?

When I started training with Sensei Nishiyama in 1962, he was 32 years old. You could say he was in his prime. He was a technician, and his techniques were sharp, clean, and powerful. His karate was very scientific, explaining applications of strategy and tactics, using combinations of uppercuts, hook punches, knees, and elbows that are not emphasized in sport karate today.

What he was teaching us was how to literally fight in close, using combinations. This kind of training was not sport karate. What he was doing was establishing the foundation for multiple combination attacks for use in sport karate. I don't see this in karate today. If you can't fight in close, then you don't know how to fight, sport or otherwise. Nobody fights standing six feet apart, except in sport karate. If you close in on your opponent, then the match is stopped.

I didn't know it at the time. All the ingredients were in place. Sensei Nishiyama was introducing a new level of karate to the United States. His teaching approach to karate had not been seen in the United States before. I was young, ready to learn, and in the right place at the right time.

### When was your last competition?

My last competition was in 1974, in Rio De Janeiro, Brazil. In the team competition, I fought Watanabe from Brazil. I won my match against him. He was very fast and was the World Champion, winning in Paris, France, in 1972. The United States Team won the gold metal in the team competition against Brazil. We fought again in the individual competition and he won.

In an earlier match against the Brazilian champion, I don't remember his name, we both hit each other at the same time. He received a cut to the face. They were going to disqualify me, until they saw me bleeding. The judges did not see my injury. I had received a cut over my right eye. The judges tried to make a big deal out of it. They told me I couldn't continue because of my injury. I protested strongly and was permitted to continue. I won my match and I walked away with third place.

I was now 30 years old, and could feel myself slipping. I was losing my edge, due to four years of no competition, along with no team training. Self-training will keep you in condition, but you have to free spar with high-level opponents to maintain your timing. After I stopped competing, I taught karate in the Los Angeles area throughout the 1970s and 1980s. Also, I taught at summer camps, instructing applications for competition training. The training was very hard. I coached the 1980 U.S. Team in Mexico City, finally retiring from active participation in 1990.

**What was your mental approach to the competition in karate?**
The philosophy in martial arts speaks of karate-do, karate-jutsu, and Zen. A karateka must have a clear mind and conscience. We must purge our egos of selfish thoughts or jealousy. I read somewhere, in Budo and Zen, "The ego is the consciousness of oneself." It's all about me. The philosophy is to suppress or defeat one's self-ego to have a clear mind. The above is all true in self-defense. In the above context, the ego is a negative thing to have… "He's got a big head, or he is conceited. He thinks he is good."

In karate, we can't have it both ways. Most athletes have big egos. They have something to prove. You have to think you're the best at what you are doing; that is what helps to motivate you. That is a positive ego to have: confidence. An example of what I am saying: If a fireman goes into a burning house to find and save a person, his training and experience tells him he can do this without being injured or killed. Is this a big ego or is it confidence in oneself?

When I was competing, there was strong social pressure in the dojo to compete. This means doing better than someone else. Your action or technique becomes a measure of superiority in both kata and kumite. That is ego; if you don't have it you will lose.

**Do you think it is positive for karate to enter in the Olympic Games or would this destroy the art and turn it into a simple sport, as it did with Judo?**
I feel karate already has turned into a simple sport. When I was competing, the national tournaments were held in stadiums, like the Olympic

Auditorium in Los Angeles, the L.A Sports Arena, Pauley Pavilion at UCLA, etc... Now national tournaments are held in high school gyms. That, my friends, is a big step backwards. In the early 70s, we were closing the gap between United States and Japan. That came to a stop with all the petty politics. History has shown there has been way too much division and fragmentation of Shotokan karate in the U.S., Japan, and the world. Karate is now worldwide, with so many styles competing for power and control. I don't see karate in the Olympics in my lifetime. A policy of intimidation, where you cannot go into a region without permission, does not work in this world today. Karate is a gift to be shared. If karate is ever accepted into the Olympics, it will require strong leadership. This requires compromise with each other for the greater good of karate in the world.

**How much of the Japanese culture do you think existed in the way the top JKA instructors taught karate in the U.S. during the 60s?**

Martial arts come from many cultures. I can only speak for my style as I can interpret it best. Shotokan Karate is a Japanese martial art. Proper manner is very important, like the purpose of beginning and ending with a bow. A major part of good manners is respect, refinement, and sophistication. This culture goes back to the roots of martial arts.

**What is your opinion of fighting events such as the UFC and Mixed Martial Arts events that we know today?**

It is great entertainment. Any fighting art can be called a martial art, old or new. These guys are professionals. They are paid to train, and they are tough and effective. You cannot compare karate to the UFC, just because they look similar. It's like day and night. The average person can take karate for many reasons for the rest of his or her life. The UFC guys are a select few of people who receive over a short period time a lot of impact to the body. If you choose to practice what is called MMA, it is fine, but it is just that—mixed arts of many versions to pick and choose from. It's a system of fighting for sport and they pay the athletes. It is as close to street fighting as a person can do under some kind of regulations and injury control.

**Have there been times when you felt fear in your training?**

Fear is a strong word that has many meanings. We have all experienced some kind of fear, at some point in our lives. In tournaments, I always had a fear of making a mistake while performing kata, due to peer pressure or embarrassment. I always had a fear of hitting my opponent and being disqualified. People and family expected a lot from me, I did not want to disappoint them.

# Karate Masters

"Karate is a part of me and will remain with me for the rest of my life."

**What are your thoughts on the future of karate?**

There are a lot of good people in karate. I have competed and instructed in many countries: Japan, Mexico, France, and Brazil. I lost so many friends due to politics. I have always said there is nothing wrong with karate. What is wrong is some of the people doing it, due to their poor leadership, politics, or greed. Karate has been around far longer than anyone living today. People will come and go. Karate will remain and evolve, as it always has done—as long as people have the need to defend and protect ourselves and our families. It is a basic human need that karate provides.

**Why did you stop training in karate and completely disassociate yourself from the art?**

I will never disassociate myself from karate. Karate is a part of me and will remain with me for the rest of my life. I have talked about karate as a martial art. The martial art aspect of self-defense will always remain with me. However, sport karate is now a fading memory from my past youth. I will always be grateful for what karate as given me.

I enjoyed teaching karate. But I never wanted to be a full-time or professional karate instructor; this was my choice. Teaching karate is not the way I wanted to make my living. It was also hard be employed and be in the instructor training program at the same time. I saw no future in this. In hindsight, I feel that I made the right decision.

After I was barred from competition in 1969, I changed direction, and joined a Fire Department in the Los Angeles area. I was a firefighter for thirty years, retiring in 2000. I was a battalion chief for nine years, and Chief of the Department before retiring.

In 1989, I attended the I.S.K.F. National Tournament to support and be part of karate that I always loved. I soon noticed that I was not being asked to judge. A few of the JKA instructors were talking to me like I was a twelve-year-old boy, not to demean twelve-year-olds. I was asked to referee

"All styles of martial arts are good if you want to defend yourself."

one time for the entire tournament. By late in the day, it was obvious that I was being blackballed. Flying home to Los Angeles the next day, in late November, I was thinking that after I had paid my own airfare, hotel expenses, and offering them my free time and 32 years of experience, that my knowledge and skills were no longer required. I was 45 years old. I resigned from the I.S.K.F. in April 1990. I directed my attention to the demands of the fire service, and going to college to further my education.

All styles of martial arts are good if you want to defend yourself. It will give you the ability to decide to act or react in any given situation. With what I experienced, I was fortunate to have the opportunity to accomplish what I achieved.

Discounting all of the negatives I encountered in karate, if I had the chance to go back and do it all over again, I would say, "Sure! When can I start?" O

# GENE TIBON

## STILL WATERS RUN DEEP

SENSEI TIBON IS A MAN OF OUTSTANDING ACCOMPLISHMENTS AND A LEADING INSTRUCTOR IN THE ART OF GOJU RYU UCHIAGE-KAI KARATE. HE HAS DEVOTED HIMSELF TO THE TRAINING AND STUDY OF MARTIAL ARTS SINCE AN EARLY AGE WHEN HE BEGAN PRACTICING UNDER THE TUTELAGE OF HIS FATHER. SENSEI TIBON'S INSIGHTS INTO THE ART ARE NO LESS EXCITING THAN THE MAN HIMSELF.

BESIDES BEING PROFICIENT IN THE TECHNIQUES OF KARATE, SENSEI TIBON HAS THE TRUE PRINCIPLES OF THE PHILOSOPHY OF BUDO INGRAINED WITHIN HIM. THIS IS APPARENT IN THE FOLLOWING INTERVIEW, IN WHICH WE LEARN NOT JUST ABOUT KARATE BUT LIFE ITSELF FROM THE KNOWLEDGE GARNERED BY THIS EXCEPTIONAL KARATE MASTER.

**How long have you been practicing the martial arts?**

I was introduced to martial arts when I was about 11 years old by my father, Gene D. Tibon Sr., who also is a martial artist in Goju Ryu, Escrima, Boxing, and good old-fashioned street fighting. Along with my brother Darren, sisters Leslie, Regina, and Jackie, and cousins, I learned from my father. So, you can say I have had over five decades of exposure and training in the martial arts, including the years with my father. My grandfather and great-grandfather also were involved in the martial arts. My great-grandfather was a highly experienced Escrimador who actually had to use his art for self-protection. He caused serious injury to seven men who attacked his family. The injuries his attackers sustained were so bad, he had to leave the country for 12 years. What is known of great-grandfather Marcos Tibon, I'm sure his father, grandfather, and his great-great grandfather also were involved or had some knowledge of martial arts. We just have no records that far back. Based on our current knowledge, it has been in my family for at least four generations with me, five generations for my sons, and six generations for my three grandsons.

**How many styles have you trained in?**

I have been involved mostly with the Goju Kai Yamaguchi system during

# Karate Masters

"I was very intrigued by the stories of the old masters who would train in the forest."

my childhood and teen years with my father, the Goju Ryu Uchiage-Kai System, then the Yamani Ryu Kobudo system, a little AAU boxing for about two years, and a little bit of Serrada Escrima Filipino stick fighting techniques.

**Would you tell us some interesting stories of your early days in karate?**

I read a lot about the old days of training in Japan and Okinawa, and I was very intrigued by the stories of the old masters who would train in the forest. They wouldn't consider themselves as having true strength in their punches and kicks until they were able to kill a tree. Well, in the front yard of my first apartment, where I lived with my wife and young son Gino, there was a very large tree in the front of my residence. I worked out every day against it, just to develop my strength in my punches and kicks. Being poor in those days, as a young man, and wanting to train hard, we used whatever we could find. One day, my landlord came knocking on the door with a major complaint, because the huge tree in my front yard was dead. All of the leaves had fallen off and it dried up. My father heard about it, laughed, and said, "Well I guess you have some power in your punches and kicks now, but you probably looked like a nut out there beating up a tree." Most people today wouldn't understand my motive.

The other story I have is the first time I broke a brick with my head. It was a six-inch thick, piece of concrete. Again, I would always revert to remember the old stories of karate: empty hand, and your whole body being a weapon. I had to test my strength in my neck and head to smash that slab of concrete, which would confirm what I could do to somebody's face with a head butt. This is even more of a test, because you are putting your life on the line with this type of psychological and physical test. You have to step over a psychological barrier with total devotion and commitment in completing this test. You have to be at your maximum level to know that you have this strength in being able to step over this line and accomplish this feat. I concentrated and put my mind into total commitment in smashing this brick with no hesitation. I knew I would suffer more with the issue of self-defeat by hesitating, or not giving my all, coupled with the injury that could result if I failed to break the brick. After smashing through the concrete slab, I almost felt as if I had discovered something more than just being able to smash this piece of concrete with my head. I felt there is nothing I cannot accomplish if I totally dedicate my whole being to it. If I believe and fully commit myself, then I will succeed in my attempt. For some reason, these two stories stand out in my mind the most but, believe me, I have other stories of different training test in my early days.

**How can the influence of training in Martial Arts help the young (kids/teenagers) generation in becoming successful as individuals in the future?**

Karate has a huge influence on young kids, if they are in a program that strives for the student to look at leadership, self-challenge, determination, honesty, integrity, discipline, and the competitive spirit of winning at life. Everyday life is a true comparative to their karate training. Life is a conflict; everything we do, including waking up in the morning, is conflict. You always want to hit that alarm clock to ring again in five minutes, just to get that little extra sleep. Once you learn that karate is life, all aspects of the work and determination in trying to perfect a movement or technique are no different than working and preparing to win at a spelling bee contest, earn that new position at work, being a great role model for others, or by attracting a new customer in business.

Our young students are engaged in their schools and challenge themselves as class officers, or high academic achievers, just as they do on the dojo floor, working on their techniques. That same pride and hard work go hand and hand with each other. The life skills that we teach in our dojos are a direct influence of the hard work and the intangibles that come with karate-do, the empty hand way. This attitude will follow the practitioner his or her whole life, if one practices long enough to understand one is the same as the other.

**Were you a "natural" at karate; did the movements come easily to you?**

I was a natural in all sports. I was a very fast runner and ran track in junior high school and on the high school varsity team, and played high school varsity soccer. I also played on the varsity football team during my senior year. Everything I did in sports, I did pretty well. If I saw something,

I was able to pick it up easily. Growing up with martial arts training at a young age, we had footwork drills in boxing training, we ran a lot, and started lifting weights just going into junior high school at age 14. That continued through my senior year in high school, when I bench pressed 450 pounds to lead the school in the 450 bench press club. There were different category clubs from 200 to 450 pound club at that time. I continued weight training until I started boxing and wanted to increase my speed.

The basic Kihon development I received from Sensei Hu was my formal concrete development in stance foundation in Goju Ryu Karate. I found this training to be what made me fall in love with Goju Ryu Karate, because of how difficult it was to achieve the stances without thinking, and to make them a natural application of the movement during kata and sparring. All of my early training with my father and sports really flourished when I started the traditional training under the *Goju Kai Yamaguchi* system.

**What do you think are the most important qualities for a student to become proficient in any art of Budo (not only in karate)?**

Especially when looking at the most important qualities in any art of Budo. I absolutely feel the qualities of humility, character, respect, manners, spirit, self-control, and being proper are very important. I think that our duty as the National Federation is to protect the Budo in our art, especially at the sport level.

One of the most important ways to do this is to not allow athletes to celebrate their own technique, rejoice at the misfortune of others, berate, or talk trash to another competing athlete during a match.

This absolutely drives me crazy, when I see some elite athletes running around the ring cheering for himself for scoring a technique, when it has not even been awarded yet. It is even worse when a referee or judge watches this sort of action with no response, allowing it to happen. In my estimation, to keep the Budo in karate, the sport aspect has to make clear not to allow any type of celebration during the match, until it is over and a winner is declared. A penalty should be given automatically for this type of behavior. Zanshin should be a large part of this, continuous mind from the beginning to the end of the match. In my estimation, it is a direct violation of the most important code of Budo in any martial arts a when there is a breakdown in humility and character for the purpose of entertainment.

**With all the technical changes during the last years, do you think there are still "pure" styles of karate?**

I think many want to think there are special pockets of "pure" styles of karate. But after so many different generations of instructors, with creative and ingenious minds, they actually take their art sometimes further from their predecessors. Many will break off from the first generation masters, after they have passed away, to create their own legacy of style or organization. Many have ideas that while locked into an organization style are held fast to that one way, until they break away and create their own version of interpretation or style, which has been happening for centuries in China and Japan. All we can hope to do is try to maintain the traditional structure of the old ways that have been handed down from previous generations to the next. I know I personally have trained with many great Goju Ryu – Goju Kai masters who all have had their own creative genius and all influenced me to the understanding I have now. I respect all of the old masters for their contributions to the art as we know it today, especially those who work to keep the essence of the traditional katas solid in movement and applications. I don't know how many "pure" styles are out there due to evolution of man's thinking and technology. Just look at the Olympics of old, in comparison to now. I would venture to say there are more styles of creative traditional interpretations of highly skilled and confident generations of masters, which styles still try to represent the original "pure" style they originated from. But who is to determine what is pure and what is not?

"I don't know how many "pure" styles are out there due to evolution of man's thinking and technology"

Take for instance the first car built by Henry Ford, the *Model A*. Even though you still have the same gas combustion engine idea with four wheels and a steering wheel to control the vehicle, you can't compare it to today's Porsche, BMW, Mercedes, Cadillac, Toyota, Honda, etc. They all have the same standard structural idea, but look what creativity, technology, and an open mind have allowed.

# Karate Masters

"I think styles are important, because the traditional essence of the kata still is defined by that group of practioners."

**Do you think different "styles" truly are important in the art of karate? Why?**

I think styles are important, because the traditional essence of the kata still is defined by that group of practioners. I look at one of history's most brilliant Okinawan pioneers, Grandmaster Kenwa Mabuni, whose magnitude of research included most of all major katas of the time. Grandmaster Mabuni tried to create a "Karate" that represented all styles by combining all the katas under one name. At the time, there was a very important reason for this. Yet, when I see a Goju Ryu Kata performed today by a different stylist outside of Goju Ryu, some very important ingredients, very specific to the style, are missing. Some of these practitioners did not research, as did their grandmaster, which could have helped preserve the essence of a kata's original style. The strength and power in some katas is enhanced by a particular stance, which in some cases may have been changed from the original style. I personally feel that the styles do work to maintain the original essence of their system, and I feel they are important to maintain. I've dedicated my life to Goju Ryu and still feel like I learn something new every day.

**Karate nowadays often is referred to as a sport. Would you agree with this definition or is "only" Martial Art?**

I think any martial art is a sport, if it is in the competition arena with rules, a referee, scoring, or a doctor who is ready to stop the match because of injuries. This is just a small part of kumite, although the test of physical control, techniques, and the attitude still has some of the vital ingredients of budo. To have all the competitive rules-based ingredients missing, and the only award for winning between two combatants is the one who survives, that is pure martial arts. The only exception is during a time of war when you are on the battlefield, or you and your family find yourself in a life-threatening situation. If you find yourself in a position of personal risk and have to protect others or yourself, you really are experiencing the true essence of the martial arts. Training for these types of situations could happen on any given day. It is when Karate is not being a sport, but again is empty hand, is a means to survive a life-threatening attack. Again, the evolution of time and laws of the land has had a great affect on the martial arts of old to the present.

**How do you see karate around the world at the present time?**

I see karate as very fragmented, and in some cases confused. Many are asking why we should support karate in the Olympics. Others are saying we need to be in the Olympics for worldwide exposure of the art. There are some who say should we stay isolated in our own world? Others say let's create our own way. Some want to get as close to full blown combat as they can get; others just want to try to preserve what they have been taught, and not change or express any more than what they were taught.

In the United States, "the land of milk and honey," creative expression is expected. Of course that is the American way. Really, what is that? I think it means the right to choose what makes you happy. There is so much diversity in the United States, a melting pot of ideas, culture, and creativity that makes us unique in the martial arts world. As for around the world, I see in South America that the styles almost all are Japanese Okinawa Karate and Korean Karate. The same strong influences exist in Europe and Africa. Canada is close to the way the United States has been influenced, by diversity. There you will find many different styles and ideas of martial arts. Due to differences in ideas and styles, I don't know that we ever can have everybody on the same page regarding martial arts. Today, especially with martial arts being run commercially, some dojos have become specialized in modified day care programs, specializing in young kids. Some dojos only teach games interjected with some martial arts drills. People are paying big money for this and some instructors are making six figures and more, teaching these kinds of programs.

Because there is a market for this type of program, and there seemingly is a strong customer base, traditional karate is having a tough time. The old style hard-core dojo never can grow larger than 30–50 students, and many traditional Senseis struggle to make a simple living, let alone support a retirement investment plan. The state of the economy also has a direct bearing on the martial arts business. To survive in the New Age, Senseis have to think outside of the box for business strategies to make their programs work, be profitable, and not compromise their teaching values.

**What do you consider to be the major changes in the art since you began training?**

I see the cost to be a legitimate dojo as the major change—cost of a building, cost of insurance, cost of utilities, cost of supplies, cost of equipment, cost of learning to run a business, and the cost of marketing just to be competitive. You have to be trained to understand safe traditional development of athletes. The last thing you want to do is have your students doing something that is outdated and become injured from it. Suddenly, you have a lawsuit filed against you for negligence. The laws have changed a lot regarding how classes are taught now from my earlier days. You have to be more sensitive to special needs of people who have many different reasons why they are training in karate.

**What is your philosophical basis for your training?**

Try to teach my students to love it as I do. It is so much a part of my life that I have been able to test myself with the idea that both my wife Yvonne and I share, that we are in a "Race for Life." How much can we accomplish before it is our time? The test in Kata "Sanchin" reminds me of my life. It means mind, body, and spirit. The test is the focus on breathing, tensing of the muscles, and focusing on the power of total concentration while your partner strikes your muscle groups to make sure your muscles are tight and strong, and that you are rooted and grounded in your stance. Every day, I work with a constant bombardment of issues, circumstances, conflicts, emotions, chaos, but yet I feel I'm just floating along handling all of those issues without a blink of distraction. I love that I can handle conflict management in such an easy manner, and I give all of the credit to Karate and Sanchin Kata. As an investigator for the 18 years, I found myself in very unpredictable circumstances every day. You are in a constant training mind of Karate-do. Technique is only real if you can use it in life applications.

**Do you have a particularly memorable karate experience that has remained as an inspiration for your training?**

I have a memorable experience from JKF 9th Dan Grandmaster Kenzo Uchiage, who was one of the Class-A Examiners from Japan testing me for my 5th Dan, many years ago. As I finished Kata Seisan, Grandmaster Kenzo Uchiage walked up to me with his son, JKF 7th Dan Goju Ryu Uchiage Kai Chairman Takeshi Uchiage, and said to me in Japanese, "Your hands are better than Japan Technical Committee." First, I was shocked, then I was honored, and then I smiled and asked, "Sensei, does that mean I passed?" Sensei Takeshi Uchiage said, "Sensei Tibon, Sensei Tibon," shaking his head, as my question was inappropriate. I smiled and bowed with respect to Grandmaster Kenzo Uchiage. I will never forget that moment as long as I live. I trained for almost three months in my swimming pool, doing kata so I could develop the fluid hands I wanted for my katas. When I did kata, I wanted my hands to look like floating seaweed in the ocean. Grandmaster Kenzo Uchiage confirmed that my training was correct. I still practice doing kata in the swimming pool to maintain the fluid hand techniques. At the end of that testing seminar, Grandmaster Kenzo Uchiage and the Class A Examiners presented me with a large poster photo of all of us together. Each examiner signed his name over his individual photo. I look at it everyday hanging on the wall in my dojo.

### After all these years of training and experience, could you explain the meaning of the practice of karate?

When you are young, you have that "I can do anything" attitude. You do all of the crazy breaking of bricks, wood, tiles, punching, and kicking trees. Your body become tempered and fast. As

"As you get even older, your mind becomes more understanding and more conscious of movements."

you get older, your body moves slower, but you are able to make strong power with less effort. As you get even older, your mind becomes more understanding and more conscious of movements, and those applications can mean so much more. I know I teach a lot more technical things now than when I was 23 years old. I think the meaning of practice is two levels, first the body and the spirit, and then with age, the mind's knowledge ultimately becomes the strongest part of the overall training experience.

### Is there anything lacking in the way martial arts are taught today compared to how they were in your beginnings?

I have to say some of the great teachers are gone; our generation is responsible to carry on their legacy. If we don't carry on and do our job to promote karate the way the old Masters did, then our way of karate will be

# Karate Masters

"If we don't carry on and do our job to promote karate the way, then our way of karate will be lost within the next two generations."

lost within the next two generations. We must work together to help preserve and instill in our future Senseis that they must pass on the old ways—the old secrets handed down to us, pass on the stories that make you think about how really deep that technique or that spiritual attitude really goes. A lot has changed since my beginnings, and my charge is to do my part to help pass on and promote our way of karate so those in the public may find us and hopefully help continue its legacy.

**Why do you think that preserving the cultural values of Budo is important in our modern society?**

I read this quote from the book "Budo Secrets" by John Stevens, "For a realization to be authentic, one must be able to apply it in the actual world. True understanding is reflected in one's technique and also in one's daily life. This is the real battlefield where one's enlightenment is constantly tested." In the book "The Way to Black Belt" by Lawrence Kane and Kris Wilder, they quote, "Etiquette and manners is an integral part of budo, for without it we would be practicing nothing more than basic violence." These statements say it all. If people really understood these quotes in our modern society and lived by them, we would have a very different world.

**Have there been times when you felt fear in your training?**

Yes, many years ago, while working for my present employer, I was loading some very large equipment. I stepped in a hole and snapped my ligaments in left ankle, where they attach to my foot. They were severed so badly they had me on the operating table for two hours, reconnecting all three of them. The doctor said: give up karate, boxing, and all I was doing in the martial arts, and that I would be a cripple the rest of my life. Well, when the cast came off my leg six months later, my left leg was two inches smaller in diameter than my right leg. I remember the doctor telling me to tiptoe to develop my strength. I thought to myself, "tiptoe" – you've got be kidding me. At that time, prior to the accident, I was bench-pressing right at 410 pounds and I was leg pressing 750–850 pounds. I tried to tiptoe on my left foot and nothing was there. I was scared for the first time in my life that I really might be done with what I loved most, Martial Arts. Well, the next day I started running – better yet, let's call it "hop-jogging" – until finally I regained my strength in my leg. So, when I went back to the doctor four months later, he measured my left leg and it was 1/8-inch bigger than my right, so I felt good and continued with my training. This also become the point where teaching became a larger part of my life. My oldest son, Gino, then 10, brought over six of his friends and asked if I would teach them karate in our garage. That's when and where our first dojo started.

"The life skills that we teach in our dojo are a direct influence of the hard work that comes with Karate-do."

**Do you think that Olympics will be positive for the art of karate-do in case that happens one day?**

The WKF is working hard to get our sport into the Olympics. It is keeping with the JKF Shitei Kata for standardized mandatory forms, so the world is seeing specific kata the way Japan deemed it to fit each system. The katas will have a standard compulsory requirement. This is much like gymnastics with compulsory floor exercises, required to be performed in front of the judges. Now, the only problem is to insure we have referees and judges who know and understand the essence of each of the standardized katas of the four major systems. This is the most difficult, because we have many referees and judges who really don't understand the systems they are judging. It's up to the Technical Committees around the world to teach or insure that the referee corps understands specific traits of the four major systems.

# Karate Masters

"The new non-traditional schools are totally commercial and look at every way to get the student in with different marketing tools."

This way, the true winner can be selected, and not the person portraying a kata that is so animated for entertainment, for that actually will be recognized as being incorrect.

Kumite is starting to transition to face shields, mostly for more of a safety aspect, and for the perception of our sport. The world will be watching. Many will not like the face shield, and it will be hard for many to get used to. I think if you look at the other contact sports, like boxing, you have mandatory head, hand, and groin protection. Tae Kwon Do has chest gear, headgear, hand, and groin protection required. Yet Kumite has only a mouthpiece, hand, shin gear, booties, and groin cup. Due to the amount of contact in our sport, many who will make the decisions may want to see more protection for this contact sport. I think it may help with the broken noses and the shattered cheekbones, so it may prove an important piece of safety equipment. The foot protection has helped with broken feet and toes, but because of the foot protection and shin protection, the kicks are coming in with full impact, and hands and arms now are suffering the injuries. I feel that as Karate goes into the Olympics, it will be good for the promotion of our art, and with the right type of marketing will help grow our art in the world.

**What are your thoughts on the future of karate?**

As far as the future of karate, it is a little frightening to me when I see how many non-traditional schools are out there versus the traditional schools. The new non-traditional schools are totally commercial and look at every way to get the student in with different marketing tools so that many in the traditional schools are used to the old idea of, "if you want the traditional dojo, you need to search for me." That has changed a lot; the attitude for karate is not the same it was back in the '50s, '60s, and '70s. There was a special mystical perception of those who were in karate and attained the black belt. Karate seldom was seen; then it became such an entertainment value in the movies that soon everybody wanted it. Unfortunately, many of the non-traditional who are very smart and know how to make money from the marketing craze on television turned karate into a jazzercise mixture of kicking and boxing, full contact, and holds barred matches that took away the mystical perception from karate. Too much of something, and pretty soon you take it for granted, and many in a world of wanting everything fast want their black belts in less than two years. Some commercial dojos promise this type of program, with kids as young as 6 to 8 years old receiving a black belt. I've even seen them on talk shows demonstrating to the masses with the quality of karate moves one would expect of a beginner in a traditional dojo.

"There was a special mystical perception of those who were in karate and attained the black belt."

I'm hoping that all Traditional Japanese-Okinawa Karate can come together and support each other in having karate represented at the Olympics, representing the United States as a united group of traditionalists working together to preserve the Budo in Karate, and at the same time helping us develop a United States Karate team to represent us in the Olympics. O

# TAKESHI UCHIAGE

## *UNVEILING THE MASTER*

Sensei Takeshi Uchiage was born in 1948 in Osaka, Japan, and made his first steps in Goju Ryu Karate-Do in his father's dojo at the age of 6. When he studied Physical Education at the Tenri University in Nara, he also practiced Kenyu Ryu under the direction of Master Tadao Nakano. After his graduation in 1971, he became trainer of the Tenri University Karate-Do team in Nara, Japan, and a technical advisor for the Taiku-kai Karate-Do team of the Osaka Keizai University.

In 1972, the first typical Martial Arts building outside Japan was inaugurated in the Steveston district of the city of Richmond, Canada. Because of the amity between Richmond and Wakayama-city, Shozo Ujita, who was mayor of Wakayama-city, also was present. He was astounded by the fact that Karate-Do would not be practiced in this new Martial Arts dojo. Therefore, being president of J.K.F. Goju-Kai and vice president of J.K.F., he requested one of his top students to leave for Richmond, Canada, as a goodwill ambassador for Karate-Do. Sensei Uchiage left for Canada in June 1973.

He is chairman of Goju Ryu Karate-Do Uchiage-Kai, which is a member of J.K.F. Goju-Kai, Chief of the Technical Committee of Osaka Keizai University since 1980, and former W.U.K.O. (WKF) Kumite referee and Kata judge. This is Sensei Uchiage, a true gem of Goju Ryu Karate.

**How long have you been practicing the martial arts and who were your teachers?**

I have been practicing martial arts for more than 55 years. In Karate, I have trained in two different styles, Goju Ryu and Kenyu Ryu. I also have a Sho-Dan in Sumo. My first teacher was my father, Grand Master Kenzo Uchiage. He was a very humble person and never showed off his skills to others. He had the ability to see and to improve the student's strengths. He also taught with the rules and teachings from his teacher, Sensei Miyagi, and he was the person who received the highest Dan from Sensei Miyagi. Also, Shozo Ujita for Goju. He was a student one year higher than my

# Karate Masters

"To always strive to become better. Not only to improve your techniques but also to improve as a person."

father at the Ritsumeikan University. He was a very gentle man, and a very strong person. Kenyu Ryu is under Grand Master Tadao Nakano at Tenri University, Nara, Japan. He always took on challenges head-on with a pure heart, and this is also the way he taught Karate.

**Would you tell us some interesting stories of your early days in karate?**

During the summer, my mother prepared ice water for after my trainings. The ice water was something I looked forward to, to get through some of the hard trainings. Also, during the summers in Japan it gets really hot, and running barefooted hurt the bottom of my feet. I was your average student to begin with. It took many hours and many repetitions to get to where I am today. When I was a white belt, in the All Japan championships for my style, I still was able to finish fourth against other black belts. I figured out that it's not the colour of your belt, but how much you know and attained through training.

**Do you think training in Martial Arts and Budo can help the young generation in becoming successful as individuals in the future?**

Yes. It teaches individuals to respect their seniors (senpais). I believe it is important no matter what profession that you respect the people who were there before you, along with the people you work with.

**What do you think are the most important qualities for a student become proficient in any art of Budo?**

To always strive to become better. Not only to improve your techniques but also to improve as a person. One's techniques reflect his or her characteristics and personality, so it also is important to strive to become a better person, not just a better martial artist. Karate is a deep martial art, and when a question arises, it takes a long time to come up with the answer. It is like a bottomless pit; the knowledge and meanings or techniques are endless.

# Uchiage

**With all the technical changes during the last years, do you think there still are "pure" styles of karate?**

I believe that the Dojo techniques have not changed much in the last years. However, techniques used and geared toward competition and tournaments have changed. The techniques have changed in order to provide judges and referees with what they're looking for to be successful in competition. I still believe that there are "pure" styles of Karate left; it's just that we don't see them as much, as they don't show in competitions.

Styles are important because each one of them has its good characteristics and its own special techniques, which no other style has. Also the different styles have developed because of where their Karate was formed and it's important to keep the history and tradition intact.

"Styles are important because each one of them has its good characteristics and its own special techniques."

**What is your opinion of fighting events such as the UFC and Mixed Martial Arts events?**

If many people support these kinds of martial arts, then I think it's a good thing rather than a bad thing. I have not personally trained in these Martial arts so I cannot comment regarding if its good or not.

**Karate nowadays often is referred to as a sport . . . would you agree with this definition or is "only" Martial Art?**

You train it as a martial art in the Dojo, but when you think of it as a sport looking to make it into the Olympics, it has to be as a sport. If you want to keep the "pure" karate, then it's still a martial art. I think that many people refer to it as a sport because people only see Karate during competitions or sports events.

**How do you see karate in North America and around the world at the present time?**

I don't know if it is lack of advertisement, but in Europe a lot of people who don't even train Karate come to watch the competitions; on the other

# Karate Masters

"The number of Katas that each style has doesn't have anything to do with mastering the art of Karate to that style."

hand, in North America, very few people who have nothing to do with Karate come to watch the competitions. I think it would be fair to say that Karate is more popular in other parts of the world.

**Do you think that the amount of Kata of the style is relevant in the mastery of the art of Karate?**

The number of Katas that each style has doesn't have anything to do with mastering the art of Karate to that style. Kata Bunkai is extremely important because otherwise you will not understand the techniques needed to be used in certain situations, and during Kata it must look like you are fighting opponents who are not there. By understanding the Bunkai, you can perform a Kata that has meaning.

**When teaching the art of karate, what is the most important element: self-defense or sport?**

It depends on what your student is there to attain through Karate. If students are there to learn self-defense, then I will teach self-defense. If students are there to train for sport and competition, then I will teach accordingly.

**Forms and sparring: what's the proper ratio in training?**

If it is someone who competes mostly in Kata, then a majority of the time should be spent training Kata. But they also must train Kumite, and vice versa. If it's someone who does not compete, then they should train both equally in order to understand all aspects of Karate.

**Do you have any general advice to pass on to practitioners?**

The results will not come right away. It is not like in movies where things can be attained at a fast rate. Take your time and be patient, and things will come with time. Karate must be studied for a lifetime as new things come up almost daily. The most important thing is to train slow and steady. You will get as much back as you put into it.

# Uchiage

"Karate must be studied for a lifetime as new things come up almost daily."

**What do you consider to be the major changes in the art since you began training?**

The techniques. Currently in competition, speed is more important than power. Also, you see that there is a reduced amount of kicks compared to many years ago.

**Who would you like to have trained with that you have not?**

Master Chojun Miyagi.

**How do you think a practitioner can increase his/her understanding of the spiritual aspect of the art?**

To not forget the roots, and keep the history in mind, but also to imagine your opponent standing in front of you and always putting forth your best. Always concentrate and do things at your best. You don't need to train long, but you must train efficiently, and concentrate.

# Karate Masters

"Always concentrate and do things at your best. You don't need to train long, but you must train efficiently, and concentrate."

**Is anything lacking in the way martial arts are taught today compared to how they were in your beginnings?**

There is a lack of emphasis on defense. People now think that offense is the best defense, and because the punches people do now are fast and have speed but lack power, there is less fear of being hurt.

**What do you consider the most important qualities of a successful karate practitioner?**

They have strong will and a strong spirit. In modern society, it's easier to attain things, so there is less patience and effort in order to get what one wants. It's important to always strive to improve, and always test your limit in order to grow as an individual and become a more well-rounded individual. The meaning of practicing Karate is to help those weaker or in need, and to head straight on with 100 percent of what you have to those who are stronger than you.

# Uchiage

**What advice would you give to students on the question of supplementary training?**

It's there to enhance your karate. If you weight train, you must weight train to help your karate. Building too much hard muscles will slow you down. But it is different for each individual, so it may be best to ask a personal trainer to train for your own body and strengthen your weaknesses along with growing your strengths.

**Have there been times when you felt fear in your training?**

When I saw someone's arm being broken when they were blocking a kick.

**Do you think that Olympics will be positive for the art of karate-do in case that happens one day?**

I stayed at Sensei Jim Kojima's house for six months when I came to Canada in 1973. Sensei Kojima was the chief

"We should try to maintain our different styles of Karate and its characteristics."

Referee for the International Judo Federation. I think Karate rules will change if it's in the Olympics, but I think this will give an opportunity for many athletes to receive funding from their respective National Olympics Committee's. However, I am not sure if you really can call it "Karate" if there is only a Kumite division in the Olympic Games. Even now in the Pan American Games, Kata is not being included. If it's truly "Karate" I think both disciplines should be included.

**What are your thoughts on the future of karate?**

We should try to maintain our different styles of Karate and its characteristics. I fear that if and when it becomes an Olympic sport, everything will become "sport karate" and we no longer will have different styles of Karate and the styles will lose its identity. O

# YUTAKA YAGUCHI

## A CUT ABOVE

SENSEI YAGUCHI WAS BORN ON KYUSHU ISLAND IN THE FALL OF 1932. HE GREW UP GOING TO SCHOOL IN HIROSHIMA AND LATER ATTENDED NIHON UNIVERSITY IN TOKYO, MAJORING IN MARINE BIOLOGY. WHILE TRAINING KARATE, HE PARTICIPATED IN A NUMBER OF SPORTS, INCLUDING COMPETITIVE SWIMMING. AFTER GRADUATING FROM COLLEGE, YUTAKA YAGUCHI WORKED FOR AN ENGINEERING FIRM. AFTER A FEW MONTHS, HE LEFT THE JOB AND ENROLLED IN THE SECOND CLASS OF THE JKA INSTRUCTOR TRAINING PROGRAM. HE TESTED UNDER MASTER FUNAKOSHI, THE FOUNDER OF SHOTOKAN KARATE, FOR HIS FIRST AND SECOND DECREE BLACK BELTS.

SENSEI YAGUCHI REMAINED IN TOKYO AFTER GRADUATING FROM THE INSTRUCTOR TRAINING PROGRAM AND TAUGHT FOR THE JKA. IN 1965, HE LEFT JAPAN AND TRAVELED TO THE UNITED STATES, FIRST VISITING LOS ANGELES AND THEN DENVER, COLORADO. IN 1966, HE RETURNED TO LOS ANGELES, WHERE HE STAYED FOR SIX YEARS. HE THEN MOVED TO DENVER, WHERE HE STILL RESIDES AND HAS HIS SCHOOL TODAY.

AS ONE OF THE FIRST GRADUATES OF THE JKA INSTRUCTOR TRAINING PROGRAM, HE HAS PLAYED AN IMPORTANT ROLE IN THE GROWTH OF KARATE IN AMERICA AND THE INTERNATIONALIZATION OF THE SHOTOKAN STYLE AROUND THE WORLD, BEING ONE OF THE MAIN INSTRUCTORS AT THE ISKF.

**When and how did you decide to visit the U.S. for teaching?**

I was requested by Nakayama Sensei to come to the U.S. to teach so I didn't have much say. I was a young 5th Dan at the time and when Nakayama Sensei asked me, I accepted, packed my bags, and moved to America.

**What was your first impression of the U.S.?**

In the beginning, I had my doubts but Nakayama Sensei told me to express myself honestly. Master Nishiyama and Master Okazaki already were here in the U.S., so to some extent that made things a little easier since people knew a little bit about the art of karate. They already had opened the doors for a young generation and I was pleased to see that in the U.S. peo-

# Karate Masters

"When you are teaching your students, the truth is...there is a limited amount of things that can be taught."

ple already knew about Martial Arts and the true spirit of Budo.

**You have a very special relationship with Sensei Okazaki and Sensei Kanazawa; what can you tell us about it?**

Yes, both Okazaki Sensei and Kanazawa Sensei have been a very important part of who I am today as karate-ka. They always were there when I "hit a wall" or got frustrated because of something. They had gone to those phases before so they knew what it was going on inside of my mind. They knew how to let me struggle and, when it was the right moment, to give me the tools to get out of that frustration. They never gave me the solution to my problems directly but pointed me in the right direction to find the solution by myself. I have found this approach extremely valuable in life because when you are teaching your students, the truth is...there is a limited amount of things that can be taught. But if you teach them to find the answers by themselves, that is when you see them growing on their own. And that is what a good teacher does with his students.

**When did you first meet Nakayama Sensei?**

It was around 1951, when I was in college. He was my main instructor but Okazaki Sensei and Sigura Sensei also taught me when Nakayama Sensei was not around.

**Did you meet Funakoshi Gichin?**

Yes, he was alive when I started, but I only saw him in testing and special events.

**How would you describe Sensei Nakayama's karate?**

He was a short person, so he based his own karate on developing strong blocks to protect himself. But he never thought of a block as a simple defense. For him, a block was an attack, with aggressive action in mind. There are offensive elements in all blocking techniques and he always emphasized those. He had a very special ability to know his own body and to work on small details to improve his technique. I think this ability made him one of the best teachers in the world because he could spot any mistake in the student's form or technique in order to correct them.

**Do you see the practice of karate as a sport?**

Karate involves more than simply sport. Therefore, it is important to fully understand the meaning of every part that constitutes the complete art. Kata is in many ways a repository of old masters' experiences and knowledge. They formatted those techniques and developed the katas we do today because of many reasons. Kata is not only self-defense. There are many other aspects intrinsic to its practice. To begin with, kata teaches body mechanics in sequences. Body mechanics are the final level of mastery when it comes to free sparring or kumite. The ability to use your body in perfect coordination and at will is the sign of a master. Well, kata training develops this important aspect. There are many elements inside of the principle of proper body mechanics, and all of them can be found in kata. The problem is that many people don't see this and they think kata is just a group of techniques put together by old karate-ka. But when you know how to look at the different segments or sections of any kata, you'll see that the true value in developing your body is in there. Different sections develop different karate principles that are the key to master the art of karate-do.

"Kata is not only self-defense. There are many other aspects intrinsic to its practice."

**What should a karate-ka never forget?**

It is important to always keep the "beginner's mind" because it reminds us that nobody knows it all. For instance, when I was young, there were times when I felt very confident of my skills and knowledge and I thought I was "getting there." Well, ten or fifteen years later, you look back and realize that you still had a lot to learn! So, it is important for martial arts practitioners to be sure that the knowledge they have at any given moment is correct and solid, but don't allow their heads to get big, because by doing it, they will be closing the doors of knowledge and their improvement will be none.

**Do you see any downfalls in the current approach of karate as sport?**

There is nothing wrong with training the sport aspect of karate and becoming a champion. This is good because it pushes the practitioners to train more and harder in order to achieve their goals. Sport is good...it is not a bad thing. The problem arises when the practitioner sees karate only as a sport; when winning or losing is the only thing it matters; when his or her training is based only on winning that tournament. Then, the practitioner's mind is focused on the wrong reason to practice karate. We need to learn how to put the sport aspect of karate in the right perspective without forgetting the true values of the art. For instance, respect is one of the most important lessons in Budo. When you beat you opponent in competition, you should show respect. How you do that? Well, go back to the line after scoring and stand there in "yoi." Show respect to your opponent by not jumping and screaming around the mat. If you lose, show respect by accepting the defeat as a warrior. Don't get upset, don't complain or protest to the referee—who even might have made a mistake in calling a point—and show proper etiquette and Budo manners. This behavior is permissible in football, tennis, or other sports, but not in karate-do. Basic and important things like these are there to remind us that karate can be used as a sport but, in the end, we should not forget that the foundation of karate is Budo and Budo implies etiquette and proper manners. Happiness in life doesn't come from external things. In karate, the mastery of the art doesn't come from winning or losing tournaments.

**So what do you think are the advantages of participating in karate tournaments?**

Well, to begin with competition always brings pressure, and it is under pressure that human beings bring the best we have. In other sports, we see how athletes run faster and are stronger. Competition will keep bringing the athletic level up for years to come and that is good. But once again...what does an Olympic medalist do after he or she retires? Karate is for life...sport just for a few years.

"Karate kata are not gymnastics. There is no need to alter the tempo or rhythm of the kata to impress judges."

**Sensei, we are witnessing these days an alteration and modification of some of the movements in kata to better fit the kata competition "requirements." What is your opinion about modifying or altering the timing of kata movements to "look" more impressive to the judges?**

Karate kata are not gymnastics. There is no need to alter the tempo or rhythm of the kata to impress judges. Every movement has its speed, timing, and cadence, so altering those to win a competition means that instead of winning, you should lose! What is happening now is that many competitors slow down movements to make their stances and forms visible for a longer period of time in front of the judges, but not to perform the kata correctly. If I slow down the movement for judges to be able to "see" my stances, then I am performing the kata wrong. If the movement is fast, then the stance should be perfect within this short period of time...and judges should be trained to see that.

**What did Sensei Nakayama represent to the world of karate?**

He was a very special person. He knew where karate was and where he wanted to take the art. He listened to everybody and took into consideration all ideas and points of view, but at the same time, he knew what was best for the art of karate. I learned many things from him, one of which was how to work on my patience. He taught me how not to get excited about things and be patient, so I could see the best way to deal with problems and situa-

# Karate Masters

"Repetition doesn't bring technical perfection."

tions. In many ways, when I look at myself in a mirror, I see things of Nakayama Sensei in me. Sometimes I act or behave in a certain way, and then I remember how Nakayama Sensei used to behave…and they are similar. In a way, I am happy that some of the lessons he taught me are still with me.

**You always stress the importance of kihon; how would you recommend approaching the training of the basics?**

Let's start by saying that running the dojo up and down doing basic techniques it is not necessarily training kihon. It seems so, but it may not be. The right way to practice kihon is to constantly test and be aware of the body in every single movement. Is that leg correct? Are the hips moving properly? Is my body vertical in the technique? …We need to constantly examine all the technical points when doing the basics. Just because you punch 1,000 times doesn't mean you are doing it right. Just because you do one more punch doesn't mean that punch is better than the one before….unless you do something to make it better. Repetition doesn't bring technical perfection. Only correct repetition does. It has to be focused in body and spirit.

**What quality do you consider the most important in a karate-ka?**

I would recommend developing patience. I had very little when I was young, and throughout the years I was taught by my teachers and by life itself that patience is an important tool for anything you do. Good things don't come overnight. They take time, and even if you think now it is the right time for something…it may not be. Patience is not only important for karate but for any endeavor in life. Parents need patience with their kids, teachers with their students, brother with sisters, and vice versa, etc…

**How should we adapt our training when we get older and develop injuries that prevent us from doing certain things?**

Karate is karate. Kihon is kihon; kata is kata; and kumite is kumite. What I mean by this is that you don't do a different gyaku-tsuki or mae-geri when you are 20 years old than when you are 50. The reverse punch is the reverse punch, and the front kick is the front kick. You simply keep doing it. Now, because of age, we need to adapt the training program to our specifics and not think we can train with the same intensity when we are 60 years old as when we were in our 20s. Also, we need to listen to our body and work around the injuries we may have. There is no need to keep doing things that will make our injuries worse. We should learn how to work around these things.

"Humbleness is not a weakness but a strength that we all should nurture inside us. Karate is for the development of the human being."

**What you consider the most important aspect of training when you reach the 50s or 60s?**

Assuming you already have a good technique—which is the way it's supposed to be—you should focus on your physical conditioning. A healthy body is always ready to train. I believe stretching is good, and muscle conditioning, too. Proper limberness and correct breathing also are important.

**Any final word, Sensei?**

Yes, I'd like to say that karate is a long-term activity. We are here because of all the efforts of Funakoshi and Nakayama Sensei, and we should make sure our conduct and manners are the proper ones to preserve the legacy and teachings of these two great masters. They were humble individuals. Humbleness is not a weakness but a strength that we all should nurture inside us. Karate is for the development of the human being. O

# KOSS YOKOTA

## *CARRYING THE TORCH*

Tetsuhiko Asai was one of the greatest JKA instructors of all time. He separated from the traditional JKA syllabus and incorporated new concepts and training principles that made his personal expression of Shotokan one of the most sought-after methods of all JKA practitioners around the world. His technical influence can be seen in other senior but top world JKA/Shotokan masters like the great Mikio Yahara.

Sensei Koss Yokota was a student of Asai Sensei. In this revealing interview, he explains for the fist time in public the fundamentals of what many have called "the highest level of JKA/Shotokan karate." He is a certified instructor as well as a certified examiner of JKS under Asai Sensei. Yokota Sensei received Roku-dan (6th Dan) from Master Asai in 2005, which made him the highest ranked JKS instructor in the USA.

**When did you meet Asai Sensei for the first time?**

The very first time was in 1982, when I entered the JKA All Japan Championship in Tokyo and I was representing my prefecture, Hyogo. At the tournament site, Budokan, I was introduced to him and we had a short conversation. I quickly introduced myself and explained that I was one of the kenshusei (trainees) under Master Sugano, the Chairman of JKA Kansai District 8th Dan then. Sugano sensei was well respected among the JKA instructors (eventually he became Vice Chairman of the entire JKA before his passing in 2002), so Asai sensei said, "You are lucky to train under Sugano sensei." I was thrilled to meet Asai sensei but I was a bit scared as he was the technical director of the JKA. Unfortunately, I do not think I made a strong enough impression on him at that meeting. In fact, when I saw him again at the championship the following year, he did not recognize me. So, I had to do the same introduction again. He told me the same thing: "You are lucky to train under Sugano sensei."

I believe it was a few years later when we met again. I had moved to California in early 1984 and Asai sensei visited California and gave a seminar in San Jose in the late 80s (hosted by Ken Funakoshi, one of the students

# Karate Masters

"There were several factors that led me to Asai karate."

in Hawaii when Asai sensei was teaching there in the 60s). I participated in the seminar and, to my pleasure, Asai sensei remembered me this time. He was very happy to find a Japanese speaking practitioner in California so he and I went out to dinner and spent several hours. Mrs. Asai was there with him so my wife enjoyed speaking with her. That was a few years before Asai sensei got in an internal political mess at JKA in 1990. At that time, two groups (Asai group and Tanaka group) were claiming the name of JKA. My group did not belong to the Asai group, so I did not see him again until 2001.

**How did you get involved in studying his style of Shotokan karate?**

Even though my membership at JKS did not start until 2003, I had been a member of JKA for 40 years. He was the technical director of JKA in the 70s and 80s, so my foundation of karate is identical to that of Asai sensei. He has "extended" the JKA syllabus and that is the difference.

There were several factors that led me to Asai karate. It is a long story but is important to share some background to understand how and why I, a staunch JKA karateka, switched to Asai style karate. I was doing karate full time and competing in the late 70s and early 80s. I was young and happy with JKA karate. My idols were Oishi sensei, for that powerful stepping punch, and Tanaka sensei, for that great roundhouse kick. When I saw Asai sensei's demonstration in the 80s, I was very much impressed, but at the same time, his style looked so different. I had never seen that whipping technique before. His style definitely was unique and I figured it was good only for him; therefore, the idea of switching to his style never entered my mind. Besides, he was one of the JKA instructors, so I would never even dream of quitting my sensei's dojo to join another JKA teacher's dojo. It may be difficult for Westerners to understand this concept, but dojo switching is not an acceptable thing to do or a common idea in Japan.

My doubts about my karate began when I was still competing at Prefecture, Regional, and All Japan championships. To be honest, I was getting bored with the point winning matches. I was not happy with the trend that the competitions were becoming more popular and mainstream. I began to think more seriously about the martial art aspect of karate. Unfortunately, in the U.S., no instructors were teaching real martial arts karate, even though they claimed Budo. I began to search for a higher level of skills that would not rely solely on pure muscle strength. I was interested in one-inch punch, to-ate (ki punch), ki-ai nage (Ki throwing techniques), etc. I moved back to Japan in 1998 and lived in Tokyo for three years to take up Ki training from Master Nishino, the world famous Ki master. In his dojo, I saw him throwing, controlling hundreds of students' body movements to his will without any physical touching. When I saw the demonstrations right in front of my eyes, I truly wanted to learn these techniques.

Therefore, I diligently went to the dojo two or three times every week and practiced Ki (no karate training) for nearly two years, until Nishino sensei told me to leave. I did not graduate or master the art. In fact, I was the only student (out of hundreds) who he not only was incapable of throwing, but also was not able to move an inch with his Ki. It was a big disappointment for me that I could not learn the martial art Ki. On the other hand, it was a huge embarrassment for Nishino sensei. He was very upset with me and asked me not to get in the line of students in front of him. He did not literally tell me to quit the training but it was the same thing. On a brighter side, I learned how to relax and turn Ki within my body. I felt very different after the two years of Ki practice in Tokyo. During that time I did not wear my karate gi even once.

When I came back to California in 2000, I decided to practice karate again, with more emphasis on relaxation. My karate was definitely different now from the standard JKA techniques. I began to tell the students to go slower and "lighter," which was getting closer to the movements of Tai chi (not quite that slow, however). Still I was not completely happy with the kind of karate I was doing. So, the foundation for a big switch was brewing in 2000.

Another factor that influenced my thinking to some degree was the negative effect of JKA karate on our bodies. Many of my co-practitioners in Japan and the U.S. are suffering from back problems and knee injuries. They call them "occupational" injuries and consider them to be something that comes with the territory. However, I remember very clearly that one black belt (nidan) in Kobe told me that he was quitting JKA because the practice itself was hurting his back so badly he cannot even walk normally without pain.

He said there was something wrong with the way we practice. As I did not have his problem, I could not totally sympathize with him, even though I felt bad that he had to quit karate. Later, I found that he switched to one of the kung fu styles and moved to Taiwan. I happened to meet him one day and he was smiling and told me that he found the right method. He said that the exercise and training was good for his body and he no longer has any more pains while he practiced. He said "the movements are natural and I can feel they are good for my body." This statement made a big impression on me. After restarting karate practice in 2000, I wanted the movements to be natural and not forced. When you move in that manner, your body tells you that you are doing it right, and you can feel it very natural and comfortable. I think by accident or a detour, I was getting closer to the concept of Asai sensei's karate.

**What details or aspects caught your attention to the way Asai Sensei was expressing the art of JKA Shotokan?**

His karate was not standard JKA or even Shotokan style. It was Asai style karate, unlike any other. There are more than a dozen points to describe his style but I will list five points here so I can share some of his techniques and teachings.

I. Understanding the human body

Asai sensei really understood the mechanism of our body. The following understanding is the key point of how our body is constructed now and its history or evolution.

a. Though it may sound far-fetched, to understand our body mechanism, we need to trace our evolution back to the fish. It is interesting to see how the fish use their backbones. The tail fin is positioned vertically and the fish moves the backbone horizontally to generate forward motion. It is amazing how fast they can move in an environment of high viscosity: water. Some fish can swim as fast as 100 miles per hour and for many hours. Another interesting point is the surprising amount of power a fish shows when we try to grab one. We have difficulty holding a rather small fish like a salmon. It is impossible to think that we could handle a bigger fish like a tuna. It shows that a tremendous amount of power can be generated using the backbone movements.

b. The fish evolved into amphibians. The alligators move their backbone horizontally and they walk with four legs. Notice that their legs are set off to the sides of the shoulders and hip joints. They are flat on the ground and their motions on the ground are rather slow.

c. The next generation is mammals. Look at horses, dogs, and cats to see how their body mechanism differs from alligators. The mammals use their backbones vertically. Look at the backbone movements of a cheetah while it is running. We can clearly see the backbone is weaving and the movements are vertical. The legs of a cheetah are not that muscular, but rather slim. Therefore, it is obvious that the tremendous speed does not come only from the leg muscles. It depends on the strong backbone movements. Also, notice that their legs are set downward rather than to the side, like an alligator. Their chest cavity is oval shaped, stretching up and downward, rather than sideways as seen with an amphibian.

d. It is very interesting to see how a human is constructed. We are so different from all the generations of the past. Fish, amphibians, and mammals position themselves horizontally. We are unique, as we stand upright. As a matter of fact, it is a very strange position—to hold the heaviest part of our body, the head, on the top. And we walk on two legs, constantly balancing this heavy object. Bipedal mechanism itself is a topic we can spend hours discussing. We just touch the fact that we humans have a unique physical construction and mechanism. Our chest cavity is unlike most mammals. Ours is elongated to sideways, which is interestingly similar to that of an amphibian. Our arms and legs also are set differently, not only from the mammals but also from the amphibians. The legs are not set downward (at a 90-degree angle) but rather parallel to the backbone. Now the body is positioned vertically (including legs), rather than horizontally. The arms are set to the sides, like those of the alligator; yet, we have much more mobility as

"I think by accident or a detour, I was getting closer to the concept of Asai sensei's karate."

# Karate Masters

"Asai sensei's training will recover the abilities we lost in the evolution process."

far as the shoulder joints are concerned. We can swing the arms in almost all directions, which is impossible for any amphibians and mammals. We gained a lot of arm mobility but we also lost some capabilities.

The main capabilities we lost are: 1) balancing of the body mass with four legs (now we have bipedalism); 2) use of the backbones to generate power for body shifting (very little use now); 3) stomach breathing (most people do chest breathing, short and shallow).

Asai sensei's training will recover the abilities we lost in the evolution process.

This challenges us to consider the changes from the fish age to our current body structure, and to appreciate the abilities we gained, but at the same time we need to understand that we lost some important ones and to figure out how to regain those lost abilities.

II. Total relaxation of the body

Asai sensei's body was very flexible. It was not just loose but it had elasticity and rebound power. In Western culture, we (mostly men) want to build and admire strong and stiff muscles. Body building is a good example of this trend. He explained that our body is 70 percent water and it is held up with several sticks, bones, and covered with a thin elastic material, skin. It is not natural to make our bodies hard and stiff. He says: look at the body of a baby; that is the ultimate flexibility. But we as we grow older, we get stiff even if we do not lift weights. He says that to be able to relax and be able to use our body to a satisfactory level, we must start by understanding why our bodies become tight or stiff as we grow old.

Bipedal is like riding a bike compared to riding a cart with four wheels. It is much more difficult to keep one's balance to stand up with only two legs. As we learn how to stand up and walk, we learn to stiffen our body in order to keep our bodies like one stick. This action applies particularly to the inner muscles that are attached to the back bones, hip joints, and ribs. Having the backbones and ribs all being stiff and not mobile, the shoulders and their joints also get tight. Therefore, the relaxation must start from the backbones, hip joints, and ribs. When those main three parts are relaxed, the entire body is ready for the whipping movements of the fists and feet. However, relaxing those three parts are not easy.

What can one do to relax those parts? You start from moving the backbones in a way a snake does (swinging or winding sideways). Then you move the backbones in a forward and backward motion as a dolphin does as it swims. You do all these moves slowly and consciously to feel the movement of different backbones. Initially, your concept or feeling of the backbones is like one long stick. After several exercises, you will begin to feel them as a long, flexible chain. At the same time, you will expand your chest cavity to move the ribs and try to make it move like an accordion. The more flexible you can move your backbones and ribs, the better it is.

III. Fist and foot whip techniques

These are Asai sensei's signature techniques. Such techniques cannot be achieved by simple arm moving exercises. One can throw a backfist strike a million times, but will not be able to achieve a whipping technique without doing it correctly with good understanding of the mechanism behind it.

To enable a true whipping action with your fist, your backbones and ribs must have total relaxation and mobility. Then, you must have relaxed shoulder joints, as well as all the muscles that are involved and connecting between the backbones to the fist. For instance, a backfist strike movement must start from the inner body with a leveraging point at the backbones and not the shoulder.

The simple exercise for this technique should be practiced with both arms simultaneously. Hold the arms in front of your chest and swing them out to the sides. There are many ways to use the hands in this exercise. The easiest is to keep the hands open. Basically, there are three ways to position the open hand here. One is to keep the palms down as you would do a knife hand strike; another is to keep the palms up as you would be doing haito uchi (ridge hand strike); a third way is to keep the hands vertical, so you will be striking the target with back of your hands. When you feel comfortable with the open hand, you can do this with fists and you can position the fist in three ways, as you did with open hands. In doing this exercise, you must bring the hands back very quickly to your chest, as fast as, or faster than, the strike out. One set of exercises is about 20 quick strikes (from the chest position and back to the original position). If you do both open hands and fists with three different positions, you will be doing 120 strikes. That would be an excellent exercise if you have only five minutes to practice. Another important point is that the extended arms must be open wider than 180 degrees (meaning your arms are in a straight line). If you tense too soon, your arms will stop before they stretch to the 180 degree point. You get better exercise when your arms are extended 200 degrees or more.

If you become good at a whipping motion with your fist, your straight punch will change. You will not stop your punch too soon. You will learn how to deliver the energy when your fist is fully extended. Check this with a simple experiment. All you need is a bunch of old newspapers. Hold a sheet of newspaper (a half of the full page) with one hand fully extended in front of you and punch it with your other hand. The purpose is to make a hole with your fist. The idea is not to cut the paper in half but punch through it. Punching through one sheet or two sheets is rather easy. Try it with three sheets or more and it becomes challenging. If your punching arm is tensed, or if you try to punch with only the arm power, you will not be able to make a hole through the sheets. You must be completely relaxed and throw a punch quickly but lightly. It is a fun experiment, and you will make a lot of trash!

For a whipping kick, the movement must start from the pelvis joint. The pelvis joint must initiate the whipping action as the backbones did for the back fist strike.

IV. Tenshin (spin body shifting)

Tenshin is a body movement that requires a high level of body shifting capability. An easy example of basic tenshin would be a forward step from left front zenkutsu dachi to right front zenkutsu dachi. In a normal step forward, you simply step forward with your rear foot (right foot). In tenshin move, you pivot on your left foot and move your rear or right foot in a clockwise direction. By doing this, your upper body will rotate 360 degrees as you move forward. In a regular step forward, your upper body will rotate very little (maybe 30 degrees or so if you start from hanmi (half hip) and end up in straight hips.

A karateka must develop a good "center," which is an ability to keep the axis of your upper body straight, thus enabling you to keep your balance after a quick turn and spin. To develop a center, we practice the turning exercise, initially with a natural stance (shoulder width), then on to kibadachi (wider stance) to rotate our body by 90 degrees (both clockwise and counterclockwise). Then, we rotate by 180 degrees, then by 270 degrees and finally by 360 degrees (complete rotation). The rotation can be initiated from the head, shoulders, midsection of the body, hips, knees, or feet. Each method has its own merits and challenges.

To check your tenshin ability, try a rotation of 360 degrees from kiba dachi. The important point here is that you will not jump to get a complete turn. You will rotate quickly by using rotational power (head, shoulders, upper body, etc.) by only floating on the floor. Once you are able to rotate 360 degrees successfully, punch chudan at the moment of the completion of the rotation. This cannot be done unless the upper body and the stance complete the rotation in a coordinated way. There are two ways of punching. One is to punch with a fist of an outside turn (meaning a side that is moving forward). For instance, if you are rotating clockwise, you will punch with your left fist. The other is to use an inside turn (the side that is moving backward) fist or right fist as you rotate clockwise.

"When Asai Sensei talked about balance of the body, he was talking about executing techniques from one leg."

V. Balancing

When Asai Sensei talked about balance of the body, he was talking about executing techniques from one leg. We find this is difficult to do as we are so used to doing things with both feet on the ground. Once a practitioner learns how to balance well on one leg, naturally, his moves using both legs will become more solid and stable.

There are some one leg moves in JKA kata, such as *Gankaku* and *Jutte*, to improve the one leg balance. Because standing on one leg is difficult, this movement of one leg stance (tsuruashi dachi and sagiashi dachi) purposely is done slowly in kata. Asai sensei wanted us to practice the one leg stance in fast motions to build our balancing ability.

**How can a "traditional" JKA Shotokan exponent benefit from the Asai Sensei's method of moving and training the body?**

I was a JKA member for 40 years, so I had always trained by the JKA sylla-

# Karate Masters

"It is very important that you stop the whole body movement after the shift and a punch."

bus. I know the benefits and what the Asai style karate can do to a JKA practitioner. Understanding the concepts and the method that I briefly covered in the answer to the previous question surely will elevate the JKA practitioners to the next level of skill.

Try some of the simple exercises I listed above; if you have a problem doing them, it means you need different training. It is very easy to get comfortable with a certain way of doing things. Therefore, it is easy for JKA practitioners (I was one of them, so I know) to do the training in the same manner and be satisfied with it. The exercises recommended here do not require any radical change in body movements. They just are different.

**Can these principles be used for any other style of karate, or only for Shotokan?**

These principles can be used not only for any other styles of karate but also for all martial arts, including Korean styles, Kung Fu, Jujitsu, Judo, Kempo, Kendo, etc. In fact, it can go beyond the martial arts. These principles can benefit all other athletics and sports, as they apply to all body movements, regardless of the activity. For instance, freer shoulder joints and arm movements (whipping motion) can be applied easily to the use of arm movements of a tennis player. Not only the whipping motion of the leg, but the quick motion of the entire body and the steps, can be applied to a soccer player.

**How did you feel in the beginning when you began to adapt your body to the principles of using the body in karate that Asai Sensei was teaching?**

Though I can never duplicate his moves, I felt quite comfortable with the new moves. It was almost like finding my old shoes: "Hey, they fit!" I understand the concepts, but being able to execute with my body is another thing. I just cannot duplicate the movements of Asai sensei yet. I need to practice a lot more, but I am not sure if I ever can catch up to him. Asai sensei got up at 4 a.m. every morning and practiced for two to three hours every day. His techniques are the best, but he did not stop training. As I train every day, I hope to find new things, and the discovery makes it so exciting.

**Why do you think Asai Sensei decided to emphasize these elements in the art of karate, and other top JKA Shotokan masters didn't?**

I cannot say why the other JKA shotokan masters did not emphasize or make them known. I only know that Asai sensei was the only one who did. I know he was not satisfied with the JKA syllabus. I guess he went way beyond the JKA syllabus and he could not help but to share his knowledge with other shotokan practitioners. He just loved karate and reaching higher levels. I believe he expected others to follow his quest, and he wanted to show the path. Even though he was secretive in some ways, he was very open and candid about all subjects of karate and martial arts. When you asked him a question, he always had a great and insightful answer. He truly was unique and outspoken. This was one of the reasons he had to leave JKA. He just did not fit in a set box of JKA.

**How much influence of Chinese kung fu did Asai Sensei allow in his JKA Shotokan style of karate?**

It definitely had a lot of influence. Mrs. Asai is originally from Taiwan and her elder brother is a master of White Crane Kung Fu. His name is Master Cheng and he is nearly 80 years old now. Asai sensei lived in Taiwan many years ago, and even after returning to Japan, he visited there many times. During this time, he spent many hours with Master Cheng discussing martial arts and exchanging ideas and techniques. Mrs. Asai told me stories of how the discussions went. Obviously, they found each other interesting enough, according to Mrs. Asai; on many occasions, they spent all night without sleeping in discussion and exchanges of techniques. Mrs. Asai also told me that Master Cheng was impressed as Asai sensei had known most of the techniques he introduced. If and when Asai sensei found a new idea or a technique from Master Cheng, he went away for a day. When he returned, Asai sensei had already mastered the technique.

**You were one of the few people who actually received instruction from him in his later years. Where was he and where he was going technically (evolution – level of skill) at the end of his life?**

I know he wanted to teach his style of karate to all shotokan and traditional karate practitioners around the world. I found a little contradiction here. Even though he wanted us to learn his karate, he was hesitant to reveal all the methods and "secrets" of his unique training. He would show

# Karate Masters

"If I teach you everything, you will not appreciate nor understand them."

you so much, but then he'd say, "You need to find the fine points yourself. If I teach you everything, you will not appreciate nor understand them." He also refused to have any private students at all (not only to the students but also the close instructors). Several individuals claim they had such training at the beach or in a hotel room or wherever, but please do not believe it. I myself asked him to give me such instruction or to train with him at 4 a.m. He said, "If I allowed you to do so, I will have hundreds of people asking for this. In order to be fair to all, I cannot give you a personal lesson." He also said, "Watch my movements very closely while I am teaching the group. If you understand what I am teaching, you will see how I use my body."

As far as the technical level is concerned, I believe he reached the top. I know he wanted to generate the power without using the energy or muscle strength. However, he did not believe in ki power that can generate physical energy (to-ate). His ki concept was within himself; it generates the power to move his body. He also was saying that he had mastered Tenketsu (vital points or dim mak) so that he could knock down a person by simply touching him lightly. I have not seen any demonstration, so I really do not know if he could do it or not. However, there is no reason why I would doubt it, as he did not need to impress someone with a lie. He always was honest and told us only the truth.

**How do you remember him?**

He was like a father to my karate life and he still is a model to me. In the late 90s, I was disenchanted with karate. I felt that I had reached my peak. I could not enjoy karate any more, so I almost gave up. Without a seminar he did in my hometown in 2001, I probably would not have come back to karate. He saved my karate life. His karate got me excited again. At the age of 70, he was moving like he was 20 years old. Unlike other karate "masters," he could move and show his techniques. He was diligent and faithful to karate by getting up at 4 a.m. every morning and do his two or three hour daily training to sharpen and improve his techniques. I wonder how many masters are committed to their training as Asai sensei was. A lot of instructors say they train every day, but most of the time they are talking about their teaching time and not their own training. They may be wearing gi and in dojo, but that is not their own training as defined by Asai sensei. He did not even wear a gi when he trained in the morning. He said a gi would be in his way and he could move better without it. He did not need to impress anyone so he trained in a gym suit or a pair of shorts. He did not need a dojo or a gym. He trained in his bedroom at his home in the morning when he was in Japan, and in a hotel room when he was traveling. When he visited California, he asked me to reserve a room on the first floor of a hotel as he made a lot of noise in the early morning hours.

"I know Asai Sensei was not satisfied with the JKA syllabus."

Time really passes fast. Though everyone admits that Asai sensei was an outstanding master and world famous, unfortunately the memories would fade unless people like me continue to talk and carry on the legacy. If we lose Asai style karate, it will be a great loss to the entire Shotokan and traditional karate. In fact, we already have lost many of his kata with his passing. He knew more than 150 kata and he probably taught only about 50 of them. Unless we discover a DVD or the manuscript of the kata steps, those other 100 kata are gone forever. O

# Karate's Finest Masters Teach

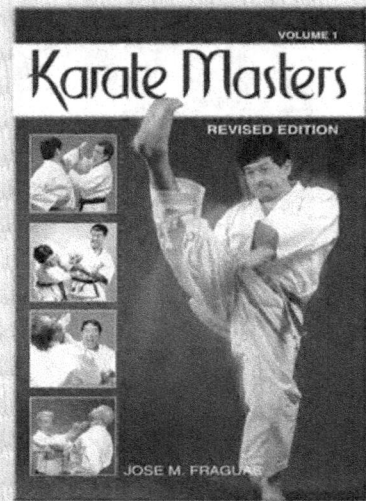

### KARATE MASTERS Vol.1 (Revised Edition)
By Jose M. Fraguas

Through conversations with many historical figures such as Osamu Ozawa, Teruo Hayashi, Kenzo Mabuni, Masatoshi Nakayama, and numerous current world-class masters such as Hirokazu Kanazawa, Fumio Demura, Takayuki Mikami, Teruyuki Okazaki, Morio Higaonna, Hidetaka Nishiyama, James Yabe, Tak Kubota, Bill Dometrich, Dan Ivan, and Stan Schmidt, the many threads of karate learning, lore, and legend are woven together to present an integrated and complete view of the empty-handed art of fighting, philosophy, and self-defense. Containing information that has not appeared anywhere else, the interviews contain intriguing thoughts, fascinating personal details, hidden history, and revealing philosophies.

#110 - $19.95 – 7 x 10 – 350 pages
ISBN: 978-1-933901-22-0

### KARATE MASTERS Vol. 2
By Jose M. Fraguas

The second volume of the series offers a new repertoire of historical figures, such as Mas Oyama, Kyoshi Yamazaki. Masahiko Tanaka, Eihachi Ota, Yukiyoshi Marutani, Randall Hassell, Keinosuke Enoeda, Richard Kim, Shinpo Matayoshi, Tsutomu Ohshima, Yoshiaki Ajari, Goshi Yamaguchi, and other world-recognized professional martial artists. In this volume, new interviews with the world's top karate masters have been gathered to present an integrated and complete view of the empty-handed art of fighting, philosophy, and self-defense.

# 111 - $29.95 – 7 x 10 – 350 pages
ISBN: 978-1-933901-20-9

**TO ORDER VISIT: www.empirebooks.net**

# Budo Greatest Lessons

### KARATE MASTERS Vol.3
By Jose M. Fraguas

Including twenty-three exclusive interviews with legendary masters, such as Gogen "The Cat" Yamaguchi, Teruo Chinen, Edmond Otis, Akio Minakami, Jiro Ohtsuka, Shojiro Koyama, Ryusho Sakagami, Katsutaka Tanaka, Anthony Mirakian, Tetsuhiko Asai, Mikio Yahara, and other karate giants, this volume contains intriguing thoughts, fascinating personal details, hidden histories, and inspiring philosophies, as each master reveals his true love for the art and a deep understanding of every facet associated with the practice and spirit of the Japanese art of Karate-do as a way of life. This invaluable reference book is a "must have" addition to your personal library.
# 112 – $29.95 – 7 x 10 – 350 pages
ISBN: 978-1-933901-04-6

### KARATE MASTERS Vol.4
By Jose M. Fraguas

After the acclaimed success of the first three volumes of Karate Masters, the author proudly presents "Karate Masters 4", with a new repertoire of historical figures, such as Yutaka Yaguchi, Hiroyasu Fujishima, Takeshi Uchiage, Kenneth Funakoshi, Kunio Murayama, Shoji Nishimura, Hiroshi Okazaki, Gene Tibon, Les Safar, Koss Yokota, Richard Amos, Taku Nakasaka, and other world-recognized Karate masters like George E. Mattson, Joe Carbonara, Tony Annesi, etc... In this fourth volume, new interviews with the world's top Karate masters have been gathered to present an integrated and complete view of the empty-handed art of fighting, philosophy, and self-defense. Containing information that has not appeared anywhere else, the interviews contain intriguing thoughts, fascinating personal details, hidden history, and revealing philosophies as each master reveals his true love for the art and a deep understanding of every facet associated with the practice and spirit of the Japanese art of Karate-do as a way of life. It's a detailed reference work, and a "must have" addition to your personal library.
#133– $29.95 – 7 x 10 – 370 pages
ISBN: 978-1-933901-49-7

**TO ORDER VISIT: www.empirebooks.net**

# Karate Masters

# Notes

# Karate Masters

www.ingramcontent.com/pod-product-compliance
Lightning Source LLC
Chambersburg PA
CBHW081343080526
44588CB00016B/2366